THE
PERSUASION
C⬡DE

THE
PERSUASION
CDE

—

How Neuromarketing Can
Help You Persuade
Anyone, Anywhere, Anytime

—

CHRISTOPHE MORIN, PH.D.
PATRICK RENVOISE

WILEY

Published by John Wiley & Sons, Inc., Hoboken, New Jersey.
Published simultaneously in Canada.

For general information on our other products and services or for technical support, please contact our Customer Care Department within the United States at (800) 762-2974, outside the United States at (317) 572-3993, or fax (317) 572-4002.

Wiley publishes in a variety of print and electronic formats and by print-on-demand. Some material included with standard print versions of this book may not be included in e-books or in print-on-demand. If this book refers to media such as a CD or DVD that is not included in the version you purchased, you may download this material at http://booksupport.wiley.com. For more information about Wiley products, visit www.wiley.com.

Library of Congress Cataloging-in-Publication Data

Names: Morin, Christophe, author. | Renvoise, Patrick, author.
Title: The persuasion code : how neuromarketing can help you persuade anyone, anywhere, anytime / Christophe Morin, Patrick Renvoise.
Description: Hoboken, New Jersey : John Wiley & Sons, Inc., [2018] | Includes bibliographical references and index. |
Identifiers: LCCN 2018023659 (print) | LCCN 2018025347 (ebook) | ISBN 9781119440758 (Adobe PDF) | ISBN 9781119440765 (ePub) | ISBN 9781119440703 (hardcover)
Subjects: LCSH: Neuromarketing. | Persuasion (Psychology)
Classification: LCC HF5415.12615 (ebook) | LCC HF5415.12615 .M67 2018 (print) | DDC 658.8001/9—dc23
LC record available at https://lccn.loc.gov/2018023659

Cover Design: Wiley
Cover Images: brain: © rustemgurler/Getty Images; background: © points/Getty Images

Printed in the United States of America

V10003070_081318

CONTENTS

ACKNOWLEDGMENTS

There are many people who helped us finish the book in record time. First and foremost, we want to thank the clients that were willing to let us share the case studies featured in this book. Without their support, we would not be able to demonstrate the value of what we do.

Second, much of the creative work featured in the book was done through a long collaboration we have enjoyed with Dr. Gail DaMert, Bryan Gray, Mike Rendel, Benson Lee, and Elliott Morin. All of them brought talent, inspiration, and arduous work making sure the principles of NeuroMap could come to life visually with stunning graphics, illustrations, videos, web pages, and more.

Finally, readers and editors of the book deserve much credit for how it flows. Both Keely Spare and Dr. Bonnie Bright gave us pointed suggestions and had many insights we included in the final work.

ABOUT THE AUTHORS

With more than 30 years of marketing and business development experience, Dr. Christophe Morin is passionate about understanding and predicting consumer behavior using neuroscience. Prior to founding Salesbrain, he was chief marketing officer of rStar Networks, a public company that developed the largest private network ever deployed in US schools. Previously, he was vice president of marketing and corporate training for Grocery Outlet Inc., the largest grocery remarketer in the world. Christophe has received multiple awards during his career. In 2011 and 2013, he received prestigious speaking awards from Vistage International. In 2011, 2014, and 2015, he received a Great Mind Research Award and two distinctions from the Advertising Research Foundation (ARF).

Christophe holds a BA in marketing, an MBA from Bowling Green State University, an MA and a PhD in media psychology from Fielding Graduate University. He is an expert on the effect of advertising on the brains of adolescents. He is an adjunct faculty member of Fielding Graduate University, where he teaches several courses in media neuroscience. He was a founding board member of the Neuromarketing Science and Business Association (NMSBA) between 2011 and 2016.

 Patrick Renvoisé is an expert in complex sales and messaging strategies that achieve spectacular results. He headed the global business development efforts at Silicon Graphics, then as executive director of business development at LinuxCare. Pushed by a fervent desire to seek the truth about messaging effectiveness, Patrick turned to neuroscience and psychology. Patrick spent two years researching and formalizing a science-based blueprint of how messages work on the brain. This became the basis of NeuroMap, which has helped thousands of companies worldwide get their messages truly understood by the brains of their customers.

Patrick received a master's in computer science from the National Institute of Applied Sciences (Lyon, France); and he is currently serving as chief neuromarketing officer and cofounder of SalesBrain.

WHY READ THIS BOOK?

Y ou may not realize this, but each day you create messages to persuade others. It could be one of the hundreds of emails you regularly send to your colleagues, friends, or customers. Or you may participate in the creation of an ad, a web page, a corporate video, and slides for a sales presentation. Often, cognitive effort and money are invested in many of these tasks. However, have you ever wondered how effective all these attempts are from the perspective of people's brains? What attention can you truly recruit? What are your chances of rewiring pre-existing beliefs and opinions? Can you trigger the "buy button" in your targets' heads?

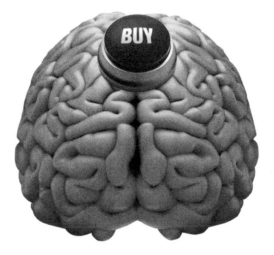

Figure 0.1   Buy button.
Source: SalesBrain. All Rights Reserved. 2002–2018.

This book will help you realize that most of your efforts to persuade others are not optimized for the brain. We are bombarded with persuasive messages throughout the day, which is why 99% of them are being ignored. They "splash" off our brains (see Figure 0.2). In *The Persuasion Code*, however, you will learn proven strategies to ensure your messages get through.

Figure 0.2   The splashing effect.
Source: SalesBrain. All Rights Reserved. 2002–2018.

Simply put, the purpose of our book is to help you use cutting-edge persuasion science to make your messages brain-friendly. This means you will be able to convince anyone, anywhere, anytime!

This book is a long-due sequel to the original book we published under the title: *Neuromarketing: Understanding the "Buy Buttons" in Your Customer's Brain*, the first of its kind to include the term *neuromarketing*. Since then, neuromarketing has become a vibrant field investigating the effect of persuasive messages on our brains. Against all odds, our first book was an international success with estimated sales of over 150,000 copies.

A few months after our book was released, we formed a neuromarketing agency called SalesBrain. SalesBrain became the first company in the world dedicated to training, research, coaching, and creative services using a proprietary neuromarketing model called NeuroMap. NeuroMap is illustrated to help you learn it with ease and is printed on the back of the book cover. Since 2002, over 200,000 executives have been trained on NeuroMap worldwide, including over 15,000 CEOs. With SalesBrain's help, over 800 companies have deployed innovative neuromarketing strategies to accelerate sales cycles, win strategic deals, optimize the effect of websites, brochures, presentation slides, corporate videos, and more. Many of our customers are leaders in their industry with large marketing budgets and teams of talented marketers: Avon, TransUnion, Paypal, Siemens, GE, Epson, Hitachi, along with many others we are not legally allowed to name but you would instantly recognize! Often, neuromarketing practices are considered too strategic to let competitors know you are employing them to sharpen the effectiveness of sales messages. Meanwhile, many of our raving fans are small to medium-sized companies with limited marketing budgets and modest marketing teams. Yet, many of these companies have generated measurable advantages by using NeuroMap. That is why we can continue to claim today that NeuroMap is the only scientific persuasion model that can explain and improve thousands of messages that are designed to trigger buying decisions.

NeuroMap is based on the dominance of the *primal brain* on our buying decisions. The primal brain is the oldest system composed of a multitude of brain structures (see Figure 0.3). The primal brain manages critical internal states that control attention and emotional resources to address survival-related priorities below our level of consciousness. Think of it as the operating system of your mind, a set of basic instructions that control how your computer receives input and output. Most users do not change their operating system. You can't really reprogram your primal brain either. Meanwhile, the *rational brain* contributes to the confirmation process of many of our decisions. The rational brain is the most recent, more evolved part of the brain. Think of it as the latest version Microsoft Office(R) for your brain. The rational brain is like a suite of enhanced applications you can learn, change or upgrade during your lifetime. This brain uses higher cognitive resources that help mediate some of the responses of the primal brain. Measuring activity in both brain systems is how we were able to decode the effect of marketing or advertising stimuli on the whole brain.

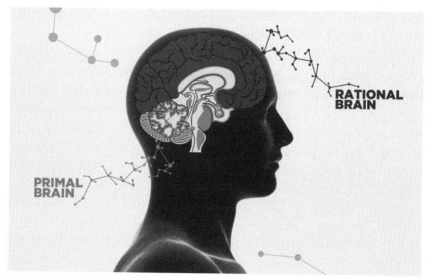

Figure 0.3   Primal and rational brains.

Surprisingly, persuasion is *not* controlled by the rational brain. Rather, it is the *primal brain* that dominates the process, a brain that is mostly unconscious, and preverbal. It appeared long before we started to use words to communicate.

The dominance of the primal brain in our decisions has only been revealed in the past couple of decades by researchers such as Daniel Kahneman, Richard Thaler (both recipients of the Nobel Prize in Economics in 2002 and 2017, respectively), as well as Dan Ariely, John Bargh, and David Eagleman, to name a few who have received public accolades. This book integrates the complex field of decision neuroscience into a proven model you can quickly use to influence the primal brain of your audience, simply but scientifically!

Despite the enthusiasm for brain-based marketing, the size of the neuromarketing industry is still relatively small. A conservative estimate is slightly under one hundred million dollars. However, recent studies conducted by Green Book suggest that marketers plan between 10 and 20% of all their marketing budgets on neuromarketing tools and methods. In the United States alone, the market research industry is a 20-billion-dollar business, which means neuromarketing research services could grab between two and four billion dollars of the potential market within a few years [1].

Even though the field is now considered more mature, a wider adoption of neuromarketing has just begun. That is the reason that the sequel to our first book is so important. It provides a deep, yet practical approach toward implementing a successful neuromarketing strategy using a tested persuasion model, NeuroMap. Over the past decade, about 60 books have covered the neuroscientific value of using neuro-physiological data to decode consumer behavior and advertising effec-tiveness. However, no book so far has demonstrated the practical and measurable value of applying messaging strategies guided by a scientific persuasion model like NeuroMap. It is our goal to take your interest in neuromarketing, scientific persuasion, sales messaging, advertising effectiveness, website conversion, and sales presentations beyond neu-romarketing basics and help you quickly apply the benefits of using *The Persuasion Code*. To achieve that, we will provide a much more compre-hensive scientific discussion on the theoretical framework supporting NeuroMap. Also, we will deliver practical, evidence-based guidance to help you apply our persuasion model daily. Armed with both a theoret-ical and practical understanding of NeuroMap, you will be able to cre-ate and deliver messages that catapult the effect of all your persuasion efforts to new record levels. Unlike our first book, in which we cited few case studies and provided limited scientific references, *The Persua-sion Code* includes hundreds of scientific references, new research con-ducted by SalesBrain, and never-published-before materials, as well as many remarkable success stories. In the past 16 years, hundreds of our customers have benefited from NeuroMap. Consequently, this book goes beyond teaching you a proven, brain-based persuasion model. It will inspire and guide you to create your own success story.

In summary, this book will help you:

- Gain a new appreciation for the tremendous amount of brain research that can be easily applied to all your marketing, sales, and communication initiatives.

- Realize how buying choices are affected by multiple brain processes that control attention, emotion, memorization, and decisions.

- Understand how the *primal brain* (evolutionary older layers controlling our automatic and survival-centric behavior), not the *rational brain* (newer cognitive layer), dominates the persuasion process and influences all buying decisions.

- Learn the working principles of the primal brain so you can assimilate how the complex process of persuasion works without a background in psychology or neuroscience.

- Discover scientific studies, customer stories, and learn scoring techniques that quickly illustrate how your brain-based persuasion strategies can deliver practical, predictable, and measurable outcomes.

Finally, note that the book is structured around three major sections presenting the science, the theory, and the process of persuasion.

The first five chapters were written by Dr. Christophe Morin; in them, he presents the scientific basis of persuasion and NeuroMap. Morin's text concludes with the presentation of the first step of our persuasion process called Diagnose the Pain.

The remainder of the book is written by Patrick Renvoisé. Patrick covers the next three steps in our process to persuade with messages that differentiate your claims, demonstrate the gain, and deliver to the primal brain. Patrick uses many examples and stories to show how you can apply NeuroMap, whether you are selling simple consumer products like toothbrushes or complex multimillion-dollar solutions. Note that this book is written in a way that allows you to skip part I and II if you want to know the HOW (part III) before the WHY (Part I & II). We do recommend, however, that you read at least the introduction before you do so.

Together, all chapters will give you access to *The Persuasion Code*!

Introduction

For over a decade now, many neuroscientists and media researchers have claimed that they can crack the neurologic code of advertising effectiveness. Yet, the adoption of scientific methods to investigate and create more persuasive ads or websites has remained curiously low.

Is Neuromarketing a Complicated Field?

First, when marketing and advertising executives discovered neuromarketing, they often felt that they needed higher education on the workings of the brain to understand and use it. It is true that neuromarketing studies generate gigabytes of information corresponding to complex mechanisms in the brain and that to manipulate this data requires the use of powerful software running cryptic algorithms. There is no question that the process of digging for neuroinsights is time-consuming and somewhat intimidating. So, you may wonder: Can I grasp this quickly? Will it radically help me improve my ability to persuade without causing me additional headaches? Rest assured that with this book you will learn enough about the brain to understand the value of neuromarketing and apply it quickly.

Will Neuromarketing Reveal Flaws of Prior Campaigns?

Marketing and advertising executives are often afraid of what neuromarketing studies may reveal. After all, a scientific persuasion model may provide embarrassing or damaging evidence on the failure of prior campaigns that wasted thousands, if not millions, of dollars. Let's face it, we all avoid confronting information that may question the fundamentals of what we believe. Often, neuromarketing findings are surprising and call into question what we have learned and applied for decades. They tell us why so many of our efforts to influence, sell, or convince did not work. They may even reveal our incompetence or flaws. Peering inside the deep unconscious parts of the primal brain is surprising if not uncomfortable, because it is information that was not available before. We keep asking people what they want, but the evidence suggests that we cannot easily articulate what we want!

As you embark on your neuromarketing journey, praise yourself for having the courage to question what you know, to challenge what you currently do, and to admit that you may have wasted time and efforts creating messages that were never going to yield any measurable results. Adopting a neuromarketing discipline is humbling, but also empowering. But remember that you may face, if not confront, economic players that are not excited about the neuromarketing revolution.

CAN CREATIVE AND PERSUASION SCIENCE MIX?

Since the inception of SalesBrain, we have met many ad executives who claim they do not need neurophysiological data to understand or predict the effect of their campaigns. Often, they consider neuromarketing research disruptive to the creative process. They do not believe that revealing what cannot be said will provide valuable insights. Worse, they often see persuasion science as limiting their creative freedom. After all, many agencies rely on the power of their creative execution to differentiate themselves. The obvious problem from our exposure to dozens of agencies worldwide (some in the top tier) is that hardly any of them uses credible persuasion theories to support the scientific basis of their messaging strategy. So be prepared to challenge advertising or even creative agencies when you start your neuromarketing journey. They may push back initially until they realize (and accept) that you want more objective measures of the effect of the creative content you buy.

WHY ARE MARKETERS ADDICTED TO WEB ANALYTICS?

In the growing digital marketing space, web and mobile analytics are so easy to produce that marketers often insist that they can easily understand the true impact of ads without more science. Companies like

Google, Facebook, and Twitter spend millions of dollars to convince us that their algorithms can reveal and predict the quality of any digital message you create. Their survival depends on it. However, ongoing events have revealed how deceptive many of the web analytics can be. Worse, they often have poor definitions, questionable assumptions, and even mathematical errors. They are based on behavioral data that give a partial view of how people respond to messages. They ignore the invisible clicks that happen in people's brains!

In 2016, the world's biggest advertiser, Procter & Gamble significantly reduced its Facebook ad strategy claiming that targeting specific audiences was expensive and did not result in a significant difference [2]. Both Facebook and Google argue that they can help advertisers target specific audiences. However, P&G insisted that there was no evidence that precise targeting was worth the effort. Meanwhile, also in 2016, Facebook admitted that it had overestimated a key video metric for at least two years. Only video views of more than three seconds were considered to compute the metric of the average duration of video viewed. That means video views of less than three seconds were not factored in the average, making it much higher than it should have been otherwise. As a result, advertisers were given higher performance scores than they should have received. Although the social network claimed that this was a miscalculation of the average time users spent watching videos on its platform, many advertisers like Publicis were outraged. Publicis was responsible for buying 77 billion dollars in ads in 2015. Keith Weed, Chief Marketing Officer of Unilever, another big advertiser, commented that companies like Google and Facebook do not allow third parties to assess their platform, which means that basically, they grade their homework [3]. Without question, the miscalculation was an embarrassment for Facebook. The company formally apologized and said that they would fix the error in their algorithm. So be warned. Web analytics have limited value and are often flawed. A neuromarketing discipline will make you a smarter buyer of digital advertising by revealing the nature and influence of invisible clicks. As a result, big data players in the advertising space may not be as excited about neuromarketing as you may be.

Meanwhile, since web analytics do not give the complete picture of what happens when buyers' brains are first exposed to ads, you are forced to constantly change your headlines, switch pictures, basically modify your message many times. This ruins your chances to understand why so many of your ads fail to produce any return. Worse, you may select an ad that is still an ineffective ad overall, although it is the highest performing message of your test. Without gaining a better understanding of how ads affect the brain, testing messages (also called A/B testing) is a trap that gives billions of dollars to advertisers and media networks. The pursuit of perfect messages via testing is inefficient, costly, and defies the laws of how persuasion works in the brain.

WHY YOU WILL LOVE A BRAIN-BASED PERSUASION MODEL

Our first book did provide a simple step-by-step process to improve any sales message using a holistic brain-based theoretical framework. However, it was not a scientific book per se; rather, it popularized the value of centering persuasive efforts on the primal brain to ignite and engage the persuasive process throughout the entire brain. Our goal with this book, however, is to demonstrate the scientific and practical validity of a fully researched, fully tested persuasion model called NeuroMap so that you can systematically reduce risk, eliminate wastes and improve your ability to convince any audience.

Part I

DECODING PERSUASION SCIENCE

CHAPTER **1**

Why Is Neuromarketing a Game Changer?

Intelligence is the ability to adapt to change.
— Stephen Hawking

This chapter will help you understand why anyone creating persuasive messages should consider using a neuromarketing model. First, we focus on the unique research questions answered by NeuroMap – specifically, an aspect not discussed in other books on the topic. Yes, it is easy to get lost under the hood of the neuromarketing engine with all its shiny bells and whistles. However, knowing the basics will help you quickly become a sharp and discriminant persuader!

In the following five chapters written by me, Dr. Christophe Morin, I bring a devouring passion for cracking the scientific code of persuasion. As you will quickly realize, I am somewhat of a brain nerd and therefore I have lots of information I am eager to share about this topic, while making this portion of the book both informative and enjoyable. I have delivered workshops on neuromarketing to thousands of people around the world for nearly 20 years. As an adjunct professor of media psychology at Fielding Graduate University, I collaborate with top academics to improve our understanding of media effectiveness in all its forms. Also, I have students from all over the world using the teachings of neuromarketing to improve movie scripts, ad campaigns, fundraising drives, and even to decode the neurobiological basis of terrorist propaganda.

Although the subject of brain-based persuasion can be intimidating at first, what you learn about the brain in the next sections may influence your life beyond what you may have imagined when you picked this book. Personally, neuroscience helped me understand complex psychological disorders affecting some of my close family members; it influenced my parenting style and much more. Be assured that choosing to read through these next pages will not just improve your ability to persuade; it may also improve your life. Often, people walk up to me after a lecture and share how learning the basics of neuroscience made it much easier for them to understand why they have struggled (sometimes for decades) to influence or to understand loved ones. I have heard powerful stories that tell desperate attempts to convince a child not to smoke, compassionate efforts to ask a friend to quit drinking, or frustrating failures to close heated arguments. Let's be clear though; our goal is to discuss the effect of sales and advertising messages on people's brains. However, I believe the value of neuromarketing can be broadened to other aspects of life for which your ability to persuade others can bring relief and hope. In fact, Patrick Renvoisé addresses a broader application of neuromarketing in his popular TEDx talk (tinyurl.com/yb3x79vq).

What Neuromarketing Can Tell You Other Methods Cannot

Right from the beginning of the creation of SalesBrain in 2002, Patrick and I suggested that *traditional marketing research* falls short of its goals, especially when it comes to measuring the effect of advertising messages. Surveys, interviews, or focus groups do not explain the neurophysiological mechanisms underlying consumer behavior. Yet, the subconscious and preconscious functional circuits of the brain are essential to explain our responses to most marketing stimuli [4–8]. That is why neuroscientific methods can generate unique insights compared to traditional research methods – a fact that is now widely accepted by marketing and advertising researchers around the world [7, 9–11]. According to many scholars, the integration of neuroscientific methods in advertising research represents one of the most significant events in consumer research over the past 50 years [12].

Despite initial skepticism and resistance to change, the advertising industry has started to recognize the importance and relevance of this movement. Why? Because collectively, neuromarketing methods go far beyond traditional collection techniques by tracing the biological, physiological, and neurological changes that arise in our brains in response to marketing stimuli. These innovative experimental settings help us analyze instinctive, emotive, and cognitive responses without placing the burden of interpretation on research subjects. You may not realize this, but anytime you answer a survey, it requires an enormous amount of your precious brain energy. Getting paid to participate in surveys does not even reduce this burden! Cognitive energy is priceless. Using brain-based methods means we no longer depend on the conscious and active participation of subjects. We are not asking them to behave like zombies but, simply, to relax and let the messages work on their brains. There is no need for the subjects to verbalize anything either. The point is to allow the exposure to a stimulus to work on their neurophysiology. Meanwhile, we maintain an environment that is safe, comfortable, and free of artifacts that could compromise the data, such as noise, moving objects, changing light, and temperature conditions.

What value do we get from these methods that traditional surveys and focus groups cannot provide? We get measures of consumer states that are difficult if not impossible for subjects to report consciously. Remember the last time you were asked what you thought of the most recent movie you saw? What a simple question, yet how difficult it would be to answer if you were forced to use emotional scales describing the degree to which it made you happy, sad, excited, nervous, worried, curious, and so on. The same is true of how we respond to advertising messages or even a website. We know these stimuli have some effect on us, but we cannot be trusted to rate with any precision their emotional and cognitive impact on our brain. Research has shown that when people are asked to describe their moods on a daily basis, they use more than three words on average to do so, suggesting that emotions are difficult to identify and report [13].

Let's go back to the key research questions that can be answered uniquely by neuromarketing research and NeuroMap. Neuromarketing research questions are designed to create insights that help you minimize the risk and uncertainty associated with the predictive effect of ads, websites, packaging labels, and more. To help you understand the relevance of these questions, it may help if you recall a campaign or a message you have recently created or used to influence someone. Think of the value of answering any of the following questions before you deployed your campaign.

There are six crucial research questions that can be answered by sound neuromarketing experiments and, of course, by NeuroMap.

Will My Message Grab the Brain's Subconscious Attention?

Attention recruits brain energy to allow your audience to focus on your message and process its content. A lot of that attention is managed below our level of awareness. Therefore, attention is difficult to measure when you ask your audience to describe how much they focused on your message. Consciousness, our ability to observe and report our immediate experience, is both slow and fragile. Your messages are narrative constructions that affect your audience at a much greater speed than consciousness allows. Consequently, we are incompetent at describing the quality of our immediate attention. Instead, collecting brain data is rather easy because it does not rely on a subject's ability to report. More importantly, it helps measure attention on a millisecond basis, which is a game changer for how you can explain the effect of any marketing stimulus. Stories produce various cycles of attention during which your audience is engaged, moved, or bored, the timeline of which can be captured by different neuromarketing techniques such as reading the conductivity of the skin, decoding facial expressions, tracking eye movements, or monitoring brain waves. A story works in amazing ways. Most of its effect is not accessible to our awareness. Neuromarketing methods are designed to show whether a message has captured any form of attention, conscious or subconscious, automatic or intentional, which makes an enormous difference in your ability to create successful messages.

Case Study #1: Which Animal Images Grab the Most Attention. A prominent nonprofit organization focusing on defending the rights of all animals wanted to find out why some of their ads work better than others to generate donations. They gave SalesBrain three ads that were produced in the past decade: one old and two new. The new ads were not doing better than the old ones, but they could not understand why. We used our NeuroLab to investigate the issue. By doing a complete assessment of the neurophysiological response from a sample of 40 subjects, we discovered that attention was dropping rapidly for any scenes that would fail to show the animals with a salient and clear expression of sadness. Also, a frontal view of the face of the animal was prompting more attention than a side view. This was related to the animal itself, and its capacity to trigger human empathy. However, a lot of the responses appear predicated on the power of the facial expression itself, and whether a scene was showing one or several animals. This hypothesis was confirmed by looking at eye tracking and emotional data on several animals, including cats, dogs, horses, pigs, cows, seals, and even monkeys. After we revealed the persuasion code of their ads, the advertising agency was able to release a new TV spot, which outperformed all the clips they had ever done before. Also, the insights produced by the study guided the photo and video team on how they use images in all their future communications.

Can People Say What They Feel?

We are good at masking and distorting the reporting of our emotions. Recent studies of social media content compared to search questions asked on Google show the extent of our capacity to deceive. Search sentences reveal concerns or interests that do not match what people are willing to disclose openly. Additionally, search data shows that we choose to share what makes us feel good and hide what lowers our self-esteem. The younger we are, the more unreliable our statements tend to be. I have conducted extensive research on teenagers that helped me realize that collecting their opinions does not begin to explain and predict their behaviors. Fortunately, neuromarketing studies do not depend on what people say, but how their brains respond. When we conduct one, we look at how the participants' neurons fire at millisecond intervals, and what they feel, measured by their brain's response to external stimuli.

The neurons in the brain respond in a fraction of a second, triggering emotional responses before the conscious mind even processes the information. Therefore, a subject may have a subconscious reaction, but once it becomes conscious, he may not feel comfortable sharing it with a researcher. Perhaps he may not feel it is appropriate or wants to be perceived favorably by the researcher. Either way, in psychology, this is referred to as the social desirability bias. Furthermore, even if the subject believes that he is reporting true feelings in response to an advertisement, the brain data may show otherwise. Neuromarketing findings help identify the distance, if not the distortions, between what people say they feel and how they truly feel while measuring the influence of our emotions on our behavior.

Case Study #2: Understanding How Consumers Feel About Banks in Morocco. Wafacash is a wholly owned subsidiary of the Attijariwafa banking group, which is the largest bank in North Africa and the sixth largest on the African continent. Over the past 20 years, Wafacash has enjoyed a dominant market share in the cash transfer and payment banking business in Morocco. The business of cash handling appeals to a majority of Moroccans who do not trust traditional banks: they value the privacy of saving and paying using cash without the requirement of owning a bank account. At the end of 2012, although Wafacash had done its share of consumer studies, the management believed that continuing to conduct focus groups or traditional one-on-one interviews would fail to generate innovative consumer insights. Wafacash commissioned SalesBrain to explore how neuromarketing methods could yield innovative consumer insights to develop and quickly deploy a more effective advertising and communication strategy. We recommended performing a study using voice analysis.

We used voice analysis during 24 in-depth qualitative interviews with customers and noncustomers. The voice analysis software extracted about 20 vocal parameters to identify emotional variables in the interviewee's voice like stress level, cognitive overload, or sadness. Through the use of voice analysis, the bank executive team received a much more objective view on what their customers felt about their services. For instance, the data revealed the presence of many frustrations and annoyances that had been historically misunderstood by Wafacash.

With a better understanding of their customers' feelings, the management was able to quickly create and deploy a new messaging campaign. The campaign was swiftly accepted and successfully launched throughout a network of 600-plus retail sites.

Which Emotions Trigger Decisions?

We experience thousands of emotions. Therefore, it is impossible to report specific emotions because they flicker, and even when they reach our consciousness, our perception is too slow and not discriminate enough to sort and label each feeling. However, some tools like facial decoding software give us the ability to reveal universal emotional expressions like happiness, sadness, surprise, anger, fear, contempt, and disgust, which are mostly triggered below people's level of awareness. Tiny movements created by our facial muscles produce micro-expressions that appear for less than 35 milliseconds. Interestingly, only self-reported negative emotions like disgust or anger tend to correlate with brain data. Negative emotions are felt in our guts and do not require the filter and bias of our cognitive interpretation.

Meanwhile, linking emotions and behavior is tricky. Understanding this critical connection requires that both emotions and behavior be defined and measured properly. Unfortunately, emotions are abstract concepts. There is not a tool ready-made to measure all emotions. For instance, there is no such thing as "an anger thermometer," so to assess anger via a questionnaire, psychologists need to develop a special scale. It is very difficult to do because once you start proposing a scale of a psychological construct, people have differing opinions about what the construct means. Fortunately, neuromarketing studies do not depend on scales or the subjective interpretation of psychological states but, rather, on known and accepted neurophysiological metrics.

Think of how we measure the weight of objects today. People do not argue about the definitions of what is light or heavy. We use standards that have been accepted and used for hundreds of years. Such standards do not exist in traditional marketing research to measure mental states like attention, boredom, engagement, comprehension, memorization, and, of course, *persuasion*. Surveys are entirely dependent on the subjective interpretation people have about the questions. Are you excited by this ad? Are you bored? These are questions that assume all people will understand the same way, leaving no room for the subjective interpretation of a given emotional state. On the other hand, neuromarketing studies scientifically measure emotional states and remove the error provided by the subjective nature of our language and the limiting processing capacity of our consciousness.

Case Study #3: The Effectiveness of Public Health Campaigns. In 2011, I investigated the effectiveness of public service announcements (PSAs) on teenagers and young adults [14]. PSA researchers have mostly relied on subjects' ability to self-report their feelings to assess a campaign's success, a severe limitation considering how emotional messages are known to produce large subconscious effects. My study tested PSAs that varied by tone. Some were positive, carrying an optimistic and humoristic tone. Others were somber and scary. Because recent neuroscientific discoveries suggest that adolescents use distinct brain circuits when processing subconscious affective responses, I predicted that the persuasive effect of emotional messages would vary between age groups. The findings supported my predictions and demonstrated that neurophysiological methods could predict the effects of public health messages targeting adolescents and young adults. Most notably, I showed that negative emotions generated by threatening fear-based messages produce more effect than positive emotions regardless of age.

Which of My Messages Work Better on People's Brains and Why?

Research subjects get quickly confused and overwhelmed by too many direct questions on the multiple ads they are asked to evaluate. For instance, the Likert Scale is commonly used in advertising research. Here is an example: To what extent do you like this ad? Use a scale of five options going from "A lot" to "Not at all" to answer. However, assessing to what extent an ad is funny or sad does not begin to represent the subconscious effect of millions of neurons firing within milliseconds in our brain. Furthermore, conventional studies ask people to express why they like or dislike various aspects of an ad. Those questions are very taxing on people's cognitive energy and rarely produce significant differences between subjects or even between stimuli.

So how good or helpful is your study if you find out that all your subjects feel the same and none of the ads appear to produce different states? I have conducted my share of such studies that yield little if any meaningful differences between subjects or worse, between the ads. Why does that happen so often? It is because we cannot begin to report the impact of the excessive amounts of information processed by different layers in our brain. Only the brain itself can do this complicated and tedious task. However, it is done below our level of awareness. By using neuromarketing tools and interpreting the data with a neuromarketing model like NeuroMap, you can assess how persuasion affects different areas of the brain and reveal meaningful differences between subjects and messages.

Case Study #4: Neurobenchmarking Multiple Ads. A large technology company asked SalesBrain to review several ads that had been airing for the past couple of years. The conventional benchmarking data on how well the ads were performing was inconclusive, so the marketing group who commissioned our study was not clear on which direction to go next. In many cases, the number of variables (tone, color, characters, etc.) involved in many advertising messages makes it impossible to isolate and measure the contribution of each variable using traditional methods. However, our neuromarketing study was able to measure the degree to which each ad was able to hold attention, create arousal, move the audience in pleasant or uncomfortable emotional states, and whether the message created any valuable cognitive engagement. The *NeuroScoring* of each ad did provide an objective way to sort the messages based on how well each activated critical persuasion stages in the audience's brains. As a result, our client was able to gain clarity and confidence on what to do next with the creative direction of a new campaign.

Can Neuromarketing Help Me Better Prove the Unique Value of My Solution?

More and more companies are turning to neuroscience to provide stronger proofs of their value proposition. You too may benefit from using a study that can demonstrate that your product or service produces stronger responses in your customers' brains than your competition does. There are many ways to design experiments that compare how subjects respond to your products, not with words but with brain signals. Consider these situations in which neuroscience can offer valuable proofs to demonstrate the strength of your value proposition.

- A Danish chocolate manufacturer wanted to promote the value of giving chocolates on Valentine's Day. In a creative study, Paul Zak [15] explored the effect of offering chocolate to loved ones while sharing romantic feelings. This experimental condition raised the level of oxytocin of men by nearly 30%.

Similarly, you could also use neuroscience to demonstrate that:

- A brand of spas is more relaxing than another by measuring how specific jets can reduce stress hormones and raise levels of endorphins.

- A noise canceling system can produce more productive office environments by monitoring cognitive effort and distraction while performing various office tasks.

- The design and color of furniture in a store may impact the emotional and cognitive state of shoppers.

Case Study #5: The Impact of Messages Viewed on Mobile. A large technology company whose revenue largely depends on selling ads for mobile platforms wanted to decode the neurophysiological difference between viewing the same ads on a mobile device versus viewing the same content on a TV. The study was focusing on distinct neurophysiological processes that are known to influence overall engagement with any form of content – namely, attention, emotion, and retention. The study objectively measured these neurophysiological states without any conscious reporting from the subjects. It did prove that there were significant differences between the two delivery platforms, some that were favorable to the mobile platform. For more on this study, visit goo.gl/XjXypL.

Can You Get Higher Returns on Advertising Using a Brain-Based Persuasion Model?

With the benefit of both neurodata and a persuasion model like NeuroMap, SalesBrain's clients can optimize how they market, communicate, and sell their products or solutions. They can also provide better advertising briefs to their agencies. By following a scientific discipline to create all their messages, they remove the risk and uncertainty that so many marketing or advertising campaigns carry. I wish I could share here some of the advertising briefs clients have shared with us. Often, advertisers recommend gigantic creative leaps of faith that put enormous amounts of money at risk. In fact, in my 30 years in marketing research, I have not seen one creative brief supported by a scientific persuasion model! Sadly, some advertising agencies are not motivated to embrace neuromarketing because they perceive that a scientific approach may limit their creative options. But why take so many wild guesses when the discipline and rigor of a tested scientific process can improve the success and ROI of your marketing and advertising dollars? Moreover, this is not dependent on the size of your company's budget. In fact, you can apply the quality and value of NeuroMap before you launched your next campaign or deploy a new website right after you have read this book!

ROI of Neuromarketing Approach: A Collection of SalesBrain Customer Testimonials

Reading this book is not worth your time unless the value of what it brings to you is proven and measurable. Therefore, we share here a few of customer testimonials. Some of the companies are large, others are medium size, but all share the same conclusion: The investment of time and money they committed to deploying a neuromarketing discipline paid off!

Note that some of the stories are transcripts of video interviews available at www.salesbrain.com.

Neuromarketing helped us deliver our solution more quickly, and helped our customers make decisions more quickly. When our customers' pains line up with our claims and our customers' gains, you can deliver on that solution. Everybody is speaking the same language, and so you get the consistency in message, you get a consistency of delivery. Neuromarketing and the SalesBrain methodology, if you go in 100%, I mean you have to do it all the way, you will find that your results will significantly improve … and it's not just your revenue, it's not just your productivity. We've had a four times increase in the number of instructors or customers since we've completely converted to neuromarketing. My customers call me back and say, "You make things so easy for me! Love your product! It's so easy!" And when your customers parrot back to you your claims, you know you've won.

Bill Clendenen
CEO, HSI
Health & Safety Training

When – SalesBrain – was able to analyze our customers' pains by using NeuroMap™, that to me was one of the most impressive aspects of the entire process. They knew what questions to ask, they learned our business … which is not an easy business to learn … they came in, learned it, and were able to get information, extract it from the people we need it extracted from. It's marketing efficiency. If you can spend a dollar on marketing and generate 10 dollars in revenue … was it worth it? Absolutely! This has one of those 10 to 1 ratios attached to it in my opinion.

HK Bain
CEO, Digitech Systems
Enterprise Content Management in the Cloud

Backed by hard science that complements excellent market research, Christophe and Patrick use their knowledge to capture your attention in creative and clever ways. Then they show you how to do the same thing with your customers and prospects. Dozens of our companies around the world have seen tangible results from this innovative approach to improving sales.

Pam Hendrickson
COO, Riverside Company
Private Equity

I think every company in America is probably guilty of focusing on what they want to say about their company, rather than focusing on what they need their customers to hear. Neuromarketing has really helped us translate our message, and what we wanted to deliver into something that the customers would want to hear. I was first introduced to neuromarketing in Chicago years ago. I was suspicious, it was the end of the day, and I was ready to move on. I can tell you today in hindsight, that presentation changed my life and our business forever. In 2005, CodeBlue was just a concept in our minds. We have used the Sales-Brain model to build this business ever since we've developed it. And today it now represents the majority of the revenue that our business throws out. For anyone who's really serious about growing their business, you've got to embrace the neuroscientific model of SalesBrain.

Paul Gross
CEO, CodeBlue
Third-Party Insurance Claim Administrator

We get asked quite frequently, "Well, why should we use Forensic Analytical?" What is it that differentiates us? How do we say it? The time we spent, just thinking back for the last 10 years of meetings, and getting other consultants, and people together, just didn't feel right. SalesBrain came around and helped us really pare it down to six words. Right people, right perspective, right now. We've been trying to do this for 10 years! The session was one afternoon, they also did our website. It's clear, simple, and it does exactly what we want it to do. It demonstrates our claims right up front. It's not like we're doing anything new, we're just expressing what we've been doing for 25 years, and we're able to say it very elegantly.

Fred Vinciguerra
CEO, Forensic Analytical
Industrial Hygiene and Environmental Health

The entire process in understanding when you're marketing to the primal brain and understanding the core emotional selling process – I realized that we weren't doing that. That we were selling our product more than we were selling feelings. I really wanted the team to adopt – the pains/claims/gains that SalesBrain talks about. Applying those principles, those core principles into an organization and just really pulling that into every aspect of the marketing that we do, whether it's on the phone, whether it's in a presentation with a big bank. Being able to identify crisply what the pain is that we're solving, and how we solve it, and what the benefits are, and create the opportunity to really close the sale is what's happening for us. People here are energized around what it is that we're doing, because they understand it better now. They understand what we're appealing to in the customers. What it is that your customers need versus the features they need.

Rene Lacerte
CEO, Bill.com
Cloud-Based Accounting Solution

I've been working with SalesBrain for nearly 10 years on refining our story and our customer pitch. Recently, we were up against some companies who are a hundred times bigger than we are. So we brought in the SalesBrain guys to help us put that pitch together and finally deliver it. I don't think we were in the running prior to that presentation. We used videos, we used big pictures, we did a whole mini-drama, which was probably funny. And we won!

Stuart Little
Product Marketing Director, Aviat Networks
Microwave Networking Manufacturer

Airgas turned to SalesBrain to help get the attention of our customers in Hawaii to make a good choice on the distributor for their Safety Fall Protection and Respiratory needs. SalesBrain was able to produce a neuromovie that uniquely captured their attention! They found the right tone and style to do that and the campaign has produced measurable results!

Jason Oshiro
Area Vice President, Airgas
Distributor of Industrial, Medical, Safety Products,
Tools, and Specialty Gases

The work we've done with Dr. Morin and his team has fundamentally changed the way we measure creative efficacy and design. As the race continues to help machines understand our world, Salesbrain remains focused on advancing our understanding of human intelligence and how marketers can effectively connect with people.

Ryan Anthony
Creative Director
Vungle

Neuromarketing hasn't just improved the effectiveness of our marketing, it's made us a better company. We were already aware of the need to translate product features into customer benefits, but we weren't going far enough. Now, we start with a concentrated focus on our customer – their fundamental needs, their pains. It's the difference between really listening to somebody versus just waiting until it's our turn to talk. We believe in the SalesBrain methodology because it works. We win in the marketplace because we bring more value to real people's needs.

Steven Hausman
President/CEO, Triumph Business Capital

To conclude, neuromarketing research can achieve better results by finding answers to critical research questions that do not require the conscious participation of people. These answers help you create messages that remove risk and uncertainty while making your advertising dollars work for your growth and profits.

WHAT TO REMEMBER

- Traditional marketing research methods fail to capture the subconscious mechanisms that affect how people respond to any form of persuasive message.

- Neuromarketing tools collect brain data that can objectively explain critical neurological processes subjects cannot self-report. It provides unique insights about how we understand, feel, engage, and ultimately become persuaded by a message.

- The strategic value of using neuromarketing comes from the possibility of answering critical research questions that have been puzzling marketers, advertisers, and media experts for decades.

- The ROI of neuromarketing dollars is measurable in multiple ways. It will reduce drastic wastes of money spent in creating and deploying messages that don't work. More importantly, it will allow you and your organization to grow faster.

CHAPTER 2

The Neuroscience of Persuasion

I have with me two gods, Persuasion and Compulsion.
– Themistocles, Greek politician 480–479 BC

There are thousands of articles and very thick textbooks discussing how the brain works. Some brain areas are known to host functional specializations, and many have evolved over millions of years. Although the anatomical borders of such key areas are often contested, the existence of three critical systems has been widely discussed for decades. The reptilian complex and the limbic system – both of which form what we call throughout the book the *primal brain* – and the neocortex, the youngest and most "rational" part of our brain.

The purpose of this next section is to present accepted definitions and discuss findings that prove that a neuromarketing model can effectively help you crack the code of persuasion. By now you should have realized that traditional methods by which we continue to assess the effect of sales messages, ads, campaigns, websites and pitches have enormous flaws. People do not have the competency to access and therefore explain what effect messages have considering the speed at which the brain processes information. That is why collecting brain data is necessary to decode why few persuasive messages work and so many fail. Brain data is complex, but a considerable amount of knowledge has been produced over the past few decades on how critical functions influence the processing of marketing or advertising stimuli. It is important to note that experienced neuromarketers have an interest in all the functions, not just a few, that can explain and predict the effect of a message. Be wary of neuromarketing agencies that claim they can explain the effect your messages have on the brain by only measuring the activity of the neocortex (typically measured with an electroencephalogram or EEG) or the autonomic nervous system (commonly measured with galvanic skin response (GSR) or heart rate variability (HRV).

ATTENTION, EMOTIONS, AND DECISIONS IN THE BRAIN

The brain is part of a comprehensive network of organs and their associated nerves that branch out to communicate to our entire body; the brain and its entire network is called the nervous system. The nervous system is responsible for processing, interpreting, and distributing millions of messages that help us sustain life, move, think, reflect, plan, and so much more. We tend to assume that many of our behaviors are guided by consciousness, intention, or free will. Think again! In his book *Consciousness and the Brain*, Stanislas Dehaene reminds us that "in many respects, our mind's subliminal operations exceed its conscious achievements" [16].

There are two anatomical subdivisions of the nervous system that control and monitor the way we react to any stimuli: the *central nervous system* and the *peripheral nervous system* (see Figure 2.1).

The Central Nervous System

The central nervous system includes the brain and the spinal cord. It hosts complex processing functions in multiple layers that have evolved over millions of years. When using a functional magnetic resonance imaging (*f*MRI) scanner, we can record and interpret brain activity that explains how we feel, pay attention, concentrate, understand, plan, remember, and make decisions or movements.

The Peripheral Nervous System

On the other hand, the peripheral nervous system rules over the motor and sensory neurons that are distributed throughout our body. The motor neurons especially respond to either voluntary movements

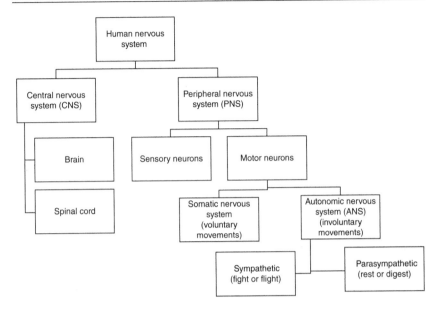

Figure 2.1   The human nervous system.

(somatic nervous system) or involuntary movements (the autonomic nervous system). The autonomic nervous system produces instinctive and emotive neurologic responses and is crucially controlled by older brain layers that are part of the primal brain. Data from the autonomic nervous system can be captured by eye-tracking devices and skin-conductance instruments, as well as from a battery of tools monitoring respiration and heart rates. Together, these recordings produce what is commonly called *biometric data*. Although we can consciously report the effect of some changes in our sympathetic (Figure 2.2) or parasympathetic nervous systems (Figure 2.3), especially in situations where we choose to fight or flight, the onset of millions of other biological responses affecting our blood flow, digestion, respiration, and sweat are largely subconscious. This is where neuromarketing studies surpass (by far) traditional methods of data collection based on self-reports. As neuromarketers, we do not estimate emotions; we measure them. By doing so, we do not compress the timeline of a response either. Instead, we synchronize dozens of neurophysiological variables to build a comprehensive time series from both the primal (oldest, subcortical) and the rational (newest, cortical) brain areas.

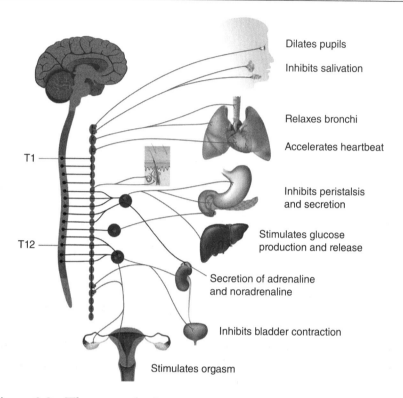

Dilates pupils

Inhibits salivation

Relaxes bronchi

Accelerates heartbeat

Inhibits peristalsis
and secretion

Stimulates glucose
production and release

Secretion of adrenaline
and noradrenaline

Inhibits bladder contraction

Stimulates orgasm

T1

T12

Figure 2.2   The sympathetic nervous system.

So why is the autonomic nervous system so central to our understanding of the biological basis of people's response to persuasive messages? It is central because it is first and foremost under the command of the primal brain. Representing approximately 20% of the mass of the brain, the primal brain constitutes the most ancient section of our nervous system. Many substructures have dedicated neurons and circuits that work on autopilot to regulate survival functions (e.g., respiration, digestion, heart rate, temperature, sweating, and instinctual facial expressions) [17]. Because of the speed at which the autonomic nervous system reacts, it precedes many aspects of our conscious behavior; therefore, the activity of the autonomic nervous system is a good candidate to assess subconscious responses to advertising messages [18, 19]. The best methods to observe changes in the autonomic nervous system include tracking the electrodermal activity, measuring the time interval between heartbeats (heart rate variability,

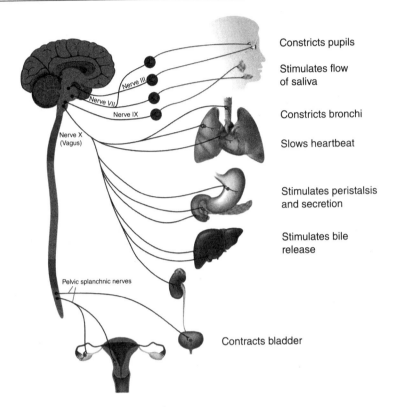

Constricts pupils

Stimulates flow
of saliva

Constricts bronchi

Slows heartbeat

Stimulates peristalsis
and secretion

Stimulates bile
release

Contracts bladder

Figure 2.3   The parasympathetic nervous system.

and recording respiratory sinus arrhythmia, which shows how heart
rate variability is affected by respiration. What matters most about
recording the autonomic nervous system activity is to extract data that
can explain how much both attention and emotions are triggered by a
message. They are the fuel of your message. Therefore, you cannot
become an effective persuader unless you have a good grasp on the
neurobiological nature of how we focus and how we feel when we
respond to persuasive stimuli.

Understanding Attention and the Brain

Attention is brain energy we recruit to process a stimulus. We can
control some of our attention willingly, which is known as *selective or
voluntary attention*. However, we also frequently allow our attention

to process novelty or events that command instant responses which are triggered by the primal brain. For instance, when we move our eyes toward a flashing light in the dark or when we become startled by a sudden loud noise. Also, think about the last time you glanced through the window of a store because a beautiful object caught your attention. This is referred to as *reflexive attention or bottom-up attention*. The speed at which we react correlates highly with the degree to which we control our attention willingly. The higher the speed, the less we control. Because of the voluntary or automatic qualities of attention, different neuronal pathways are at play in the production of higher or lower states of attention.

The idiom *paying attention* says it all. Attention burns valuable oxygen and glucose in the brain, which is why it is both precious and fragile. We often pretend to pay attention because it is socially expected that we do. However, our studies show that marketers always underestimate the amount of brain energy people need to spend to comprehend their messages. In other words, assume that people are not biologically motivated to read your emails, understand your ads, listen to your pitches, browse your website, or remember anything about your selling arguments. That is why the principles we teach you in this book will greatly enhance the probability your message will trigger initial attention, so the primal brain of your audience notices and focuses on your message without thinking about it first.

How can we measure attention in the brain? It is done by recording neurophysiological reactions while people are exposed to a message. That could last for milliseconds, seconds, or minutes. Such reactions generate electrochemical signals that are traveling to thousands of neurons. Neurons are brain cells that initiate and control all forms of activity in the brain. We have 86 billion neurons and over 100 trillion connections (called synapses) between those neurons. Neurons connect with their axons and dendrites (see Figure 2.4). Neurons represent only 20% of brain cells. The balance of the cells are called glial cells and, they support neurons while also playing a crucial role in speeding information transmission.

The process of *synaptic transmission* directly enables neurons to receive, send, and integrate information throughout the entire nervous system (see Figure 2.5).

Human Neuron Anatomy

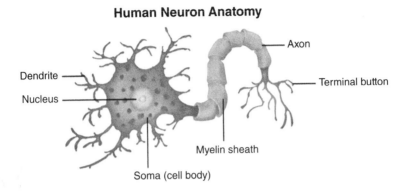

Figure 2.4   Neuron.

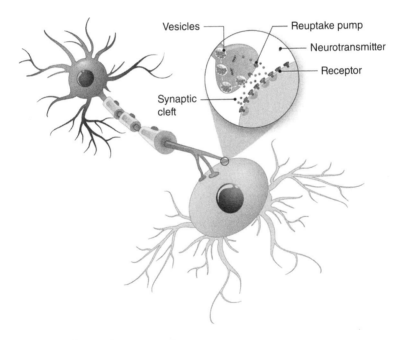

Figure 2.5   Synaptic connection.

There are many types of synaptic connections; some excite neurons, whereas others inhibit them. When a neuron is excited, it is more likely to fire, that is, to send an electrical signal to the neurons with which it is connected. If it is inhibited, it is more likely to stay neutral. Inhibiting neurons does not mean they do not change behaviors though. Both types of synapses enhance or neutralize specific responses generated by the nervous system. Thus, the basis of any movement, action, or decision in the brain is ultimately related to the biological nature of our synaptic connections. Donald Hebb [20] was one of the first psychologists to offer a compelling model of how neurons work. He hypothesized a revolutionary theory with disconcerting simplicity:

> When an axon of neuron A is near enough to excite neuron B and repeatedly or persistently takes part in firing it, some growth process or metabolic change takes place in one or both neurons such that A's efficiency, as one of the cells firing B, is increased. (p. 62)

Hebb's law is often paraphrased by saying, "When neurons fire together, they wire together" and by doing that, they form the basis of neuronal circuitry. Now, remember this law because it will impress your friends! Though Hebb's theory was proposed decades ago, neuroscientists have confirmed the importance of neural networks in all instinctive, affective, and cognitive functions, and especially in the role of attention, emotions, learning, and decision making [21].

Thankfully, the measurement of excitatory (more) or inhibitory (less) signals in our physiology has been possible for decades and is typically done by recording electrodermal activity, which is also called galvanic skin response [22]. Meanwhile, the thalamus (Figure 2.6) is a subcortical region of the brain considered to be highly responsible for how we orient our attention. This structure is also part of the limbic system, a critical brain structure of the primal brain.

In the thalamus, special neurons called *attention-grabbing neurons* are sensitive to visual stimulation and can direct our attention instantly [23]. The visual response is a key component of how attention and emotions affect our brain. In fact, approximately 55% of the cortical surface is dedicated to vision-related processes, which is more than any other sense [24]. Also, an estimated 10% of our optic nerves terminate in a subcortical structure of the primal brain called the *superior colliculus* (see Figure 2.7), confirming that we orient our early visual attention without any consciousness.

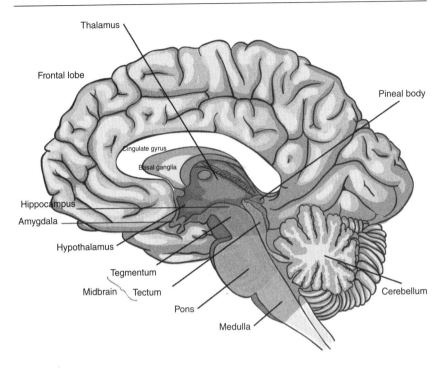

Figure 2.6   Key brain areas.

Understanding Emotions and the Brain

Emotions play a huge role in our day-to-day lives. They create the rhythm of our moods. We feel happy or discouraged because billions of neurons release specific chemical messengers call neurotransmitters that affect our conscious interpretation of our emotional states. In my view, not enough is taught about emotions and their role in guiding our behavior. I would argue that many business books have given a bad reputation to emotions by suggesting that emotions may be in the way of good decisions. I believe that it is the exact opposite.

The word *emotion* comes from the Latin word *movere*, which means to move. Emotions precede a movement and influence the direction of behavior [25]. Long before functional magnetic resonance imaging (*f*MRI) could verify which areas of the brain light up when we experience fear or anger, Darwin and Ekman [26, 27] identified that many of our emotional responses translate into facial expressions

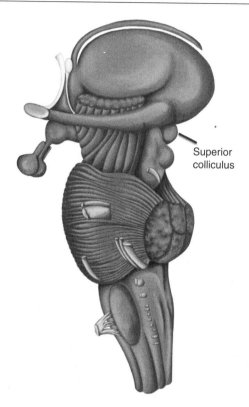

Figure 2.7   Superior colliculus.

that appear instinctual rather than learned. Emotions shape the way we feel about the world and ourselves and they directly influence our decisions. As the neuroscientist, Antonio Damasio said, "We are not thinking machines that feel, we are feeling machines that think" [28]. Recent neurophysiological discoveries show that strong emotional responses generate a powerful mix of neurochemicals that strengthen synaptic connections between neurons; a condition known to influence behavior and to enhance memory marking in the brain [29]. Fundamentally, the biological reason why emotions have such a profound effect on our behavior is that they change our *homeostasis*, a state of physiological balance our brain naturally seeks to maintain. Emotions can raise our heart rate, increase our blood pressure, and disrupt other autonomic functions such as sleep, perspiration, respiration, and even digestion. Likewise, they can help us calm down, become contemplative, relaxed, or joyful.

Primitive life forms found in unicellular organisms such as bacteria typically only worry about *getting closer* to sources of energy like sugar and *moving away* from toxic substances like an acid. Human emotions have evolved from this primary function to get closer to positive stimuli, or further away from negative ones [30]. So, when we experience an emotion, regardless of its strength or valence (i.e., positive or negative), a cocktail of various molecules (neurotransmitters, neuropeptides, and hormones) floods our brain, causing a cascade of neurophysiological changes in our body. Not surprisingly, we have a limited conscious experience of our emotions. The limbic structure (subcortical) is considered largely responsible for mediating our emotional life. Jank Panksepp, a prominent affective neuroscientist, claims that our feelings – the ability to report the effect of emotions on our psychological states – is an unconditional gift of nature rather than an acquired skill [31].

Studies have shown that whereas the amygdala is involved in most emotional situations, other primal brain structures modulate specific emotional responses. For example, the anterior insula, a subcortical area deeply nested in the brain, is responsible for mediating our experience of disgust [32]. Emotions instantly influence how we feel and how we think. To the degree that emotions last, they create moods that are transient psychological states that color how we perceive events. We all can relate to feeling sad or happy for an extended period. Words alone may not easily reveal our underlying emotional patterns. Fortunately, by using neuromarketing tools, we can create a more objective and accurate recording of the affective states that can be associated with a stimulus of interest.

Evolutionary psychologists, as well as cognitive neuroscientists, tend to view emotional response as an adaptive mechanism that has evolved over millions of years to ensure our species could survive in a difficult environment. In his book, *The Expression of the Emotions in Man and Animals* [26], Darwin insisted that emotions are hardwired and produced by the nervous system of all animals. Meanwhile, at a physiological level, the emotional system of an Asian person is not different from one of a White Caucasian. Likewise, there are no significant anatomical differences between the limbic system of an Italian and a French person (though French people would argue otherwise, no doubt!). However, some studies showed cultural differences in the subjective reporting of physiological responses, which confirms that our conscious interpretation of physiological responses is not as reliable as direct measures of the primal brain [33].

Measuring Emotional Neurophysiological Responses from Advertising Stimuli

Numerous scientific studies have now solidly confirmed that changes in emotional states can be traced in our neurophysiology [21, 34–37]. We sweat when we get excited, our pupils get bigger when we are interested, our heart decelerates when we concentrate and our neurons fire when we think. However, reading the peer-reviewed papers describing these neurophysiological changes would quickly give you a headache or, worse, put you to sleep. Fortunately, we have done the challenging work for you, by identifying the most important insights that relate to the effect of emotions on the brain.

In fact, three important constructs can help you assess how emotional messages affect the nervous system: *emotional valence*, *emotional utility*, and *emotional encoding*. These terms are central to how a neuromarketer can measure and optimize the effect of messages on the brain.

Emotional Valence. Valence is the direction of an emotion. Emotions that have positive valence help us approach a stimulus, whereas emotions that have negative valence make us withdraw from a stimulus. Valence is mediated by neurotransmitters, neuropeptides, and hormones, which are brain chemicals responsible for how we experience emotions, such as fear, surprise, or even happiness. Humans experience a range of approximately 5,000 emotions that can all be individually coded on a valence scale [38]. Valence is also explained by the importance of a decision. For instance, choosing a car may impact the valence more than buying a toothbrush. We activate a limited set of emotions on a daily basis, sometimes referred to as primal emotions [39]. Also, research has shown that a limited set of primal emotions produce universal facial expressions [27, 40].

Emotional Utility. Utility is a quick measure of gain or loss calculated by our brain to assess the importance and urgency of a decision. When the brain evaluates the relevance and value of a persuasive message, it quickly computes the likelihood that expected benefits exceed the costs. Although you may not realize this, a sales offer, your brain is busy figuring out if the sum of the benefits that is above the cost you must pay. The net difference is commonly referred to as the utility of that decision [41] or its gain, a critical concept of NeuroMap that is extensively discussed in Chapter 7, Demonstrate the Gain.

More importantly, there are two powerful emotions that affect the *perception of the utility* of any buying decision: the *fear of regret* and the *fear of loss*.

The fear of regret may arise when the outcome of a situation is not what we expect. This happens when you consider the utility of the decision to fall short of your expectations. On the other hand, the feeling of loss appears when we no longer own or control something we value. In fact, Knutson and his colleagues [41] from Stanford produced convincing neuroimaging evidence showing that we use distinct circuits when we expect a gain or a loss. The fear of loss activates the insula (which also fires when we experience disgust) and deactivates the medial prefrontal cortex, whereas the expectation of gain generates more activity in the nucleus accumbens. The nucleus accumbens is a subcortical structure considered part of the basal ganglia, a key component of the reward system controlled by the primal brain. Knudson's research confirmed that, when facing difficult choices, we tend to display loss-avoiding behaviors rather than use rational thinking, a scientific fact that is central to the fundamental tenet of NeuroMap and explains primal brain dominance.

Meanwhile, Hare and his colleagues [42] also revealed that two specific brain areas are involved in computing utility or the gain of a decision: the ventromedial prefrontal cortex and the ventral striatum. The role of the ventral striatum (also a substructure of the basal ganglia) is especially interesting because it is involved in reward learning and novelty decision making. More activity in the ventral striatum also translates in excitation of dopamine-rich neurons located in the brainstem, a key subcortical structure of the primal brain!

Emotional Encoding. Emotional encoding represents the effect a message has on memory, which is often a measure of how a persuasive message ultimately succeeds. Being able to remember an advertisement does correlate positively with the probability of selecting a brand [43, 44]. After all, how can you decide if you do not remember which brand you are supposed to pick and why? The study of how information encoding is performed in the brain has received considerable attention from neuroscientists since the mid-1990s. Though it is still very difficult to crack the neural code of memory in general, it is clear that subcortical areas of the brain such as the hippocampus and the amygdala have an important role in creating and maintaining our long-term memories [32]. This may surprise you, but crucial functions such as remembering our short-term and long-term experiences are largely controlled by the primal brain and without much of your awareness involved.

Also, research conducted by Bogdan Draganski and his colleagues [45] demonstrated that gray matter volume increases as a result of learning, offering scientists more tangible ways to measure the neuroanatomical correlates of emotional marking. How cool is that? The more you store information, the more you create circuits in your brains! In fact, a famous study conducted on London cab drivers [46] confirmed that by having to remember the names and location of London's 25,000 streets, their brains had a larger hippocampus than most people. That is because the hippocampus is responsible for storing and organizing our long-term memory. You can think of your long-term memory as a muscle: the more you work it out, the stronger it will be.

The Neuromarketing Research Matrix

You now understand the research questions that neuromarketing can uniquely answer plus how important it is to collect data from various subdivisions of the nervous system.

Let's put all the conventional marketing research methods in perspective by comparing them to the most popular neuromarketing methods (see Figure 2.8). Except voice analysis, which is not supported by much peer-reviewed research, the other neuromarketing methods listed have all been used and accepted by the research community for quite some time.

Researching advertising stimuli is a probing exercise. You are investigating the underlying causes that can explain how people react. There are multiple levels in this probing journey. The most primal responses are the way we orient our attention and respond emotionally. These responses are mostly controlled by subcortical brain structures that form a system we call the primal brain, one that is operating mostly below our level of consciousness. Meanwhile, the rational brain or cortex is what we use to access higher cognitive functions like reasoning, language, and predictions. A lot of calculations and predictions humans perform are not entirely conscious. For instance, most of the visual processing calculations performed in the visual cortex happen below our level of awareness. However, thanks to the cortex, we do have the ability to observe and report many of our experiences. For

	PRIMAL 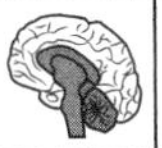	RATIONAL 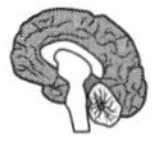	
Probing level	Attention and Emotions	Cognition and Recall	
Measures	Approach or Avoidance Arousal Visual attention	Associations/Intentions/ Beliefs/Attitudes/Awareness/ Memorization Retention/Decisions	
Consciousness level	Subconscious	Subconscious (Implicit)	Conscious (declarative)
Layers voice analysis (LVA)	X		
Biometrics (EDA-HRV-RSA)	X		
Facial decoding	X		
Eye tracking	X	X	X
EEG	X	X	X
fMRI	X	X	
Self-reported data (panel, surveys, interviews)			X

Figure 2.8   Neuromarketing research matrix.

example, we can speak a language and perform critical thinking with awareness and intention. We can also solve math problems, engage in self-reflection, and, more importantly, we can assess risk and formulate predictions.

Activity of the primal brain can be monitored by performing voice analysis, measuring galvanic skin response or EDA, heart rate variability (HRV), Respiratory Sinus Arrhythmia (RSA), tracking eye gaze, decoding facial expressions, frontal lobe dominance (EEG) and recording blood flow changes (fMRI). High-resolution fMRI can also measure early visual processing activity performed in the superior colliculus (SC). Briefly introduced earlier, the superior colliculus is a poorly known yet critical visual processing station that is located at the top of the brainstem; it helps us see without knowing we see before it reaches more evolved cortical areas [37].

Activity of the rational brain can be measured by EEG, fMRI, and eye tracking for the portion of the visual activity that is processed with more intention (consciousness) in the visual cortex. The visual system located in the cortex has at least two dozen distinct regions where neurons perform extensive computation before passing the information to another region. Visual perception is generated first through intuitive and automatic decoding performed in the primal brain below our level of consciousness, whereas visual cognition is only possible with the more specialized neurons of the visual cortex located in a large area at the back of our rational brain.

As a persuasion expert, you need to accept that you cannot fully decode the effect of a message on your customers' brains unless you probe multiple levels of consciousness. The good news is that, with neuromarketing tools, cognitive psychologists and neuroscientists have already defined most neurometrics measuring attention or emotions for over a decade. For instance, we know that subcortical areas drive our attention, and we can use arousal data coming from the conductivity of the skin to measure it. We also know that our emotions produce tiny contractions of our facial muscles that can be detected and decoded in real time. Furthermore, we can measure variations of intensity and frequency of certain brain waves. We can assess cognitive effort from electrical activity and use tested algorithms to predict cognitive engagement. I could easily argue that there are less heated debates between neuromarketers on what we measure than among conventional marketers when they discuss ways to measure attention, emotions, awareness, and engagement.

Indeed, for neuromarketers, the definitions of constructs like attention, emotion, retention are dictated by patterns of neuronal activity, not by words with subjective interpretations that may vary from one research company to another. Moreover, questions that are used in surveys to measure these states require complex cognitive processes that often distort the answers. Considering the critical importance of the subconscious mechanisms that control and influence decisions, it is easy to recognize that self-reported methods offer an incomplete and often inaccurate picture of consumer behavior and buying decisions.

To conclude, the promise that marketers can fully decode the effect of ads by solely engaging in dialogues with an audience is a complete fallacy. That is why polls do not predict elections [47] and between 75% and 95% of all new products fail [48]. Only neuro-marketing methods objectively assess the effect your messages have on the brains of your audience, information that they are not able to share consciously. Meanwhile, you do need to make sure your research considers two brain systems that implicate multiple critical brain structures. Although we do not currently directly measure the activity of many of these substructures, we know that they influence the subconscious and conscious processing of persuasive messages. Figure 2.9 identifies the most critical brain substructures that play a significant role in how our brains process persuasive messages.

Although there are numerous methods by which you can collect brain data, we argue that a competent neuromarketer must combine sensors that probe multiple areas of the brain to decode how persuasion works. At SalesBrain, we use voice analysis, galvanic skin response, facial decoding, EEG and eye tracking to monitor the primal brain activity, and we use again EEG or electroencephalograms to record activity from the rational brain. We have developed proprietary algorithms to score primal and rational activity, as well as one overall score of neuropersuasion called the NeuroMap Score. To collect the raw data, we use a software developed by Imotions. The configuration of the neurolab we use is presented in Figure 2.10.

PRIMAL	RATIONAL
The pons: control of sleep and arousal	**Frontal lobes:** control important cognitive skills such as problem solving, working memory, goal setting, concentration, emotional control, predictions. Often assimilated as a "personality control panel."
The medulla oblongata: regulation of critical survival functions like breathing and heart rate. Houses **the reticular activating system**, which controls sleeps and mediates arousal.	**Parietal lobe:** sensory integration. Contains the primary sensory area where impulses from the skin and touch are interpreted. Is also involved in spatial and mathematical processing functions. Responsible for handwriting and body position.
The cerebellum: mediates automatic movements. **The cingulate gyrus:** involves many autonomic, emotional, and basic cognitive responses, including early forms of language. **The basal ganglia:** supports learning habits and sequence of movements. **The amygdala:** mediates fear and hijacks body to confront or avoid situations. **The hippocampus:** serves to organize and store long-term memories. **The hypothalamus:** directs many responses to keep body in a state of balance. **The thalamus:** relay station for motor and sensory signals between the brainstem and the cortex. **The midbrain:** allows rapid processing of responses to external stimuli.	**Temporal lobes:** include primary auditory cortex. Critical for memory association and formation. 90% of all humans have their language functions hosted in the left temporal lobe. Many structures of the limbic system are located in the temporal lobes. Important structure for processing conceptual representations for semantic knowledge. Also include the fusiform area, which is essential to decode faces and associated expressions.
	Occipital lobe: contains most of the anatomical region of the visual cortex. There are more than 30 distinct cortical visual areas. Simple cells of the primary visual cortex calculate edges while complex cells use the information of simple cells to represent shapes. Visual perception is like an analytic process, with neurons sensitive to colors, others to contours, but an overall visual impression is created to form a coherent representation.

Figure 2.9   Critical substructures of the primal and rational brains.

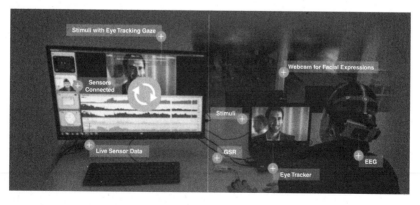

Figure 2.10   SalesBrain neurolab (Imotions)

WHAT TO REMEMBER

- The brain is a complex network of areas that have evolved over millions of years.

- The cognitive functions have appeared relatively recently during our evolution, whereas the neurological circuitry of our most basic survival-centric responses is ancient.

- In the past three decades, numerous studies have clarified how attention and emotions affect us and their dynamic role in influencing our decisions.

- Neuromarketing helps marketers measure neurophysiological activity arising from autonomic and mostly instinctual responses, but also cognitive and emotional activity mediated by the central nervous system.

- Recent research suggests that neuroscientific methods generate valuable insights on the hidden processes that affect the ways messages work on our brains.

- A wide variety of tools are now available to produce data that complement information that is critical to our understanding of consumer behavior, persuasion, and media effect.

- Individually, each method can provide important insights. However, without measuring both the subcortical activity (primal) and the cortical (rational), the interpretation of brain data is inaccurate and ineffective.

- You do not need to be a neuroscientist to understand the critical importance of measuring more than what people can tell you about the effect of your messages. Neuromarketing is designed to help you figure out once and for all what a brain-friendly and persuasive message is.

- Neuromarketing research has helped us develop a convincing theoretical model that you can learn and apply without conducting complicated studies. It is called NeuroMap.

Part II

DECODING PERSUASION THEORY

CHAPTER 3

NeuroMap: A Brain-Based Persuasion Theory

In theory, theory and practice are the same. In practice, they are not.

– Albert Einstein

We have spent almost two decades researching how sales and advertising messages affect our brains. This work led to the creation of NeuroMap, the persuasion model you are about to discover. Persuading is not easy and until recently it was considered more an art than a science. By deconstructing the effect of messages on the brain, we have created a simple, yet scientific model to help you develop and deploy persuasive messages targeting anyone, anywhere and anytime. Using NeuroMap will make all your attempts to persuade more successful and less risky. So how widespread is the use of persuasion models in advertising to begin with? You would expect that companies that spend millions of dollars would always use scientifically based persuasion models to guide the creation of their campaigns. Well, most don't.

Recently, I decided to thoroughly research the effect of public health messages and propaganda campaigns on adolescents [49]. Each year, hundreds of millions of dollars are spent to warn us that smoking is dangerous, drugs can kill, or texting and driving is not just an imprudent behavior but dangerous. What I found (sadly) is that most of the public service announcements (PSA) campaigns do not use persuasion models to guide their creative development process and hardly any use brain-based models. According to a meta-analysis conducted by Whitney Randolph (the only one we can find!), less than one-third of empirical articles on PSA report using any persuasion theory at all [50]. From our experience dealing with many Fortune 500 companies, this trend is not specific to PSA campaigns; it appears to be the norm among most advertising campaigns. I believe that is why such a large majority of advertising campaigns fail. So let's clarify what a persuasion theory is and why it matters to use one to save time and money.

POPULAR PERSUASION THEORIES

A persuasion theory is a model that can explain and predict the probability messages have to influence or convince. Presumably, good persuasion models help creators of messages be more systematic in the way they approach the development of a narrative to convince. Reviewing popular persuasion theories can be confusing. There are several models that have been cited for decades, yet there is little evidence that any are effective. The differences between the most popular models highlight the challenges faced by researchers to deconstruct the critical processes involved in explaining and predicting the effects of persuasion. Although the following brief review explains why there is often confusion and discord among persuasion researchers, it also shows that emerging neurocognitive models offer the best hope for creating and testing radically more powerful advertising messages.

Here are summary descriptions of the most popular persuasion models of the past two decades. You may be familiar with a few of them, but usually, only academics or persuasion researchers have heard of them.

The Elaboration Likelihood Model

Inspired by the cognitive theoretical movement, this model [51] states that a persuasive message will trigger a logical succession of mental processes that engage either a central (cognitive) or peripheral (emotional) route. Both routes represent the levels of thinking performed by recipients to understand the meaning of the information. The central route ensures that the message is considered further (or elaborated), in which case the message has achieved its persuasive intent.

However, if a message is processed by the peripheral route, the effect is predicted to be mild. According to the Elaboration Likelihood Model, a good message is only elaborated if it appeals at a deep and personal level. Advocates of the Elaboration Likelihood Model argue that an effective campaign must include strong proofs to establish the credibility of the claims used in a persuasive message. However, despite its wide popularity, the critical flaw of the Elaboration Likelihood Model is to assert that persuasion is possible if recipients only engage cognitively with the content of a message, a fact that is not supported by NeuroMap and by most neuromarketing research studies of the past decade.

The Psychological Reactance Theory

According to this theory, humans are deeply motivated by the desire to hold themselves accountable and free from other's rules and suggestions [52]. The psychological reactance theory predicts that if people believe that their freedom to choose how they want to conduct their lives is under attack or manipulated, they will experience an ardent desire to react as a way to remove the pressure. Reactance is believed to be at its peak during adolescence because teens have a strong drive toward independence and form beliefs and attitudes that often compete with those recommended by their parents. This model further predicts that explicit persuasive messages trigger more resistance than implicit attempts. Also, Grandpre [53] demonstrated that reactance to persuasive messages increases with age. This may further explain why campaigns invoking the role of parents discussing the dangers of smoking are not effective [54]. The major flaw of the model, however, is the suggestion that persuasive messages are always recognized consciously, a fact that is clearly no longer defendable based on the evidence generated by neuromarketing studies.

The Message Framing Approach

This model is based on the notion that a persuasive message can be framed in two ways: either *a loss* if recipients fail to act/buy or *a gain* if recipients agree to act/buy [55]. Loss-framed messages are typically effective when they raise consciousness on the risks or loss associated with a lack of action. For instance, you may kill people by texting and driving, or you may be financially ruined if your house is destroyed by a fire and you have no insurance. Experiments using this approach have demonstrated that loss-framed messages are better at preventing risky behaviors than changing them, suggesting that the effect may only be short-term [56–58]. Our research also shows that loss-framed messages work better than gain-framed messages because of the role played by the primal brain.

The Limited Capacity Model of Mediated Message Processing

The Limited Capacity Model is another model inspired by the field of cognitive psychology. It provides a conceptual framework based on a series of empirical studies examining the relative effect of message elements on key cognitive functions such as *encoding, storage, retrieval, information processing,* and *limited capacity* [59]. The model suggests that allocation of brain resources may be equally distributed among several cognitive subprocesses leading to inconsistent results in recall and general effect on recipients. Studies using the Limited Capacity Model indicate that adolescents remember more details from public service announcements than college students do and require more speed in narratives to stay engaged. This model did confirm that key cognitive differences exist between adolescents and adults and that these differences may alter the subprocesses involved in processing persuasive campaigns [60]. However, it lacks scientific credibility and is largely ignored by the persuasion scientists today.

Kahneman's Two-Brain Model

The dual processing theory was originally introduced by Stanovich and West [61], and is also known as the System 1 and System 2 theory. It was eventually popularized by Daniel Kahneman through his seminal book *Thinking, Fast and Slow* [62], for which he received the Nobel prize in economics. The tenets of this approach are both simple and profound. Although the research supporting this model was done to study rationality and explain cognitive processes in a multitude of decision-making tasks, the value of the theoretical framework extends

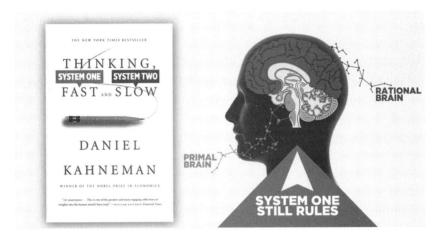

Figure 3.1   Thinking, fast and slow.

far beyond cognitive psychology. In fact, it speaks directly to the nature of human cognitive biases and how they affect our day-to-day choices. For Kahneman, humans regularly access two decision systems that have different if not opposing priorities. System 1 is the most primitive part of the brain. It is automatic, unconscious, and requires low computational resources. System 2 is the newest part of our brain. It is more intentional, needs more consciousness, and has access to more cognitive resources to establish goals and calculate consequences of our decisions. Kahneman argues that System 1 rules over most of our decisions (Figure 3.1).

SALESBRAIN'S MODEL OF PRIMAL DOMINANCE: NEUROMAP

NeuroMap expands the dual system model in profound ways (see Figure 3.2). First, we recognize that even though anatomical borders of each system are the subject of ongoing discord among neuroscientists, they have gained wide acceptance among members of the neuromarketing community. At SalesBrain, we call System 1 the primal brain and System 2 the rational brain, but we consider that the primal brain not only rules our decisions, it dominates the persuasive process. There are key differences between the primal and rational brains we have already introduced but need to reemphasize.

Figure 3.2   The primal and rational brains.
Source: SalesBrain. Copyright 2012–2018.

The primal brain only "lives" in the present because the notion of time is too abstract for a survival-centric brain. Also, it is much older in terms of evolution, but it can process information at remarkable speed because your life depends on it! We are not conscious of what the primal brain does most of the time. For example, we do not think about our breath, even though we can, but for the most part, it just happens. It is all regulated below our level of consciousness. So, the primal brain cannot think much, it certainly does not read, write, or perform arithmetic. It is guided primarily by vigilance, intuition, and senses that guide our short-term actions. Because it is the fastest brain to respond and it oversees our survival, we believe that the primal brain also dominates the persuasive effect. The default processing style of the primal brain is instinctive, intuitive, and preverbal. Unfortunately, most persuasive messages are seeking to motivate people to make long-term decisions and use text to convince; therefore, they are not primal brain friendly!

Meanwhile, the rational brain is much younger, much slower, and does have the capacity to think, read, write, and do complex math to predict, assess risk, and engage in long-term goal setting. The rational brain can travel through time. Although memory is a highly distributed system, critical circuits of the rational brain allow us to file, organize, and retrieve information over a considerable amount of time. With the help of our frontal lobes, we also project a lot of our attention and thinking in the future. In fact, you could argue that few of us truly live in the present because we get lost in our worries of the past or the future. Thankfully, we do have some level of consciousness because of the rational brain; we can reflect on our experiences and even share them with others. That gives us more ability to control the rational brain than the primal brain.

NeuroMap: The Bottom-Up Effect of Persuasion

When we first published our persuasion model in 2002, we suggested that the reptilian complex was the ultimate decision maker. The model was radical, if not controversial. At the time, we did not have as much scientific evidence to support the theory as we do today. Indeed, the research and case studies we have accumulated since 2002 confirm that persuasive messages do not work unless they first influence the primal brain – that is, System 1 [14]. In fact, the primal brain is largely influenced by the reptilian complex, a system composed of the brain-stem and the cerebellum. NeuroMap is based on the dominance of the primal brain over the rational brain. NeuroMap predicts that when a message is friendly to the primal brain, it will quickly radiate to the upper sections of the brain where the information will be elaborated using critical thinking and logic. In short, NeuroMap supports the dual processing model proposed by Kahneman and his argument that System 1 rules, but also provides enhancements that can be directly applied to a persuasion model. Indeed, we have convincingly identified that successful persuasive messages *capture* the primal brain first and *convince* the rational brain second. We call this the *bottom-up effect of persuasion*. Both conditions are necessary for a message to work on the brain! In our view, the reason why so many persuasive messages fail is because they do not trigger the bottom-up effect. Worse, they try to appeal first and foremost to the rational brain.

Here is an example of an ad for an insurance product (Figure 3.3). Because text cannot be processed by the primal brain, it can only be processed by spending much cognitive effort. Because the rational

Figure 3.3   Rational message.

brain does not control the initial flow of cognitive energy, the message will be quickly discarded.

Instead, this next message has far better chance to trigger a primal brain response. As provocative or shocking as this next message may be (Figure 3.4), it does recruit attention and activates the bottom-up effect. We do not really want to think about the value or importance of getting life insurance. However, once reminded that we could die quickly, we do.

Figure 3.4   Primal Brain Friendly message.

Proving the Dominance of the Primal Brain

Here are other ways by which we can quickly demonstrate the ongoing dominance of the primal brain. For instance, try to solve the equation shown in Figure 3.5 quickly: How much is the candy if the cookie costs one dollar more than the candy?

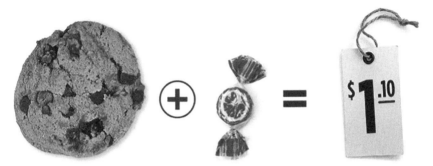

Figure 3.5   Candy equation.

The answer is 5 cents, not 10 cents! It seems so weird that you and over 95% of people we have tested on this question fail to solve a seemingly easy math equation. However, the error can be explained by the dominance of the intuitive and fast nature of the primal brain, which made you jump to the wrong conclusion. Here is another test demonstrating primal dominance (Figure 3.6). Which bet would you favor?

YOU <u>MUST</u> BET

OPTION 1:   50% CHANCE TO WIN $1000

                    50% CHANCE TO WIN $0

OR OPTION 2:   100% CHANCE TO WIN $500

Figure 3.6   Gain maximization bet.

Most people pick option 2, a more attractive positive outcome created by using the number 100%. This option "frames" a perception of choosing the option with the highest probability of gain, even though both options have the same mathematical gain expectancy.

However, notice how you feel about the next two options now. Which one would you pick (Figure 3.7)?

YOU <u>MUST</u> BET

OPTION 1:   **50% CHANCE TO LOSE $1000**
                 50% CHANCE TO LOSE $0

OR OPTION 2:   **100% CHANCE TO LOSE $500**

Figure 3.7   Loss-avoidance bet.

You probably picked 1, and you most likely did so faster than when you evaluated the two options of the first bet. Option 2 frames the perception that you will lose $500 for sure, whereas option 1 creates the perception that you may still have a chance not to lose anything at all. When facing such options, the primal brain instantly activates a loss-avoidance bias, a bias that is central to most of our buying decisions.

The loss-aversion bias was first discovered by Kahneman and Tversky. In fact, some researchers even quantified the loss-aversion bias at 2.3 times the value of winning. This means that if you lose $1, it takes winning $2.3 to offset it. Note that this explains why it is always hard to sell something: the negative emotion your customers will experience to pay $1 for anything can only be overcome by the positive emotion generated by receiving something they would perceive as being worth at least $2.3. This also explains why offering a 50% discount is so effective: it compensates for the 2.3 loss aversion bias. Meanwhile, many other so-called cognitive biases can be explained by NeuroMap.

Cognitive Biases Explained by NeuroMap. A cognitive bias can be defined as a predictable pattern of deviation from logical reasoning. Cognitive biases prevent us from making systemic and completely rational decisions. Psychologists have studied the nature of these biases for centuries, and most recently Buster Benson, a software engineer with a passion for decoding human behavior proposed an interesting nomenclature of *188 such biases* [63]. Many social biases, for instance, preserve our self-esteem and stem from our ego-centrism [64–66]. A full discussion of this topic is beyond the scope of the book. However, we believe that many of these biases can be explained by the dominance of the primal brain over the rational brain: if all our behaviors were rational, these biases would not exist.

Error Management Theory and Cognitive Biases

Psychologists Martie Haselton and Danie Nettle [67] proposed a very powerful model to integrate most cognitive biases based on the theory of evolution called the error management theory (EMT). According to EMT, we collectively suffer from "paranoid optimism" a dynamic tension that pushes us on one end to "play safe" and on another to "seek risk." The paradoxical nature of this tension is a function of our drive to survive. For instance, men tend to overestimate how much women desire them. Haselton and Nettle argue that this tendency may have been reinforced over thousands of years to increase the number of sexual opportunities, and therefore increase the number of children from one pool of genes. They also argue that decision-making adaptations have evolved to make us "commit predictable errors." They posit that EMT predicts that human psychology contains evolved "decision rules that are biased toward committing one type of error over another."

NeuroMap can also explain and predict the same biases. The dominance of the primal brain is crucial during events that compromise our survival. In the absence of enough cognitive energy and the required need to act quickly, we activate programs that minimize risk. Now let's go back to the tendency to be overly optimistic. This does not easily reconcile with the drive to avoid risk. For instance, people tend to be overly optimistic about health problems they face [68]. In that case, EMT states that we have more sensitivity to harms that may arise from external sources (others) than harms that can come from internal sources (us). This suggests that we have different biases based on the origin of the risk. Once again, this is predicted by NeuroMap. External threats are urgent for the primal brain to process and trigger our instinctive response to avoid risk and uncertainty. However, internal threats are typically more complex to assess and therefore are more likely to engage cognitive resources from the rational brain, which may be more naturally inclined toward optimism and hope. Haselton and Nettle call this phenomena "paranoid optimism." They observe that we appear fear-centered about the environment (primal) but optimistic about the self (rational).

Top Cognitive Biases

We summarize next some of the top cognitive biases that have been popularized by successful thought leaders and authors like Malcom Gladwell, Dan Ariely, and Buster Benson.

The Bias of Thin-slicing

Malcolm Gladwell's book *Blink: The Power of Thinking Without Thinking* [69] tells curious stories in which people make seemingly absurd decisions using a limited amount of information. He calls this bias "thin-slicing" and draws examples from a wide range of situations involving scientists, doctors, executives, art experts, and more. In all these cases, logic and rationality are missing. Choices are made in the "blink of an eye" even though they may involve smart and educated decision makers. Although Gladwell does not investigate the neuroscience of "thin-slicing," NeuroMap can explain many of the situations he describes. For instance, in the presence of too much information, the primal brain takes over while the rational brain stalls. Furthermore, when our primal brain dominates plenty of emotional factors influence our decisions beyond our level of consciousness. Although there are clear benefits from allowing the primal brain to control an enormous number of our decisions, it can lead us to make very bad choices. Remember the example of trying to find how much the candy was worth? Your primal brain took over, and most likely you did not get the right answer!

Another important book discussing the faulty nature of many of our decisions is *Predictably Irrational* by Daniel Ariely [70]. The book presents several cognitive biases that affect many of our decisions, basically because the primal brain controls the process below our level of awareness. Following are a few cognitive biases.

The Bias of Relativity

To decide, we need to be able to contrast options that appear radically different. By offering two options that are about the same, and a third that is radically different, most people will choose the third. The primal brain is wired to make quick decisions, and contrast allows that level of efficiency. When we easily compare and contrast options, we are allowing the dominance of the primal brain to rule our choices.

The Bias of Anchoring

Our first decisions may considerably influence the rest of the decisions we make regarding the same product or solution. This suggests that we are wired to repeat decisions we find satisfying. That is why habits are so addictive. We argue the reason we do that is because the primal brain wants to reduce cognitive effort by retrieving old patterns of behavior. It also explains why it is so difficult to change our behavior in general or shift to another brand of toothpaste!

The Bias of Zero Cost

We always prefer *free* options over *fee* options because we perceive that there is no risk when the item has no price. According to Ariely, the reason free shipping offers are so effective is that it lifts the objection of adding any cost on top of the price of an item. In fact, the zero-cost bias reflects the loss-avoidance bias of the primal brain. It is not logical and rational to wait in line for a free ice cream, yet thousands of people do it because they are under the dominance of their primal brain, which seeks instant gratification!

The Bias of Social Norms

We act based on what is expected of our community of reference (social norm), and this may influence the way we respond to market offers. If the offer is aligned with the social norm, we accept the offer. If it is not, we reject it. What this explains is that incongruence between our primal brain (compliance reduces risk or regret) and the rational brain (evaluation of a market offer) disrupts the bottom-up effect. NeuroMap predicts that for messages/offers to work, they must stimulate both the primal and the rational brains.

The Bias of Multiplying Options

According to Ariely, we pretend that we prefer more options than fewer. Paradoxically, to survive, we are better off reviewing a limited number of options. We will discuss this bias when we elaborate on *contrastable* as a persuasion stimulus later in this chapter. We argue that the primal brain hates too many choices. The rational brain does not mind going through an extensive evaluation process, but it may delay decisions in the process. This creates a paradox in many of our decisions. We tend to say we want options, but at a deeper level, we do not want to face the cognitive burden of choosing among many. NeuroMap posits that a persuasive message can trigger decisions when it asserts that there is only *one* good decision: the one you suggest!

The Bias of Expectations

What we expect influences our behavior. This bias is the direct consequence of the dominance of the primal brain over the rational brain. What we want is known to emerge in primal subcortical areas of the brain. What we want shapes what we expect, and what we expect does overrule what we logically and rationally report we need.

The Cognitive Bias Codex

Completing an inventory of the most common cognitive biases is challenging. Academics have not agreed on key definitions, so the topic remains the subject of heated debates. In 2016, however, Buster Benson, a software engineer with a passion for decoding human behavior proposed an interesting nomenclature of 188 biases [63]. The result of his work is one visual you can see in Figure 3.8. The picture does not do it justice, so I recommend you visit the website, which you can easily find by searching Cognitive Bias Codex.

Even though Benson's work is arguably exploratory in nature, we find it impressive. More important, NeuroMap can explain and predict all categories of the cognitive biases that are identified by the model. They are as follows:

Too much information: The dominance of the primal brain is based on survival priorities that are deeply anchored in our biology. Cognition came later. We are not wired to process a lot of information, spend ample time finding patterns, or agonize over decisions. Too much information freezes the primal brain.

Not enough meaning: Our primal brain does not have the cognitive resources to compute and resolve complex arrays of data. If the pattern of a situation is completely new, and not urgent or relevant, the primal brain will not be able to retrieve a previously stored set of commands that would accelerate the processing of the information. We love cognitive fluency because it conserves valuable energy.

Not enough time: Time is directly related to how much energy the brain needs to process information. In the primal brain, faster is always better. Therefore, situations that require time do not appeal to our older brain structures and receive low priority.

Not enough memory: Our brain is not designed to store much information. The reason is simple. Encoding is costly, because of the energy required to store but also to maintain and retrieve our memories. Recent research demonstrates that memorizing attaches specific neurons to our memories. In fact, by using light to stimulate nerve connections, Dr. Malinow and his team successfully removed and reactivated memories by stimulating synapses in rats' brains [71]. This only proves further that the brain welcomes situations or events that make it easy to hold information in working memory and not highly dependent on long-term encoding. The primal brain favors such conditions over others.

To conclude, NeuroMap provides a simple yet practical model for developing and deploying persuasive messages: it helps you consider cognitive biases by following a linear creative development process.

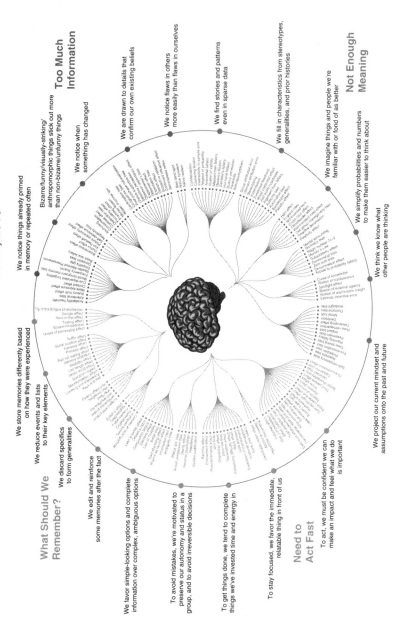

Figure 3.8   Cognitive Bias Codex.
Source: Used by permission from Buster Benson.

It is designed as a sequence of steps to maximize the impact of your persuasive arguments. Igniting the primal brain requires using only six stimuli in the brain. The six stimuli will provide you with simple guidelines for the creation of any persuasive message. The value of the six stimuli model is now supported by nearly 20 years of scientific and empirical evidence.

WHAT TO REMEMBER

- Persuasion has been studied for decades, but old models have ignored for too long the dramatic role played by subconscious brain structures.

- Persuasion is a bottom-up effect between two main brain systems named the primal and rational brains.

- NeuroMap shows that persuasive messages do not work unless they first and foremost influence the bottom section of the brain – the primal brain, which reacts to emotional, visual, and tangible stimuli (see Chapter 4) and can amplify or abort any persuasive attempt.

- Once a message has "engaged" the primal brain, persuasion radiates to the upper section of the brain where we tend to process the information more sequentially and confirm decisions in the frontal lobes.

- Most of the 188 cognitive biases can be easily explained and predicted by NeuroMap.

CHAPTER **4**

Applying Six Stimuli to Persuade the Primal Brain

> *Some balance of the emotional and rational systems is needed,*
> *and that balance may already be optimized by natural selection in*
> *human brains.*
> — David Eagleman, neuroscientist and author

We learned in Chapter 3 that persuasion can be explained and predicted from the quality of messages that appeal to the primal brain. Table 4.1 will help you make the transition from the science of NeuroMap to its practical application. Although we recognize the value of identifying 188 cognitive biases [63], we believe there is a limited number of meta-biases (biases above other biases) that can explain and predict why we are so irrational in our choices. We have identified six primal meta-biases that mediate the way persuasive messages work on the brain. These meta-biases can all be explained by the dominance of the primal brain. The term *stimulus* means a detectable change in the environment that will elicit a predictable response from the primal brain of your audience. We suggest that, together, the six stimuli (Figure 4.1) work as a system of communication you can use to influence the primal brain.

That is why we call it a language. This analogy is important because it points to the value of using *all* six stimuli to maximize the persuasive power of your messages. After all, when you learn to speak a foreign language, using just verbs will not take you far in a conversation.

Table 4.1   Primal biases.

Primal Stimulus	Primal Bias	Primal Goal
Personal	To survive	Protect from threats
Contrastable	To speed up	Accelerate decisions
Tangible	To simplify	Reduce cognitive effort
Memorable	To store less	Remember limited information
Visual	To see	Rely on the dominant sensory channel
Emotional	To sense	Let neurochemicals guide action

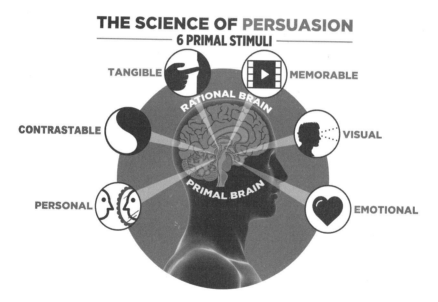

Figure 4.1   Six stimuli.

Another way to understand NeuroMap is to consider the six stimuli as a creative checklist that has already been used successfully by thousands of persuaders over the past 16 years.

Now, let's explore each stimulus in more details.

PERSONAL

PERSONAL

"Let's try to teach generosity and altruism, because we are born selfish."
– Richard Dawkins, Evolutionary biologist and author of
The Selfish Gene

The first stimulus to activate the primal brain is to make sure your message centers fully on the person or group you are trying to persuade. Because the primal brain is driven to help us survive, humans are fundamentally wired to be self-centered and to attend first to what affects us personally. Jaak Panksepp, a neurobiologist who has studied the emotions of animals extensively, argues that "the utility of selfishness has promoted the evolution of many self-serving behaviors" [39].

The primal brain evolved over millions of years. As such, it still rules our most primitive, survival-centric behavior. The primal brain is the oldest structure of our nervous system, and some parts are believed to be nearly 500 million years old. Although the primal brain is ancient and rather small (about 20% of the mass of the entire brain), it remains largely in control of all the functions that are critical to our life like respiration, digestion, and automated motor commands – essentially all the functions that are regulated by the autonomic nervous system. The primal brain also produces a multitude of key neurotransmitters like serotonin, dopamine, and norepinephrine, all part of a special group of molecules called monoamines. Monoamines are chemical messengers that form the basis of how networks of neurons fire and wire during brain activity. Because they influence so many affective responses, they have been intensively studied for decades. Each neurotransmitter has its complex network linking older regions of the brain (primal) with newer ones (rational).

In a brilliant paper discussing how hard-wired selfishness and altruism crosses, evolutionary psychologist Gerald Cory [72] suggests the existence of a dominant "self-preservation" program that can explain our tendency to seek power, attack, and express less empathy for others. His approach is inspired by the triune theory of Paul McLean [73]. Although many neuroscientists contest the triune theory, it has the merit of suggesting the existence of three main brain structures that evolved over a considerable amount of time. McLean first coined the term *reptilian complex* to describe the function of a group of brain structures that is mostly involved in regulating critical survival functions like breathing, eating, and sexual reproduction. He suggested that the limbic system, which hosts many important networks involved in emotional processing, developed when the earliest mammals appeared and, therefore, called it the *paleomammalian complex*. Finally, McLean observed that the uppermost layer of the brain, which enables the highest cognitive abilities like thinking, planning, predicting is found in all mammals' brains but, more importantly, is especially large in the human brain. He called that layer the *neomammalian complex*.

The reason that the McLean model has been largely abandoned is that we know now that older brain structures like the basal ganglia (considered part of the limbic system) are not only found in reptiles but also in the earliest jawed fish. We also know that the earliest mammals had neocortices and presumably some ability to use higher cognitive functions as well. Finally, and more importantly, the three layers do not operate independently from each other. However, taking all that into account, the evolutionary nature of our brain development is a biological reality that was well-captured by the McLean model, and it is continuing to influence important psychological theories such as the Triune Ethics Model.

The Triune Ethics Model

Davide Narvaez [74] developed a theory of ethics based on the McLean model, which is appropriately labeled the Triune Ethics Theory. It is a psychological theory based on the neurobiological roots of our multiple moralities. The Triune Ethics Theory suggests that there are three types of moral orientations that have evolved over millions of years: the ethic of security, the ethic of engagement, and the ethic of imagination. The ethic of security is based on the critical urgency of attending to any threat and is driven by the dominance of primitive systems hardwired into our primal brain. Therefore, fear and anger urge us to feel safe and practice self-centeredness. Narvaez confirms that the primal brain is very self-focused. It seeks routines and avoids novelty, a view that explains the importance of making messages *personal* to grab attention. Gerald Cory, another acclaimed psychologist who spent his lifetime investigating the role of evolution also asserts that we are under the influence of critical survival and emotional forces that we cannot consciously control [75]. He further states that from "the predominantly survival-centered promptings of the ancestral protoreptilian tissues, as elaborated in the human brain, arise the motivational source for egoistic, surviving, self-interested subjective experience and behaviors."

Meanwhile, this discussion on personal would not be complete unless we highlight the seminal contribution of Freud to the topic of ego dominance in our daily behavior.

Freud's Psychoanalytical Model

For Sigmund Freud [76], the basic nature of humans was instinctual (primal), largely controlled by innate forces that act below our level of consciousness. He established that our core instincts are sexuality and aggression. Instincts are automatically activated when we experience an unpleasant tension. In his psychoanalytical model, the sexual instinct ranges from pure erotic pleasure to satisfying thirst or hunger, whereas the instinct of aggression refers to the destructive need to return to a state of nonexistence, a concept that he simply labeled the *death instinct*. According to Freud, drive reduction brings the body back into a natural state of homeostasis.

For Freud, the price we pay to live in a civilized society is to feel and hold a permanent psychological tension [77]. According to him, all behavior has underlying psychological causes, an idea that he called psychic determinism. He proposed a structural model of personality based on our ability to manage our psychic energy, which consisted of the *id*, the *ego*, and the *superego* [78] (Figure 4.2).

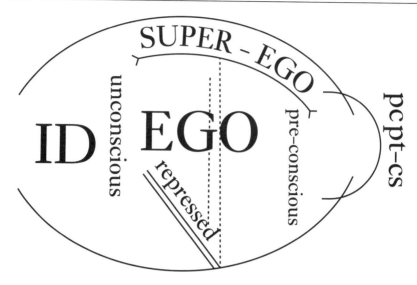

Figure 4.2   The id, the ego and super ego (1933 Illustration by Freud).

The id is present at birth and is entirely unconscious during our entire lifetime. It controls the total supply of our psychic energy and transforms basic biological drives into *pain avoiding* psychological tensions. The id is also called the primary process and can be described as the biological component of personality. We would argue that the influence exerted by the id reflects the dominance of the primal brain on our behavior. The ego develops out of the id by the time a child is eight months old. In Freud's terms, the ego is "a kind of facade of the id, like an external, cortical, layer of it."

Even though the model presented by Freud is over 100 years old, it is still regarded by many psychologists and psychiatrists as the most important building block to understanding human behavior. It focuses on the predominant role of the unconscious, what we consider to be the direct influence of the primal brain. Since Freud was a highly regarded neuroscientist during his time, it is not completely surprising that even contemporary neuroscientists have taken a special interest in his model. In 2008, Mark Solms conducted an interview for the magazine Mind in which he discussed Freud with Erik Kandel of Columbia University [79] (2000 Nobel laureate in physiology), who confirmed that one of Freud's biggest contributions is the suggestion that the same unconscious mechanisms are at play in a healthy mind as they are with someone struggling with a mental disorder. Kandel also claimed that psychoanalysis is "still the most coherent and intellectually satisfying view of the mind" [80]. Like Kandel, Mark Solms also believes it is possible to link specific brain areas to the three components of personality defined by Freud: the id, the ego, and superego. The instinctual id maps nicely to the primal brain, whereas the emotional ego is best associated with the higher limbic structures and the posterior sensory-centric part of the cortex (both considered part of the rational brain).

Although many of us struggle with the idea that selfishness may drive so much of our behavior and is one of the key drivers of our decisions, for Richard Dawkins [81], the most plausible answer to this puzzling question is in our genes. In his famous book *The Selfish Gene*, Dawkins convincingly presented a gene-centered view of evolution that has continued to rock the scientific community since the book was first published over 40 years ago. Dawkins wrote, "genes are in a sense immortal...our basic expectation by the orthodox, neo-Darwinian theory of evolution is that genes will be selfish."

Applying the Personal Stimulus to Persuasive Messages

There are two ways to make your message more personal and, in doing so, more persuasive:

Focus on Your Audience First. Make sure you put your audience, prospect, or listeners at the center of the message. So many ads or presentations forget this simple rule. Admit it: Have you not ever started a presentation by saying, "Good morning, ladies and gentlemen. Today I would like to tell you about *our* company, *our* values, *our* mission statement, *our* technology..."? The image in Figure 4.3 is indicative of just how interested and excited the primal brains of your audience will be while listening to your introduction.

In a matter of a few seconds, you only prove that you have no intention of putting your audience at the center of the story because it is all about *you* instead of *them*!

Figure 4.3   Man sleeping during pitch.

According to Kahneman [82], we experience 20,000 psychological "present" moments per day, each three seconds long. Since the primal brain craves input that is personal, a substantial portion of these moments is spent thinking about us!

Focus on a Pain That Is Relevant to Your Audience. Our primal brain seeks to protect us. Therefore, in your attempts to persuade, highlight, if not magnify, a threat, a risk, or a pitfall that your solution can solve. As a result, you will command immediate attention. Too often, messages focus on the solution (business centered) and not the problem (personal). NeuroMap suggests that before offering a solution, you need to remind your audience of a pain they have experienced or do not want to face. This is not to manipulate or create undue stress. It is simply to recognize that the primal brain will not dedicate energy unless your message is both urgent and relevant to the person you are trying to engage.

The Neuroscience of Personal

Since there are no studies testing the neurophysiological effect of making a message more personal, we decided to create our own. We recruited 30 participants, half males, half females with an average

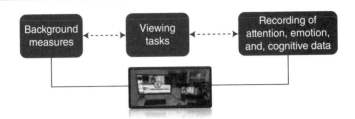

Figure 4.4   SalesBrain's neuro study.

age of 33 years old. We collected data from their skin (GSR), their hearts (ECG), their faces (facial coding), their cortex (EEG), and their eyes (eye tracking). The neurophysiological variables helped us measure how much each persuasive stimulus (a total of 12) sustained visual attention, triggered emotions, produced cognitive effort, cognitive distraction, and cognitive engagement. The experimental design is presented in Figure 4.4.

For personal, we tested the following research question:

Can making an ad more personal improve its persuasive effect on the primal brain?

We used the following advertising stimuli to test our hypothesis:

- Video footage of people flying a wing suit. The video was filmed from two perspectives:

    - Personal (objective) perspective: watching this footage makes the viewer see the landscape as if he/she was flying in a wing suit.

    - Impersonal (subjective) perspective: viewer is observing others jump and fly in a wing suit.

- Fishing Print Ads

    - A first ad featured a fishing boat and promoted business-centric claims, like the boat is safe, comfortable, and so forth.

    - A second ad featured someone catching a big fish and highlighted customer-centric claims like the joy of bringing a fish home.

The results supported the hypothesis:

- The personal video segments making the viewer experience flying in a wing suit triggered much more attention (+14%) and more emotional arousal (+25%), as well as more negative emotions (+143%) than the video segments giving a more impersonal experience of the flight.

- The ad featuring someone catching a fish triggered much more attention (+39%), far more arousal (+520%), more positive emotions as well as more cognitive engagement (+52%) than the ad focusing on the fishing boat. It also captured more visual attention in critical areas of interest.

Personal Neuroinsights: Raise the impact on the primal brain by making your message personal. When putting your customers at the center of the narrative, you can quickly transport your audience in the story of your value proposition.

What to Remember About Personal

- We are wired to be selfish.
- Perceiving something as personal makes us proactively scan our environment for what is relevant and urgent to us.
- If you cannot magnify a pain that matters to the members of your audience, you will not grab their attention.

CONTRASTABLE

CONTRASTABLE

"We are so constituted that we can gain intense pleasure only from the contrast, and only very little from the condition itself."

– Sigmund Freud, neurologist *and founder of psychoanalysis*

The priority of the primal brain is to accelerate decisions, and we do that best when we have limited options. This points to an important paradox in consumer behavior: customers tend to tell you they want lots of brand options, even though they *subconsciously* resist using valuable energy to evaluate and sort the best ones. I did not discover this paradox by practicing conventional marketing. Rather, I detected this puzzling contradiction nearly 20 years ago by observing shoppers in grocery stores. At the time, I was the vice president of marketing of a grocery chain called Grocery Outlet. Grocery Outlet sold top brands at bargain prices in 12 US states. Our products' variety was somewhat limited given the nature of our retail concept, so I wanted to know if we could increase our sales by adding additional brands for certain categories of products. I conducted focus groups, and sure enough, when I asked customers if they wanted more choices, they always *said* yes. However, when I observed them shopping in the stores, they systematically froze in front of too many possible choices. When faced with too many options that were not immediately *contrastable* with one another, customers were unable to quickly and easily differentiate among assorted brands. This explained why our category sales did not move quickly when we added brands. Customers were overwhelmed by being in front of so many options.

That is the paradox of choice. It is also the title of an excellent book by Dr. Barry Schwartz [83], in which Schwartz demonstrates that we do not get happier from getting more choices, and therefore we subconsciously seek to have fewer options. Even though we may complain when we have limited choice, this response is a function of the thinking routine of our rational brain. After all, it is logical to assume that in the presence of more choices, we have a greater probability of finding what we want. However, since the primal brain dominates our decision-making process, we want to avoid *at all cost* the time, energy, and risk of a lengthy decision cycle, which is what more choices will bring.

Schwartz's book cites many studies proving the bias for our preference to have limited choices. For instance, a study performed in a gourmet store featuring 24 varieties of jam in one experimental condition and only six in another demonstrated that presenting fewer varieties could increase sales tenfold [84]. Meanwhile, according to renowned Yale medical doctor Jay Katz [85], we choose to outsource many of our decisions in order to escape the burden of making decisions, even when our lives are at stake. According to Katz's research, a majority of patients prefer others to make decisions about their care, rather than making their own choices. We recommend the contrastable stimulus to push customers toward a simple and obvious choice: the best solution to their pain!

The Use of Contrastable Offers in Comparative Advertising

The most common use of contrastable in advertising is *comparative advertising*, where one brand compares itself to another. There are many research papers on the effect of comparative advertising, but few make any reference to consumer neuroscience and none provide a brain-based interpretation of its results. According to Professor Fred Beard, a general conclusion we can draw, though, is that comparative advertising works! – especially for "products of high quality," where claims are well substantiated and focused on salient benefits that are believable [86]. Beard explains that comparative advertising works especially well for companies that have a smaller market share. This makes perfect sense! How can you convince anyone to buy your product unless you do the challenging work of finding what your unique differentiators are first?

Although infomercials have a less than positive reputation because consumers often say they do not like them, this unique format of advertising has a remarkable effect on us. Infomercials work on the primal brain because they use customer stories to present evidence of a sharp before-and-after contrast. For instance, they typically feature individuals with serious problems (such as being overweight or having acne) who went through a radical transformation thanks to a "miraculous" product. There are very few studies on the effect of infomercials because formats and products vary greatly. However, one experiment conducted by a group of researchers from Southern Illinois University [87] managed to provide clarity on why infomercials work so well. They decided to create messages formatted in three ways: an advertising (aspirational) message, an infomercial, and a direct experience. The researchers hypothesized that the level of credibility gained by viewing or experiencing these three different formats would follow a continuum from low credibility (advertising message), to medium credibility (infomercial) to the highest credibility (direct product experience). Presumably, direct experience would have the highest level of credibility because people tend to believe and remember more what they do than what they see. The results support what we would predict with NeuroMap. The superiority of infomercials over regular television ads was striking. In fact, infomercials' scores placed them very close to the direct experience format. Furthermore, the more infomercials used contrast between the pain of the products they solved and the solution, the more effective they were. The contrastable stimulus acts as a catalyst for consumer decisions, and if the success stories shared are credible, it pushes the primal brain to decide in seconds.

Applying Contrastable to Persuasive Messages?

There are easy and practical ways to make your message more contrastable: increase the saliency or prominence of your benefits and compare them against other brands or, if you don't have competition, compare them to the losses of not buying your solution at all.

Find the Salient Benefits of Your Solution. The primal brain will not accept the burden of making complicated decisions. Too often, sales messages spew a list of reasons that customers should consider a solution. However, these reasons do little to motivate the primal brain to commit the energy required to consider them all. Therefore, you need to distill a limited number of benefits, and then demonstrate that no other brand or company can deliver a solution that is as unique and as effective as yours. Later in this book, we will elaborate further on how you can find your claims. Claims represent the compact list of the top benefits you offer. They can accelerate the decision and create contrastable situations that make immediate sense for the primal brain. Typically, claims will provide direct solutions to pains and grab attention to make your message completely relevant to an urgent threat or risk that your audience faces. Once you magnify a pain and show how your solution can solve it, customers will beg to buy your solution. As David Ogilvy famously suggested, selling is easy: "Just light a fire under people's chairs, and then present the extinguisher!"

Compare Your Solution to a Competitor. Contrasting your product or solution with that of a competitor is a good strategy. "Before and after" stories can do that as well. Show the life of one of your customers before they own your product or solution – it should be painful to see! – and then show the relief of their pain as the contrast. This scenario is the typical story that you see in an infomercial and for a good reason: it works!

The Neuroscience of Contrastable

For contrastable, we tested the following research question:

By comparing two products, two services or two situations, can we raise the persuasive impact on the primal brain?

We used the following advertising stimuli to test our hypothesis:

- Video advertisement for a dental discount card
    - One ad featured customers of a dental-care plan but did not show any form of contrast between "before" becoming a member and "after."
    - One ad featured a short story of two people who had to face the urgent need for dental care. One had a discount plan, the other did not.
- Weight-Loss-Supplement Print Ads
    - Two ads featured a man who lost 39 pounds using a leading weight loss supplement.
        - The first ad showed a man who had already lost the weight and showed the product.
        - The second ad showed a man who had lost the weight but also showed a picture of him before he lost weight.

The results supported our hypothesis:

- For the dental discount card ads, the ad featuring the contrast between before and after scored much higher on the primal brain than the other ad (+119% on the NeuroMap score)

- For the weight loss supplement ads, using a contrastable picture drew 38% more attention than the other one. It also produced less distraction and less cognitive effort.

Contrastable Neuroinsights: By making your ads more contrastable, you can raise the impact on the primal brain. Using contrast will also reduce cognitive effort by easing the choice customers need to make.

What to Remember About Contrastable

- Despite what we say, we do not like multiple buying options because it overwhelms our primal inclination to decide quickly and to do so with the least amount of brain energy.

- Comparing two situations makes decisions easy for the primal brain.

- Rather than stating: "Choose us because we are one of the leading companies in the XYZ industry," highlight only a few unique benefits (claims).

- Contrast stories of before and after, or your brand against the competition, to help your customers decide.

TANGIBLE

"It is hard to explain just how a single sight of a tangible object with measurable dimensions could so shake and change a man."

– H. P. Lovecraft, American author

TANGIBLE

Making something *tangible* means to achieve simplicity and minimize the cognitive energy necessary to process your message.

The primal brain does not have the cognitive resources offered by the rational brain, yet it dominates the initial review process of any persuasive message.

Our Brain Is Green

The brain conserves energy all the time. You are looking at an organ that's only about three pounds – 2% of your body mass. However, it requires 20% of our entire energy to run properly, more than any other organ in the human body. Two thirds of that energy is used to fuel electrical impulses, and the remaining third is to perform cell-health maintenance. At rest, our bodies consume about 1,300 calories per day of which the brain burns about 260 calories. Interestingly, the stomach is second in energy consumption. Indeed, we use 10% of our energy to digest, absorb, metabolize, and eliminate food. Why do you think there is such dynamic tension between the brain and the stomach right after lunch? That is why it is not recommended that you try to close a deal while people are still chewing on their food! There is a fierce competition between the brain and the stomach for precious energy.

So, the quality of making things tangible is the quality of serving information to the brain that does not require much mental effort. We welcome speed and simplicity because we welcome the opportunity to not waste cognitive energy. Let's simply reflect on one idiom that says it all: *paying attention*. What does this expression imply? That you are asking people to "spend something," which is effectively brain energy. The reason we are so bad about consciously controlling our attention is that the primal brain is the guardian of that spending. Before you can even think of selling anything, you must sell the value of using your audience's energy to process your message.

When was the last time you were attending a workshop and found yourself thinking, "I wish this were harder on my brain?" It does not happen. The teachers we loved are those that made it easy and fun for us to comprehend their message. The same is true for your persuasive messages. Your audience is not prepared to read or hear all your explanations. You must take the burden of making your message crisp and simple so that they will know within seconds there is not a better option or a better decision than the one suggested by your message.

EEG data measures how much messages create cognitive effort. We do that by recording and analyzing brain waves, especially in the frontal lobes, where we control our concentration and use our working memory. Irrespective of how smart research subjects are, we always find that they do not enjoy exerting cognitive effort when processing advertising messages. Nobody will ever complain that your message is too easy to understand. On the contrary, people will stop paying attention if your message is too abstract, or too intangible. If you sell a physical product, arguably it might be easier to get people's attention from the primal brain, because that product has a physical form. It is real, concrete. However, if you sell software or a financial service, clearly you have a much bigger challenge to make it tangible.

Since our primal brain is biased to make quick decisions, we avoid complexity all the time. For instance, a 2012 study from Google and the University of Basel demonstrated that web visitors judge the aesthetic beauty and the perceived functionality of a website in about 50 milliseconds [88]. That is less time than it takes to snap your fingers or trigger a smile. First impressions are formed in the primal brain. Speed is inversely related to complexity. The research on the neurobiological basis of first impressions is rather scant. Aesthetic perception is an arduous process to understand and testing messages that have different aesthetic styles is tricky. Most of the media research on the subject comes from web analytics collected from websites that have varying degrees of complexity. However, a study confirmed that web pages of moderate complexity receive more favorable consumer responses [89]. Another one further established that web pages that are perceived as visually complex produced negative arousal and increased facial tension [90].

The Power of Cognitive Fluency

The value of making your message more tangible is supported by the study of how much we enjoy *cognitive fluency*. Cognitive fluency is the subjective experience of ease or difficulty to complete a mental task. It is a well-researched bias that explains how much we favor processing information that is easy to understand. For example, we prefer people whose names are easier to pronounce than others [91]. Also, we remember better what is easier to learn [92]. Shares in companies that have easy-to-pronounce names tend to outperform others. The fluency of many cognitive processes is "pre-assessed" by the primal brain. Anything that appears complicated within the first few milliseconds is likely to be rejected by the rest of the brain. For instance, whenever I talk about our persuasion model, I hold a brain in my hand to establish that I am passionate about the topic. Doing so increases people's attention and reinforces the perception that I am competent to talk about neuroscience! More importantly, it makes the SalesBrain model easier to understand because I am not just relying on words to explain it. It makes a complex topic more cognitively fluent.

In fact, using less energy to comprehend anything may be the ultimate expression of the brain's intelligence according to a fascinating study examining how much energy chess players consume [93]. Using an EEG to study the patterns of neuronal activity while playing a game, expert chess players were compared with beginners, and the results were very surprising. Master players had lower brain activation, and therefore displayed more neural efficiency than beginners. Experts use less brain energy than a novice. They also perform many tasks subconsciously [94]. Some scholars suggest that this study may unveil the neurobiological basis of intelligence. By that, they mean that intelligence may well be the ability of the brain to minimize the amount of brain energy used for a particular task.

Applying Tangible to Persuasive Messages

There are three effective ways to make your messages instantly more tangible:

1. Use analogies and metaphors as shortcuts that help people grasp the essence of what you communicate.

2. Use familiar terms, patterns, and situations when you explain. We learn best by pointing to what we already know.

3. Remove abstraction by providing concrete evidence to prove what you say.

The Neuroscience of Tangible

For tangible, we tested the following research question: *Can concrete evidence create more persuasive impact on the primal brain and reduce cognitive effort on the rational brain?*

We used the following advertising stimuli to test our hypothesis:

- Dental discount-card video ads
    - One ad featured customers of a dental care plan without showing real customers as tangible evidence that the service was as good as the ad suggested.
    - One ad featured several video testimonials of the dental care plan customers.
- Duct tape billboards
    - One ad featured the product and one unproven claim: "It holds."
    - Another ad featured the tape as if it was holding a billboard together.

The results supported our hypothesis:

- The ad for the dental discount card featuring the testimonials produced a primal brain score 10 times higher than the basic ad, which did not include tangible evidence from customers.
- The billboard demonstrating the value of the duct tape received a primal brain score that was twice the score of the billboard demonstrating nothing concrete about how strongly the tape could hold.

Tangible Neuroinsights: By making your ads more tangible, you will create more impact on the primal brain and reduce cognitive effort on the rational brain.

What to Remember About Tangible

- The primal brain is the guardian of our cognitive energy.
- Don't expect messages that create cognitive effort to persuade.

- Making a message complicated is easy but achieving cognitive fluency is difficult.

- You need to work hard to create a simple, yet persuasive message.

MEMORABLE

MEMORABLE

"I'm trying to make sure that there's comedy as well as sadness. It makes the sadness more memorable."
– Rick Moody, American novelist

Memory, or how information is encoded, is a complicated function of the brain. First, it is largely distributed across many brain areas, some located in the primal brain (hippocampus, amygdala), but also in newer cortical areas like the temporal lobes or the prefrontal lobes. A full discussion on memory is beyond the scope of this book but discussing short-term memory and how you can improve your ability to impress upon your audience to make your messages more memorable is extremely important.

The U-shape Curve of Memorable

First, the effect of a message on our short-term memory is very much like a U-shape curve. For example, do you remember your first car? We all typically do. Do you remember your last car? Not that difficult either. However, do you remember your fourth car? Not that easy! Discovered more than 60 years ago and proven by countless studies, the U-shape curve effect is also known as the *recency and primacy effect*. We tend to remember the first occurrence (primacy) of an event and

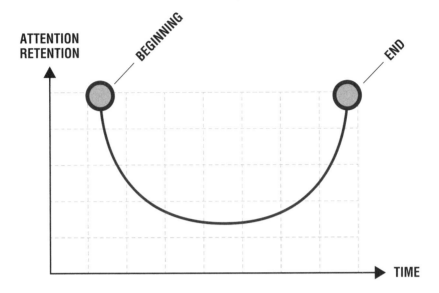

Figure 4.5   Beginning and end effect.

the last occurrence of an event (recency), but we forget what happened in between (see Figure 4.5).

Psychologists have shown that the primacy effect plays not only a role in the recall but also in decision making. For instance, the result of the reward we receive for a first experience greatly influences our subsequent behavior, a phenomenon called *outcome primacy* [95]. Thus, beginning and end points are important aspects of what happens with a message over time. It is because we have a unique – yet fragile – ability to remember. Therefore, the introduction of your message and its conclusion represent special opportunities to amplify the effectiveness of your story. You cannot afford to talk as much about your business, your mission statement, your products, and your services at the onset of your presentation or advertisement, because this part of your story is of *no interest* to the primal brain (Figure 4.6). Additionally, explaining your value from your perspective will inflict undue effort on your audience's brains. By communicating too much about your technology, your people, your products, you are on a mission to fail.

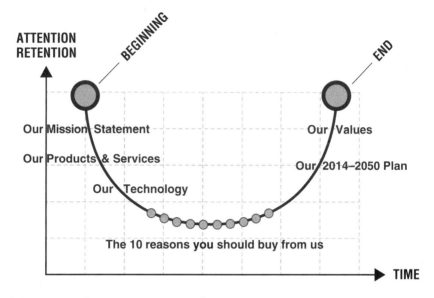

Figure 4.6   Spraying reasons to buy.

The Neuroscience of Message Recall

Message recall is the ability to retrieve and report information that has been presented to you for a few milliseconds, seconds, or minutes. There are three subsystems involved in this process:

1. Sensory memory, defined as the retention of information by your sensory structures

2. Short-term memory

3. Working memory

Sensory Memory. Our senses can store information for a very short period. For the auditory sense, it is called *echoic* memory. For vision, it is referred to as *iconic* memory.

Physiological recordings allow researchers to measure the trace of sounds in our brain. Echoic memory is critically influenced by the saliency of sounds we hear. For instance, a scream will tend to be remembered more than a whisper. Also, emotion is likely to influence how much we remember what we just heard. Indeed, we may retain entire sentences when our attention is heightened by a strong emotional response. This can help us retrieve several seconds of auditory information. On the other hand, our immediate recollection of visual stimuli is very poor. Estimates coming from visual studies suggest that we typically recall between 300 and 500 milliseconds of visual information we have just received. So, although both echoic and iconic memories are only able to hold information for a very short period, these forms of memory *can* store much more information we may not be able to recall consciously. Therefore, building a strong emotional beginning, especially re-enacting a pain is critical. And finishing with a strong emotional "close" in your message is very important. Both techniques will be further developed in Chapter 8, Deliver to the Primal Brain.

Short-Term Memory. Compared to sensory memory, *short-term memory* can retain seconds and minutes from any interaction. It has long been proposed that short-term memory is directly dependent on the stimulation of sensory memory first [96]. In other words, short-term memory does not work well unless our senses have engaged in the recording of tiny fractions of our experiences. Meanwhile, long-term memory is also highly dependent on short-term memory, confirming that memorization is a complex process, distributed in multiple areas of the brain, but organized at its core by the primal brain.

In the 1950s, many psychologists were investigating how much we could effectively store in our short-term memory. Studies from George Miller [97] initially suggested that no matter what information people were asked to remember (digits, words), the number of items that they could easily remember was around seven. However, there was a critical flaw in this conclusion. Although some information can be classified as "bits" – elementary pieces of information – other types of information represent groups of bits, commonly labeled "chunks or packets." Using chunks makes us more efficient than remembering bits. For instance, we can easily remember a word of 13 letters, like "neuromarketing." However, whereas some of the chunks (like words) may pass on to long-term memory, a large majority won't. In fact, recent research suggests that long-term memory may not be as dependent on short-term memory as once thought. Instead, long-term memory may be critically influenced by sensory memory. This further suggests that using seven reasons (or more) to influence your customers is not optimized for their short-term memory. On the contrary, it confirms that your first goal should be to strongly activate their sensory memories. To achieve that, you cannot exceed three chunks of information (typically three words) to describe your value proposition – that is, your *claims* – and you need to make them visual, the dominant sense in the brain!

Working Memory. The concept of w*orking memory* is critical to how you can make your message more memorable. Working memory holds information in our brains for a short period (short-term memory), and transforms the information to guide a decision, a thought, or a movement. Working memory can be stimulated by input coming from your senses (the ringing of your alarm clock), or from your long-term memory (retrieving the address of the restaurant where you are meeting a friend). As you realize by now, the whole point of presenting a persuasive message is to make sure it is easy for people's brains to manipulate the information they receive. Therefore, your ability to persuade is completely dependent on the activation of your audience's working memory. Studies prove that the frontal lobes are extensively involved in activating the process by which we hold and manipulate short-term information we receive. And SalesBrain's research shows that only messages that engage the primal brain first are successfully processed by our working memory.

Applying Memorable to Persuasive Messages

- To make your message memorable, create a narrative that will have limited and short attention dips.

- Narratives that work on the brain grab attention at the beginning and the end of each segment.

The Neuroscience of Memorable

For memorable, we tested the following research question: *Can concrete evidence create more persuasive impact on the primal brain and reduce cognitive effort on the rational brain?*

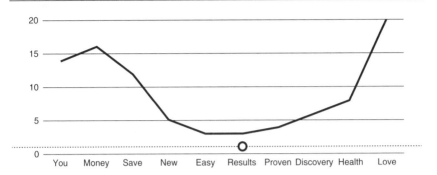

Figure 4.7   Beginning and end recall.

We used the advertising stimuli shown in Figure 4.7 to test the hypothesis that the beginning and end of an event matter more than the middle. We presented a list of 10 words to our subjects and we measured their recall after 20 seconds. We use words that are known to be influential words. The data does confirm the U-shape curve of recall.

Memorable Neuroinsights: Recognize that memorization is a complicated process for the brain. Make sure what you say is easy to retain and put a special emphasis at the beginning and the end of your message.

What to Remember About Memorable

- We are wired to remember basic information to guide our short-term actions.

- Message recall is affected by sensory memory, which further influences both short-term and working memory. Both are critical systems that make encoding fragile.

- The primal brain needs a solid narrative structure with a strong beginning and strong end to create attention and retention.

- Messages imprint better in the brain if they focus on the pain first.

VISUAL

VISUAL

"Dialogue should simply be a sound among other sounds, just something that comes out of the mouths of people whose eyes tell the story in visual terms."
– Alfred Hitchcock, Filmmaker

When we conduct a neuromarketing experiment, data we collect from the visual system gives us crucial information on the effectiveness of persuasive messages. Why? Because the visual sense is the dominant channel through which we perceive the world around us.

The Visual Sense Is Dominant

Nearly 30% of the neurons in the brain are visual neurons. Researchers have confirmed for decades that the visual sense dominates other sensory processing systems. This phenomenon is commonly referred to as the Colavita effect [98], named after a researcher who was able to prove the superiority and speed of visual processing over auditory processing when subjects were asked to consider bimodal stimuli. In a recent study, researchers examined the neurophysiological correlates of visual dominance using EEG and confirmed the Colavita effect in multisensory competition [99]. They found that irrespective of the intensity of a stimulus, its type, its position (before or after audio, for example), the demands on attention, and arousal, the subjects committed more energy to the visual sense than any other sense. What is interesting about this research is that auditory stimuli tend to accelerate visual responses, suggesting that the brain looks for other sensory inputs to enhance visual processing. Also, while the visual sense is the fastest to engage, it has a longer processing cycle than auditory information.

The visual system is activated when we see and imagine while being conscious or unconscious (includes dream activity). Most persuasive messages rely on the direct delivery of visual information, which is typically processed by our eyes first. Eyes are sensors that convert photon particles (light), into information that the brain can understand – that is, electrochemical signals. These signals travel along the optic nerve, through the optic chiasm, and enter the brain first in the brainstem. From there, visual data travels to reach neurons that are located at the back of the brain in the occipital lobe, also called the *visual cortex*. There are over 30 columns of neurons responsible for processing color, motion, texture, patterns, and so forth. They are organized in visual areas that attend to basic information first, and more complicated interpretation next. However, what's really important, and rarely discussed in textbooks or research papers, is that before all this visual information goes to the back of the brain, some of it is processed by the primal brain ahead of the visual cortex [100]. Indeed, the first point of connection of the optic tract is in the brainstem. The brainstem houses critical visual stations – namely, the lateral geniculate nucleus and the superior colliculus. The lateral geniculate nucleus (considered part of the thalamus) plays a critical role assessing the importance and urgency of a visual stimulus, while the superior colliculus gives us the capacity to see without consciously knowing we see. Meanwhile, right above the superior colliculus is a tiny brain structure considered part of the limbic system called the amygdala. The amygdala has the power to control our entire body and move us away from danger in about 13 milliseconds [101]. Joseph Ledoux, a prominent neuroscientist and researcher on emotions and responses to threats at NYU showed that it takes about 500 milliseconds for the neocortex to recognize the legitimacy of a threat. Therefore, the primal brain is nearly 40 times faster than the neocortex to respond to a visual stimulus [102].

After the information has been processed by the lateral geniculate nucleus and the superior colliculus, visual data typically follows a ventral stream and a dorsal stream, each serving different processing functions. The ventral stream is called the *what* pathway because it processes the urgency of recognizing objects or situations we encounter. Upon the stimulation of the ventral stream, we may receive enough information to act. This is what Ledoux calls the "low road." Low-road processing demonstrates the importance of relying on visual data to survive. When we see something that looks like a snake, we do not think about it; we move away from it by shortcutting any engagement with the rational brain. Meanwhile, a dorsal stream, engaging primarily the parietal lobe to prepare and guide our behavior, also interprets visual data. Therefore, if we see something that looks like a snake, we use the dorsal stream to decide if we should change our walking course. The dorsal stream is called the *how* network because, without a healthy parietal lobe, we cannot figure out what to do with an object, or how to respond to a situation. In fact, the dorsal stream is also responsible for re-assessing the self-relevance of a situation confirming the critical importance of making a visual stimulus personal. However, let's be clear: visual dominance is not just a function of how much we fear death. It is truly our default decision-making system.

Even Voting Is a Visual Decision

Some surprising research has demonstrated that we tend to cast our political vote for people who have the most visual impact on us. In a study conducted by Princeton University in 2006 [103], subjects were asked to "use their guts" to confirm which of two gubernatorial or senatorial candidates they would pick. With no prior knowledge of who these candidates were, they could only rely on the candidate's facial appearances. Yet, researchers were able to predict their picks over 70% of the time. The conclusion of the study is obvious: we are guided by the visual dominance of our primal brain, and we later rationalize choices made below our level of consciousness. Although none of the stereotypes attributed to how beauty or attractiveness is portrayed in media today, there is clear and undisputable evidence pointing to the importance of how we perceive the character of a person based on the way they look. For instance, we are better at judging personality traits of people we consider attractive after we meet them briefly than doing the same for people who are perceived as less attractive [104].

The Four Types of Visual Stimulation

There are four types of visual stimulation that are important to consider when you are on a mission to persuade an audience.

3D Moving Object. The most potent visual stimulus for the primal brain is a three-dimensional object moving in space. The onset of motion captures the most attention of all [105]. Think about the impact of a lion starting to run toward you! Consider that, when you present in front of people, you are a live being moving in space, which is why you can trigger more attention than a video or an email ever will. Also, faces and their expressions capture more attention than any other object [106]. That is why using your body language is a critical visual stimulus. Face familiarity detection in the brain only takes 200 milliseconds according to a recent study using EEG [107]. Researchers have also shown that a lot of the visual processing of objects is "pre-attentive." This means that it happens mostly below our level of consciousness [108].

3D Static Object. The second-best visual stimulus is a static three-dimensional object. It could be an object you place on a table in front of you during a presentation, like a prop, a mock-up, or a 3D model. Alternatively, the object can be you facing an audience while remaining still. In all these cases, even though the object is static, it may be of great interest for the primal brain, if the object is relevant to your audience and to the story of the value of your product, company, brand, or message.

2D Moving Image. The third most effective visual stimulus is a two-dimensional image moving frame by frame. Of course, we are talking about a video. We enjoy them simply because visual frame changes are entertaining for our primal brain. This is true as long as the changes are not happening too fast. In the era of digital editing, video producers can display many frames in a very short period. However, studies we have conducted on the effect of videos on the brain show that our primal brain stops processing the meaning of a narrative when the speed of change is above three frame changes per second or below 35 milliseconds per frame. Above that speed, the information may still be processed below the threshold of consciousness, in which case the effect is called *subliminal*. Although the subject of the effect of subliminal stimuli has garnered much attention over several decades, the effects are minimal [109]. However, we now know that text and visual stimuli produce distinct subliminal effects – namely, because reading text requires complicated computational operations that involve not only the eyes but also the auditory cortex. Although subliminal perception is possible from either type of stimuli, visual primes receive more subconscious attention than words do. This, of course, is due to the dominance of the primal brain. Many scholars also explain this phenomenon by considering that language has evolved over a very short period compared to our biological ability to decode a visual stimulus, which predates the development of the cortex by millions of years [110]. Also, as we mentioned earlier, our ability to acquire visual information without conscious effort is enabled by old subcortical areas (like the lateral geniculate nucleus, the superior colliculus, and the amygdala), which process visual signals before they reach higher, more evolved cortical areas [111]. Finally, negative emotional videos produce more brain response than those featuring positive emotions, regarding both intensity and speed. To be persuasive, we recommend that a video should use a persuasive narrative with a pain-centric drama. Also, you learned earlier that we need about 200 milliseconds to recognize a familiar face. So to recognize or connect with the characters of the story, remember that your audience needs at least 200 milliseconds of footage to do so [112].

2D Static Image. The fourth most effective visual stimulus is a picture – a two-dimensional set of pixels. Notice I did not mention text or charts. Photos (objective form) are better at grabbing attention than illustrations (subjective form) because they require less time and energy to be recognized by the primal brain. Illustrations are not as effective because they are less concrete and potentially less familiar than real scenes captured by a camera. Using custom photography of situations that are unusual is effective if the objects, the context, and the nature in each photo are familiar to your audience.

The Power of Colors

Primates started to see in color –trichromatism – about 35 million years ago as the result of a mutation of the seventh and X chromosome [113].

As a result, they developed an evolutionary advantage to pick up fruits, detect predators, and become better at reading facial expressions. Colors have a specific effect based on their wavelength:

- For example, visible colors of longer wavelength (reds) have an innate effect of stimulant because they are associated with dangerous stimuli like fire, blood, lava, and sunsets [114].

Although the physiology of vision cannot explain all responses to colors, there are still many similarities among diverse cultures on how colors are perceived. For instance, in a study performed on 243 people from eight different countries researchers confirmed that blue, green, and white are always associated with calm, serenity, and kindness [115]. Another study performed in the United States showed that different colors and different shapes – circles, squares, angles, and waves – of lines communicated the following affective values [116]:

- Red is happy and exciting.
- Blue is serene, sad, and dignified.
- Curves are serene, graceful, and tender.
- Angles are robust and vigorous.

Once consumers have started to make a strong association between a product and a color, the evaluation of a new product that contrasts with the original color may fail [117]. For example:

- Pepsi introduced Crystal Pepsi a transparent drink whose color was too far from the regular brown and was quickly abandoned.
- Palmolive tried a new color for its dishwashing soap. The consumers considered it less "degreasing" than the yellow one and less "fresh" than the green.

Researchers have also demonstrated that colors play a role on memorization: red strongly increases memory for negative words, and green strongly increases memory for positive words [118].

Beyond a simple color association for a physical product, researchers have also established that certain colors impact the cognitive performances – for example, green stimulates creativity, whereas red inhibits intellect [119, 120].

In conclusion, the choice of packaging color, color of the product itself, color of the background where the product is presented, or color of the fonts in text will all affect the brain of your audience. As an effective persuader, make sure to use colors effectively.

Applying Visual to Persuasive Messages

Maximizing the visual appeal of your message is a priority. There are many ways to apply this core stimulus when you craft an ad, a corporate video, a commercial, a web page, and, of course, a face-to-face presentation.

First, always remind yourself that your audience will not process the entire visual stimuli. Only a fraction of what you show will be seen. Less is more. Eye-tracking studies confirm that only a fraction of a web page or a packaging label will be processed by most people, regardless of age, gender, or education. There are 100 million receptors in the eye, but only a few million fibers in the optic nerve. Fifty percent of our visual brain is directed to process less than 5% of the visual world. It is as if our eye movements curiously help us see more of small areas, not more of big areas.

Second, focus on improving the saliency of your images. Visual saliency is the inherent quality your visual stimuli must have to capture and captivate your audience. We typically process details in the center of the visual field, but the contrast between an object and its surroundings makes it more salient. For example, when we designed the home page of the SalesBrain website (see Figure 4.8), we made sure that the key message elements would be salient. The pictures featuring the brain are complex, but the dark background helps the viewers focus their attention on the critical elements (water splash and funnel). The icons are simple, with clear white lines around three illustrations introducing our claims. The visual opacity map (Figure 4.9), which shows only the areas that are predicted to receive visual attention, confirm that

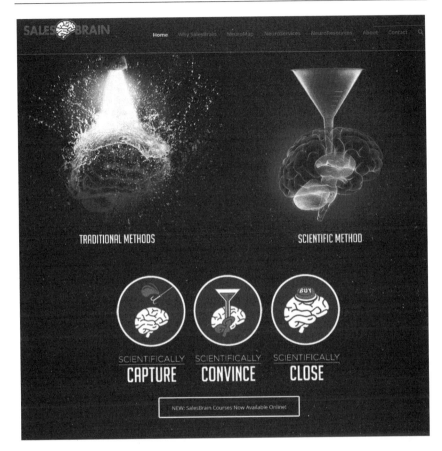

Figure 4.8   SalesBrain home page.

the overall design is well balanced because the most important message elements have good saliency.

On a web page, identifying a pop-out object can take less than 100 milliseconds. However, that time will increase if you design objects that have more than three levels of differences from each other – namely, their sizes, their colors, and the speed of their motion.

Third, visual processing is done in stages. You must appeal to early processing stages where neurons are busy sorting the easiest elements to recognize first. Avoid using too many colors, for example, because this makes separating salient elements difficult to achieve. As the Sales-Brain example demonstrates, using lines around objects helps the brain

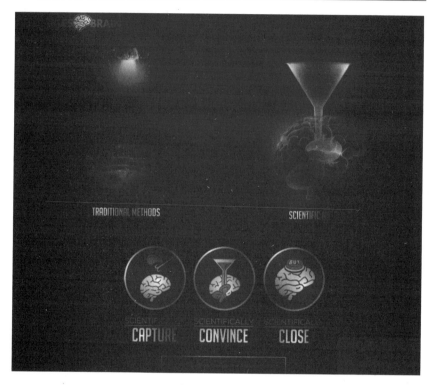

Figure 4.9   Opacity map of SalesBrain site.

perform a pattern detection with less cognitive energy. The more visual your messages, the more persuasive they will be.

Sometimes, your messages might even save lives. Such as in the field of public health. There's been some interesting research showing the superiority of visual warnings over text (Figure 4.10). They are called *picture warnings*. More than 40 countries around the world are using such visuals, and they produce better results than text warnings, especially on young brains and brains of light smokers [121]. The younger the brains, the more important employing visuals and emotional content to influence behavior. This is important because lives are at stake, and you want to make sure that your message is communicating urgency.

To conclude, most people do not understand what making a stimulus visual really means, especially when you consider how visual data

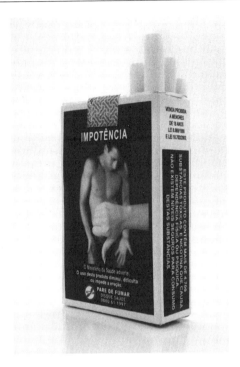

Figure 4.10   Poster for World No Tobacco Day, May 31, 2009, Tobacco-Free Initiative, World Health Organization.

is processed in the primal brain. For instance, if you use bullets with text on your presentation slides, none of that data is visual! The primal brain sees letters as of if they were hieroglyphs, which mean they will trigger no meaning or urgency!

The Neuroscience of Visual

For visual, we tested the following research question: *Can you make a message easier to process and more memorable by making it more visual?*

We used the following advertising stimuli to test our hypothesis:

- Insurance print ad:
  - One ad explaining the value of life insurance using text.
  - One ad showing someone about to be eaten by a shark.
- Pictures and words of animals flashed for 10 seconds.

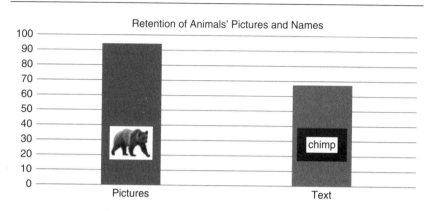

Figure 4.11   Visual retention.

The results supported our hypothesis:

- The insurance ad using a visual grabber instead of text triggered more attention (27%), more arousal (+697%) and much more emotional valence (100x) while reducing cognitive distraction by 25%.

- The retention of animal pictures was over 90% of the list and 40% higher than the retention of the animal words (Figure 4.11).

Visual Neuroinsights: By making your messages more visual, you will create more impact on the primal brain and make your message more memorable.

What to Remember About Visual

- The visual sense dominates all other senses.

- It takes only 13 milliseconds to process an image, but about 10 times more to process a word and nearly 500 milliseconds to process a decision that engages the rational brain.

- Making a message visual delivers the fastest and most important persuasive stimulus of all.

- Objects in movement attract the most attention.

- Saliency of objects is key.

Emotional

EMOTIONAL

"We are not thinking machines that feel, we are feeling machines that think once in a while."

— Antonio Damasio, neuroscientist

Emotions play a critical role in making your message persuasive because emotions are the basic fuel that trigger decisions. The role of emotions in decision making is well-researched, but the topic has often been highly controversial. What are emotions? Do they derail us from making good decisions? Can we control them so that they do not affect our choices? These are just a few of the questions that have been debated for hundreds of years.

Let me introduce the seventeenth-century French scientist, philosopher, and mathematician largely responsible for this discord among today's scholars and researchers, René Descartes. Descartes, one of the greatest scientists, gave us modern mathematics with the Cartesian representation of data (Cartesian comes from the name Descartes). For instance, when you plot x and y on two axes, you use Descartes's model. Descartes believed that reason drives the best of our decisions and it is only through logic and deduction that humans can pursue a path to a greater truth. He promoted a philosophical model called "dualism" in which he argued the mind and the body be two separate entities. For Descartes, the mind thinks like a god and is imbued with the capacity to use logic and reason, while the body cannot think and responds like a machine to basic instructions. In a famous book titled *Le Discours De La Méthode* [122], he suggested a step-by-step process to make the best rational decisions and developed the notion that only humans have rational souls: "I think, therefore I am." So, Descartes inspired a long-held view that humans are always driven by rationality. Hence, scholars have supported for decades the notion that emotions have little influence on the way we decide.

In fact, many argue that we systematically use reasoning to compute the *utility of a decision*. Introduced earlier, the pursuit of more utility assumes that we seek to maximize the value of our choices by increasing the number of options. Doing that increases our probability of finding what we want. Supporters of the utility theory further believe that bad choices are caused by limited choices, not by inherent flaws in our decision-making process [123].

However, behavioral economists, neuromarketers, and decision neuroscientists have revolutionized our understanding of how choices are made in the human brain. Their findings disprove the rationale of the utility theory because neurotransmitters affect our behavior in ways that revolutionize our understanding of decisions. One such transmitter is dopamine, which plays a critical role in emotional states related to predictions and rewards. For instance, in one study, participants who received synthesized dopamine were better at optimizing their choices than others. Other studies have shown that choices under uncertainty are difficult to make for patients with prefrontal and amygdala damage, confirming that emotions play a crucial role in making complex decisions [124]. Neuroscientist and prominent expert on the neurobiology of emotions, Antonio Damasio, is a fervent opponent of Descartes' dualism as well as any decision-making model theory based on the dominance of rationality. In the book *Descartes' Error* [125], Damasio showed the fallacy of Descartes' argument by revealing the neurobiological processes underlying our decision-making processes. For Damasio, emotions are the basic fuel that our brains need to make decisions.

According to Damasio, there is no such thing as a rational decision, because older evolutionary systems influence and often dominate our choices by recruiting the guidance of our emotional system. He claims that "Nature appears to have built the apparatus of rationality not just on top of the apparatus of biological regulation, but also from it and with it." For Damasio, emotions play the role of a biological bridge between subcortical layers and higher-level cognitive functions such as thinking or goal setting. In fact, there are more neurons extending from the limbic system (subcortical) to the neocortex than the other way around. Clearly, emotions influence our wants below our level of awareness. This explains why we cannot easily report our emotional states. All we can report is our interpretation of how rapid changes of key neurotransmitters make us feel.

To summarize, we make emotional decisions first and rationalize them later. Richard Thaler, recipient of the 2017 Nobel Prize in Economics, a prominent behavioral economist, behavioral economics, also claims that humans systematically avoid rationality and recruit emotions to make decisions. He coined this phenomenon *misbehaving* [126]. Our research also supports the notion that we decide emotionally and that the primal brain largely controls this process. Like Damasio, we argue that we cannot make decisions without the guidance of physiological clues provided by older regions of the brain. In fact, studies on patients with lesions in their orbitofrontal frontal cortex (OFC) show that they are not able to make good decisions because they fail to interpret the biochemical changes they experience after being emotionally aroused [127]. As a result, they perform poorly without the guidance of the emotional clues [18]. Meanwhile, neuroscientist and prolific author David Eagleman also argues that "emotions are also the secret behind how we navigate what to do next at every moment" [128]. Eagleman supports his statement by describing the case of patients such as "Tammy" who damaged her orbitofrontal frontal cortex, and as a result cannot receive emotional feedback from her body. She, too, was unable to make any decisions. To conclude, Eagleman insists, "physiological signals—are crucial to steering the decisions we have to make."

Which Emotions Influence Most of Our Decisions?

Although the evidence coming from studies done with healthy or unhealthy subjects largely support the critical role of emotions in decision making, we need to recognize that we experience thousands of emotions in any single day. Most theoretical models on emotions are complicated and, to date, there are many different models of emotions attempting to measure, evaluate, and rationalize emotions. One of our favorite models of emotions was proposed by Robert Plutchik [129], a psychologist who developed a psychoevolutionary theory of basic emotions. The major tenets of Plutchik's model are as follows:

1. Emotions affect animals as much as they affect humans.

2. Emotions help us survive.

3. Emotions have common patterns and can be categorized.

4. There is a small number of basic or primal emotions.

5. Many emotions tend to be derivative states from the primal states.

6. Each emotion has its own continuum of intensity.

Plutchik created an organized view of emotions illustrated in Figure 4.12 as the wheel of basic emotions. Even though the model was introduced nearly 40 years ago, it is regarded as one of the most elegant ways to organize emotions from eight core critical states: anger, disgust, sadness, surprise, fear, trust, joy, and anticipation.

The wheel of emotions helps you realize that creating a strong emotional cocktail is a function of activating a limited set of primal emotions that have opposite and negative effects (valence) on our responses. At the time Plutchnik developed his model, neuromarketing research did not exist, so researchers could not easily measure and predict the impact of a persuasive message on emotional valence.

Based on this model, the most effective emotional lift you can create should first include an avoidance emotion – such as reminding the prospect of their pain – followed by an approach emotion – such as letting them experience the gain. Producing a good emotional lift is challenging for most of our clients. For instance, many tend to resist starting a message with a negative emotion. Yet, it is the best path to a successful persuasive message, because the primal brain attends to negative events before positive events. Failure to act in front of a negative event has more dramatic consequences for our survival than ignoring a positive event. That is why the fear of regret is the most powerful negative emotion to amplify the effect of any persuasive message.

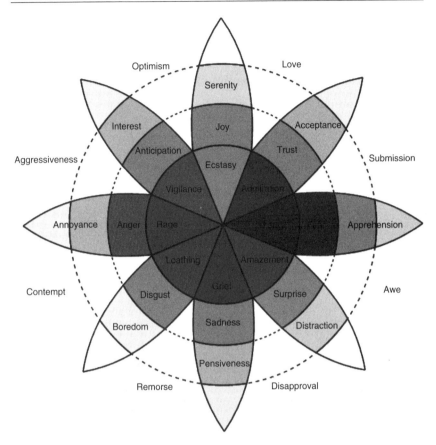

Figure 4.12 **Plutchik wheel of emotions – first published in** *American Scientist.*

Table 4.2   Primal Emotions.

Avoidance Emotions	Approach Emotions
Fear	Anticipation
Sadness	Joy
Disgust	Trust
Anger	Surprise

Source: Adapted from Plutchik.

The Fear of Regret. Briefly discussed earlier in the book, the fear of regret arises when we expect outcomes to fall short of our predictions. We experience regret when we choose an option that turns out badly, or when we pass on an option that turned out to be better than the status quo. In both instances, there is a sense that we have lost something that we can no longer experience, and more importantly, that we have prolonged the risk of the threat of making the wrong decision. In their paper on the impact of regret on decision making, researchers from both France and the United Kingdom [130] demonstrated that there is an intricate neural network involved in decision-making situations where regret is a key factor. They collected *f*MRI data while subjects participated in a gambling task. The data showed that the fear of regret generated higher brain activity in the *medial prefrontal cortex,* the *dorsal anterior cingulate cortex,* the anterior hippocampus, and the amygdala. The anterior cingulate cortex is considered a general center of emotional processing with projections to the amygdala and the *anterior insula,* a brain structure that lights up when people experience disgust. In all studies focusing on the impact of regret, the same neural circuitry appears to mediate both the experience of regret and the anticipation of regret. Meanwhile, the stress produced by the fear of regret induces the release of noradrenaline from the *adrenal medulla* and the *locus coeruleus* in the brainstem. Noradrenaline is responsible for the fight or flight response managed by our autonomic nervous system [131]. Additionally, a slower system, the *hypothalamus-pituitary-adrenal (HPA) axis* releases both cortisol and adrenocorticotropic hormone to calm our body when we experience stress from regret. However, cortisol starts working only 30 minutes or so after the onset of a stressful event. Therefore, studies show that the immediate effect of a negative event is better recalled right after it occurred rather than later, presumably because cortisol lowers cognitive processing and retention. This only reinforces the importance of producing messages that include "regret stressors" right at the beginning to heighten your audience's attention and retention but finish with a positive emotion at the end. Indeed, the best way to lift your message after re-enacting the fear of regret is to generate more *anticipation* in the brains of your audience.

The Power of Anticipation. Anticipation is a prediction that we will receive excitement, joy, pleasure, or happiness if we engage in a specific experience. Such prediction is rewarded by a powerful neu-rotransmitter called dopamine. Although a healthy dose of dopamine can create the fuel of our day-to-day motivation, it can also lock us into addictive habits [132]. Psychologist and popular author Adam Alter argues that addiction is a pattern of behaviors we reproduce because they stimulate our dopaminergic system. For instance, when we look at our cell phone over 300 times a day, drink too much alcohol, or consume mind-altering substances, the chemical effect of dopamine is gradually less potent, hence it pushes us to continue a potentially destructive habit. Practically, persuasive messages can directly stim-ulate a healthy dose of anticipation. By magnifying the power of an excellent product or an innovative solution, you can stimulate a safe level of dopamine in your audience's brain.

To conclude, both the fear of regret and the power of anticipation can help you create the simplest, yet most powerful emotional lift.

Emotions and Memory

Triggering an emotional lift is crucial to hijack attention and to jump-start the decision-making process of the primal brain. However, there is another critical benefit from making your message more emotional – retention and recall are improved. Curiously, emotions not only affect both our decisions and behaviors, but also the encoding of all messages and events that mark our lives. According to neurobi-ologists, emotions have a direct effect on what and why we remember anything at all. Research performed by Jim McGaugh has confirmed that emotional arousal enhances the storage of our memories [133]. That is why we call emotions the glue of your message. Without them, what you say, present, or show will not stick. By the way, this explains why we recommend that you first activate a negative emotion. Stress hormones participate in this process. The ability to retain information is essential to our survival, and negative events tend to be remembered more than positive events [134]. It is as if we have a "record" button in our brain that is automatically activated during noteworthy events. It does make sense that we would be wired to remember events that produce a strong impression on us, and especially those that could cost us our lives.

By creating emotional cocktails, you simply ensure that your messages are optimized to activate these automatic mechanisms. Meanwhile, emotions also produce physical movements on people's faces that are crucial to helping you monitor the effect of a presentation in front of a live person or audience. The visual cues you may receive from their micro-expressions can confirm that you are successful at capturing their attention, that your message is triggering an emotional response. With the help of Dr. Wallace Friesen, Paul Ekman developed a comprehensive inventory of such movements over a 13-year period (1965–1978). They called it the Facial Action Coding System (FACS). The FACS is a catalogue of 43 facial movements called action units (AUs). Each AU is anatomically unique and has its visual signature. According to Ekman, a limited set of emotions produce the same facial expression anywhere on this planet (see Figure 4.13).

Applying Emotional to Persuasive Messages

To ensure that you properly guide your audience to the behaviors you want, your message should first activate negative emotions that prompt us to avoid a situation. For instance, a negative surprise is one the most commonly used avoidance emotion to sell products or solutions that reduce risk or uncertainty, like insurance. If this negative emotion is relevant to your audience, then it will grab their attention and prime people to ask for a solution. In fact, at best, their *mirror neurons* will kick in to sample the stress that this situation may represent for them. Neuroscientists consider the existence of mirror neurons a crucial step toward understanding the basis of empathy and learning functions in humans [135]. It is now widely accepted that mirror neurons help us learn and sample people's emotions by simply observing their behavior. Later you will learn that one of the most effective ways to stimulate mirror neurons is to act out the pain of your prospects so they can personally relive it for just a few seconds. Once you have done that, simply activate an approach emotion by presenting your solution to their pain. This, of course, will liberate your audience from the tension you created by re-enacting their fears. The emotional lift will produce more trust, more sense of safety, more joy, more love, or more excitement for the value you can bring. Never forget that a good

Figure 4.13   Universal facial expressions.

emotional lift directly impacts the chemical balance of the brain. Stress or fear may indeed raise levels of noradrenaline, adrenocorticotropic hormone, and cortisol in the brain and throughout the body. Love and trust may produce elevated levels of oxytocin; laughter will raise levels of endorphins; happiness may raise serotonin levels; and anticipation will boost dopamine. Making your message emotional means using the power of brain chemicals to make your message more persuasive (see Figure 4.14).

The Neuroscience of Emotional

For emotional, we tested the following research question: *Can you make the message more persuasive by increasing arousal using negative or positive valence?*

Figure 4.14   Emotional response to a message.

We used the following advertising stimuli to test our hypothesis:

- Don't-drink-and-drive print ad.

  - One ad showed a text warning.

  - One ad showed the face of a victim of a drink-and-drive accident.

- Video of protective products.

  - One version of the ad featured the value of wearing a respirator.

  - Another version showed a man at home using a barbecue recklessly and the same character at work wearing a respirator in complete control of the situation (safe versus unsafe).

The results supported our hypothesis:

- The ad featuring a victim of a drunk driver generated a huge spike of valence (+2600x) and a remarkable boost of cognitive engagement (+70%) compared to the text warning ad.

- The video featuring the emotional contrast between a character unable to use a barbecue safely but using a respirator at work also produced a huge spike of valence (+3800x) and reduced workload (−5%).

Emotional Neuroinsights: By making your messages more emotional, you will create more impact on the primal brain and make your message more memorable.

What to Remember About Emotional

- Emotions are chemicals that affect all our decisions.
- We need emotions to make buying decisions.
- The most powerful emotions are the fear of regret and the pleasure of anticipation.
- Emotional lifts are needed to pay attention, retain, and decide!

INTEGRATING THE SIX STIMULI

Individually, each stimulus has limited effects on the primal brain. However, triggering all stimuli with NeuroMap will catapult the effect of your persuasive attempts (Figure 4.15). That is why we use the language metaphor here. The combined effect of all six stimuli works like a powerful sentence. First, let's briefly review what each stimulus does to ignite activity in the primal brain. Repetition is good for your memorization!

The dynamic nature of the persuasion process creates activity in the primal brain first, then stimulates the rational brain second. We suggest that this effect is like a path, a way through which persuasion radiates upward in the brain.

The Path of Persuasion

The illustration in Figure 4.16 can quickly help you understand the path of persuasion and the step-by-step effect of each stimulus. Your

Personal

> Think of the primal brain as the center of ME. It has no patience or empathy for anything that does not immediately concern its well-being. It scans for threats before it attends to pleasure. Vigilance drives the speed and nature of its response.

Contrastable

> The primal brain is sensitive to solid contrast such as before/after, risky/safe, with/without, and slow/fast. Contrast allows quick, risk-free decisions. Without contrast, the brain enters a state of confusion, which delays a decision.

Tangible

> The primal brain is constantly looking for what is familiar and friendly; what can be recognized quickly, what is simple, concrete, and immutable. The primal brain cannot process complexity without a lot of effort and skepticism.

Memorable

> The primal brain remembers little. Placing the most important content at the beginning and repeating it at the end is imperative. What you say in the middle of your delivery should be brief and convincing. Don't go over three claims. The primal brain loves stories because a good narrative construction is easy to remember.

Visual

> The primal brain is visual. The optical nerve is physically connected to the primal brain. Therefore, the visual channel provides a fast and effective connection to accelerate decisions. No other sense is more dominant than the visual sense. It is the super highway of your messages to the primal brain.

Emotional

> The primal brain is strongly triggered by emotions. Emotions create chemical events in your brain that directly impact the way you process and memorize information. No emotion, no retention, and no decisions!

Figure 4.15   Summary role of the six stimuli.

message is like a rocket that you are launching in a vast and crowded persuasion space. You need to rely on six different fuel tanks to put it into the "orbit of persuasion." To do that, you need to make sure that each stimulus is moving your audience to the right coordinates of the persuasion space, from neutral to engaged. The six stimuli represent your Persuasion Code!

This process will happen in sequence if you apply the power of each stimulus to your message. People are busy attending to competing priorities and are typically not excited when they receive sales messages. Therefore, you should first activate an emotional lift by triggering engagement in the primal brain, moving the persuasive emotional state of your audience from *neutral* to *aroused*. However, the persuasive process cannot be just about creating an emotional lift such as

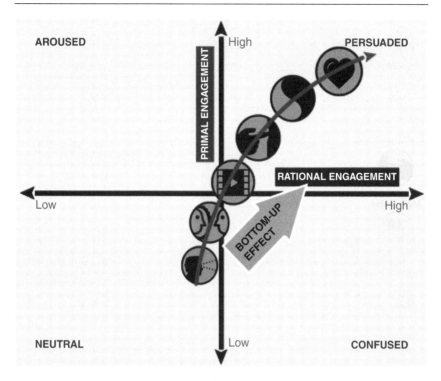

Figure 4.16   The persuasion map.
Source: © Copyright 2002–2018, SalesBrain.

making a situation surprising, painful, or even shocking. The message must help your audience move from the emotional engagement to the rational engagement. For that to happen, brain energy must radiate to the upper right section of the persuasion map to activate higher cognitive functions. By doing so, the message can then be confirmed as not just relevant but important so that it becomes elaborated by the frontal lobes of the rational brain. At that point, you can consider that your message has successfully created cognitive engagement and can persuade. This entire process is what we call the *bottom-up effect* of persuasion. We discussed how the dominance of the primal brain controls the path of persuasion earlier. However, now that you have learned the role of the six stimuli, we can explain how each one can progressively help you persuade.

The Gradual Effect of Each Stimulus. Visual and personal are central to how a message can quickly CAPTURE attention. Next, your message must be able to share memorable elements that provide a structure to the narrative of your value proposition. However, your story must be tangible to be easily understood and believed, which is why you need to present evidence. Making your message memorable and tangible help you CONVINCE. By then, your message should reach higher cognitive areas. It means that the effectiveness of your message now depends on the dynamic relationship between the primal brain and the rational brain: the bottom-up effect. So, by using contrastable and closing with a strong emotional cocktail, you are providing the catalyst and the glue to CLOSE the persuasive cycle. Meanwhile, NeuroMap can also help you assess how your messages perform without having to conduct extensive neuromarketing research. You can use our *NeuroScoring* tools and see how well you are currently using the six stimuli on a home page, a print ad, or a commercial. See Appendix A.

NeuroQuadrant Analysis. Additionally, performing a Neuro-Quadrant analysis helps you confirm the degree to which your message stimulates both the primal brain and the rational brain (Figure 4.17). Once you get your *NeuroScores* from Appendix A, you can find out where your message is on the persuasion map. Each quadrant reveals the existence of four persuasive states that have different potency of emotional and cognitive effect.

Conclusion from the Neuroscience of the Six Stimuli. The neuro study we conducted did confirm that each stimulus can produce measurable change on the neurophysiology of an audience. Table 4.3 summarizes the direct impact of each stimulus on the primal and rational brains. The + sign shows the degree to which a stimulus is likely to activate specific functions in the brain. For example, personal creates a lot of arousal in the primal brain, whereas memorable strengthens retention in the rational brain.

The NeuroMap scores we computed for each stimulus suggest that they have different individual contribution to the overall persuasion effect. Understanding that this neuro study has methodological

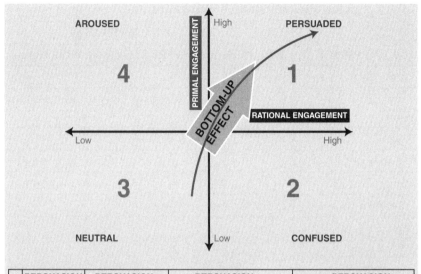

#	PERSUASION STATE	PERSUASION EFFECT	PERSUASION PREDICTION	PERSUASION RECOMMENDATIONS
1	PERSUADED	Strong primal appeal. Strong rational appeal. The bottom-up effect is working.	Ads from Quadrant 1 can be liked or disliked but create higher retention and action than any other Quadrants.	Optimize toward upper right corner by maximizing the contrast and emotions.
2	CONFUSED	Poor primal appeal. Strong rational appeal. The bottom-up effect is not optimized.	Ads from Quadrant 2 can be liked or disliked but tend to overwhelm because they lack emotional relevance and are not memorable. While they activate cognitive processing, the effect is temporary and typically leads to high cognitive effort and distraction.	Raise primal appeal by optimizing the six stimuli and especially by making your message more relevant to a specific pain, more visual and more emotional.
3	NEUTRAL	Poor primal appeal. Poor rational appeal. The bottom-up effect is not working at all.	Ads from Quadrant 3 tend to be disliked and rated worse than any other Quadrants.	Rebuild the message from scratch using the six stimuli.
4	AROUSED	Strong primal appeal. Poor rational appeal. The bottom-up effect is aborted.	Ads from Quadrant 4 tend to be liked but generate lower retention and action compare to Quadrants 1 and 2.	Improve narrative structure to raise cognitive engagement, use sharp contrast and a strong emotional close.

Figure 4.17   NeuroQuadrants.
Source: © Copyright 2002–2018, SalesBrain.

limitations that do not allow us to be statistically conclusive, we still believe that the data supports the predictions of NeuroMap. For instance, it confirms the importance of using all six stimuli to achieve the highest possible persuasive impact. Table 4.4 shows that visual is the highest, most potent stimulus of all six according to our data, while personal is the lowest. Together, however, they all

Table 4.3   How stimuli influence both brains.

	PRIMAL			RATIONAL		
	Attention	Arousal	Valence	Workload	Engagement	Retention
Personal	+++	+++				
Contrastable	++		+	++	+++	
Tangible			++			
Memorable						+++
Visual		++	+++	+		+++
Emotional		+	++	++		

Table 4.4   Rank effect of each stimulus.

	NeuroMap Rank Effect	Recommended Sequence	Persuasion Stages
Personal	6	2	Capture
Contrastable	4	5	Close
Tangible	3	4	Convince
Memorable	5	3	Convince
Visual	1	1	Capture
Emotional	2	6	Close

contribute to three critical stages in the persuasion path which we introduced earlier (Figure 4.16): the first stage is to *capture* the brain's attention (visual and personal), the second stage is to *convince* (tangible and memorable), and the final stage is to *close* the persuasive process (contrastable and emotional). The persuasion path explains the logic of using six stimuli and the role each one plays to move an audience from the neutral state to the persuaded state.

WHAT TO REMEMBER

- To improve your ability to persuade, you need to use six stimuli that speak to the primal brain first and can ultimately engage the rational brain as well.

1. The message must be personal and able to relate quickly to a relevant frustration or pain.

2. The message needs to be contrastable, so that a decision can be accelerated by comparing two situations that make the best choice obvious.

3. The message must be tangible to achieve cognitive fluency and allow the primal brain to accept the truth of the argument.

4. The message must be memorable so that retention is done effortlessly and designed to encode the part of the message that will trigger a decision.

5. The message should be visual because the primal brain is visually dominant in the way information is first considered and integrated into our decision-making process.

6. The message must produce a positive emotional uplift, to reach the higher cognitive areas and trigger a decision.

7. Together, the six stimuli can propel your message to success, achieving the optimum path of persuasion, as explained by NeuroMap.

8. NeuroScoring your message on the six stimuli will help you correct and improve the course of your message on the path of persuasion.

9. NeuroQuadrants also provide a simple tool to optimize the effect of any message.

Yet again, we are making a very important transition, which is the critical importance of maximizing the use of six stimuli by following a four-step PERSUASION PROCESS. You cannot achieve the benefits of NeuroMap by skipping anyone of the steps. The four steps are the fundamental pillars of your persuasive strategy. They ensure a proper articulation of your message by:

1. Diagnosing the top pains of your customers

2. Differentiating from your competition by identifying unique claims

3. Demonstrating the gain of each claim

4. Delivering to their primal brain by following the blueprint of a killer presentation, a sticky website, a stunning ad, or a compelling video.

PART III

DECODING YOUR PERSUASIVE NARRATIVE

CHAPTER 5

Diagnose the Pain

DIAGNOSE THE PAIN™

"Most people want to avoid pain, and discipline is usually painful".
– John C. Maxwell Clergyman

WHY PAINS DRIVE BUYING BEHAVIOR

First, your message must target the elimination of fears, threats, or risks that the primal brain prioritizes to eliminate. As humans, we aspire to reduce or remove anxiety to survive and to feel safe. As we learned in the section on personal, our brain has evolved over millions of years. Even today, we need to pay attention to events that matter most to our survival so that we can thrive as a species. According to Stanislas Dehaene, a foremost expert on the neuroscience of consciousness, our ability to navigate a complex array of decisions is driven by the level of vigilance we apply to critical states of consciousness. As vigilance rises (as threats increase), the brain recruits more brain areas in a bottom-up process that results in recruiting more cerebral blood flow [136].

Since vigilance is so critical to how brain energy radiates from emotional to cognitive layers (from subconscious to more conscious), it is why we are anxious beings, not only when we wake up every day, but also when we make buying decisions. It is part of our default processing mode. Our brain is like a car that is always in an idle "anxiety" state. Vigilance is the basic program that helps us cope with this idle state. Starting the engine is not an option when you need to drive away quickly! Our state of vigilance is central to our capacity to face the challenges life throws at us. Sigmund Freud famously suggested that human anxiety was responsible for most mental disorders. For Freud, anxiety came from worrying about the future, without having a very precise idea of what could cause harm. The top expert on fear and anxiety in the neuroscientific community, Joseph Ledoux, supports this view [137]. Ledoux insists that there is a critical difference between anxiety and fear, in that anxiety is mostly produced by subcortical brain areas of the primal brain and typically does not involve or require the conscious, more rational, and more recent layers of our cognitive machinery. He reminds us that the root of the word *anxiety* is the Latin word *anxietas* that itself comes from the Greek word *angh*, which was used to describe unpleasant physical sensations like tightness or discomfort.

In fact, today anxiety disorders affect more than 20% of the US population. Many of the people who suffer from anxiety-related diseases cannot naturally cope with the psychological and sometimes physical impact of the ongoing rumination of their worries. I am not suggesting that buying a product may produce as much anxiety as experiencing the dread of not being able to afford a house, find a job, or break a cycle of bad relationships. I am, however, claiming that anxiety is generated largely by the dominance of our primal brain. As a result, we tend to use the same neural networks to assess the relevance and value of a purchase as those we use to cope with a life-threatening situation.

The iceberg in Figure 5.1 helps you recognize the hierarchy of decision drivers that influence how and why we buy. For instance,

Figure 5.1   Iceberg of decision drivers.

the motivation that directly influences a buyer's brain often arises from fearing devastating consequences, such as the fear of regret or the fear of disappointment. Fear causes frustrations or pains, which ultimately affect what we say we need, want, or even like. Note that many of our worries and fears may be completely unconscious, while we can typically articulate what frustrates us (pains), what we need, want, and like.

The iceberg of decision drivers is a powerful metaphor to explain how critical psychological and neurophysiological states affect our response to persuasive stimuli. Traditionally, marketing research has focused on what people say they like or think they want. However, neuromarketing studies have now proven that customers cannot be trusted to articulate or even confirm what they like or want.

That is why both likes and wants are poor predictors of buying behavior. Likes and wants are vague conscious interpretations of what we think we need to be happy and safe. They tend to shift over short periods based on lifestyle changes, trends, and even moods. On the other hand, our core fears and pains are more permanent. As such, they become the best predictors of how people make decisions.

Since we formed SalesBrain nearly 20 years ago, we have designed numerous surveys, conducted hundreds of focus groups, and facilitated thousands of in-depth interviews. We have collected self-reported feedback from thousands of people from over 10 countries. Collecting data on what people *want* systematically yields confusing if not misleading insights. What we have learned over nearly two decades of neuromarketing research is that nothing is more powerful than asking people what they fear. What they fear comes from our human nature of being anxious and vigilant to survive.

The Nature of Fear

According to Ledoux, fear is associated with emotional events for which we can identify a specific threat. The semantic difference between both terms may appear pointless until you realize that anxiety is more diffuse and more permanent than fear, while fear is more precise and typically more imminent than anxiety. Ledoux argues: "To experience fear is to know that YOU are in a dangerous situation, and to experience anxiety is to worry about whether future threats may harm YOU" [137].

The Nature of Pains

We understand that in most cases, it is very difficult if not awkward, to discuss anxiety and fears with your customers directly. When we conduct a neuromarketing experiment, we can assess the level of arousal and fear that people may experience watching an ad without requiring conscious feedback. However, for many of SalesBrain's clients, identifying the neurophysiological basis of fears associated with the purchase of a product or a solution is both costly and challenging to execute.

On the other hand, engaging in PAIN dialogues that can specifically focus on what people consider their biggest frustrations associated with the purchase of a solution is relatively easy to do.

Diagnosing the top pains is a critical step because it will later help you select a few benefits of your value proposition that can directly eliminate the top sources of frustrations. It is like putting the dozens of reasons why customers should buy from you through a strainer. Only those that offer a direct, unique, and credible solution to the top pains should stay in the strainer!

Often, pains are simply correlated to complaints, pet peeves, or grievances that customers have once they have purchased or used a product or a solution. When you sell something new, pains can predict future complaints. Here is some valuable data to help you further understand the power of diagnosing the top pains to increase customer satisfaction [138].

- Sixty-six percent of customers switch to another brand because of receiving poor service.

- Fifty-eight percent will never use a company again after they experience a negative experience.

- Forty-eight percent of customers with negative experiences will tell ten people or more, whereas good experiences are shared with five or fewer.

These data points stress something obvious: we are more affected by negative customer experiences events than we are by positive ones. This is why we tend to spend more time sharing our customer nightmares than we do sharing our pleasant experiences.

The Nature of Needs

Psychologists investigating how personality traits explain and predict our behavior popularized the term *needs*. Needs typically describe what we seek to acquire or do to protect and enhance our lives. The field of personality studies has debated for decades the psychological (and most recently, the neurophysiological) basis of our needs or, more simply, what drives us on a day-to-day basis. For our discussion, though, let's review one of the most important models explaining the importance and usefulness of having needs: the Maslow Theory [139].

The Maslow Theory. Abraham Maslow [140] had a rather optimistic view of human nature. He believed that Freud had identified "the sick half of psychology" (p. 5) and suggested that his own model would provide "the healthy half" (p. 5). His view of motivation was dualistic. He believed we have two types of motives: *deficiency motives* and *growth motives*. Deficiency motives are common to all people and address physiological and emotional needs such as hunger, safety, love, and esteem from others. Growth motives are specific to some individuals and explain the unselfish pursuit of knowledge or love we can provide to others. He proposed that humans must, in fact, satisfy some basic needs before they satisfy higher needs like self-actualization. His famous ladder of human needs (Figure 5.2), known as "Maslow's hierarchy of needs," shows physiological needs at the bottom, followed by safety needs, belongingness and love needs, esteem needs, and self-actualization.

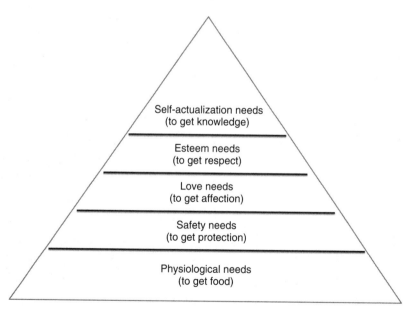

Figure 5.2   The Maslow hierarchy of needs.

Moreover, Maslow believed that human needs vary with age and map our personal development stages as illustrated by the graph in Figure 5.3.

Clearly, the primal brain is implicated in the pursuit of the first three needs of the pyramid, whereas the last two require more influence from the rational brain. At a deeper level, though, the theory of needs proposed by Maslow is a theory of human motivation. To that extent, because buying a product or solution requires motivation, Maslow's model is both relevant and important to understand. However, the model does not integrate the complex routine of neural processes that trigger the expression of all basic needs. Additionally, the model posits that human development follows a well-planned progression of sequential and logical psychological stages, as if they were like rungs on a ladder. Obviously, this is simplistic and is no longer supported by today's understanding of developmental psychology. To conclude, asking consumers what they need is not enough to predict their behavior. This is why marketers have relied on measuring another decision driver to understand consumer behavior: the nature of our wants.

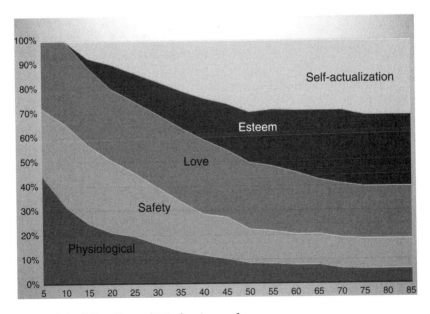

Figure 5.3   Timeline of Maslow's needs.

The Nature of Wants

The nature of our wants points directly to the consumerism movement and the well-accepted idea that our wants are insatiable. There is, again, a subtle difference between needs and wants. Wants articulate desires that can go beyond what we would consider basic needs. Most researchers on the subject argue that wants are outcomes that make us more influential or more powerful, like money, power, or public attention [141]. Frankly, the theoretical discussion on the subject has been blurry for decades because it has relied for too long on what people are willing to say they want. Fortunately, recent studies coming from the field of neuromarketing and neuroeconomics have provided a more credible theoretical framework to understand our wants.

In his book *Introduction to Consumer Neuroscience*, Thomas Ramsoy presents his theory for the neurophysiological basis of our wants. He claims that "wanting" is mediated by a brain structure called the nucleus accumbens (NAcc), a brain structure we have discussed several times already in this book when we discussed the emotional stimulus. It is tucked deep in the primal brain. Ramzoy suggests that "wanting is the unconscious approach and avoidance evaluation related to items, organisms, and events." He uses a well-known study from Knutson and colleagues to support his theory [41]. We already cited this source, but to remind you, Knutson claimed that he could predict what people "want" before they decide by looking at the surge of blood flow to their nucleus accumbens. Unfortunately, although we have a better understanding of which areas of the brain predict the want signal, there is still no reliable scale to collect people's self-reported evaluation of what they want. In other words, unless you put people in a fMRI, your ability to measure what people want is very difficult and mostly unreliable. This is why we suggest that collecting pain data is easier and more predictive of purchasing behavior.

The Nature of Likes

The concept of liking may be less ambiguous than the concept of want. After all, we can usually report whether we like something or not. Liking is typically captured by asking people to rate something, which is a way of providing a grade or a numerical assessment of how much you enjoyed a product or an experience. As such, you would think that measures that come from liking or rating are more reliable than measures of what we want. Think again! A famous study conducted by Gregory Berns on the popularity of songs revealed that the liking data was not predictive of the neural response [142]. For instance, the data collected from the nucleus accumbens activity, which also correlates with what people choose (or buy), did not correlate with the liking data. Even Facebook considered the importance of going beyond collecting like data by adding emoticons a few years ago. This provides the social media company more emotional granularity that their data scientists can use to analyze the sentiment expressed by millions of users.

AN INTEGRATED VIEW OF DECISION DRIVERS

The process of how consumers assess, respond, and eventually decide after they are exposed to persuasive messages is complex and the source of extensive debate among scholars and researchers. Our proposal for an integrated view of decision drivers considers neurophysiological research and traditional research performed on a wide range of products and industries, as well as over 20 countries. We believe that decisions are influenced by the dominance of the primal brain and especially the pains we strive to eliminate.

Buyers typically start their journey in a basic state of ignorance or anxiety about a product or solution, a situation in which risk is potentially high (the fear of regret), and the cognitive involvement is typically low. However, to the extent that a product or solution is made relevant, urgent, and useful by re-awakening pains, specific fears become activated. For instance, if a message is making you realize that you could die abruptly and leave your loved ones with massive debt by not having life insurance, you face multiple fears you feel you need to address quickly. By considering the value of having life insurance, you now move from a neutral state to a state of interest. Two possibilities happen next. If you are not willing to engage cognitively with the topic, you will choose to forego a decision, which means do nothing or else evaluate another option. However, if the message or the value proposition is successful at activating cognitive engagement, you will move to a "want" state and feel the motivation to buy (anticipation), rewarded by a nice dose of dopamine in your brain. So, as you can see, diagnosing pain is a central construct persuasion step that increases the likelihood you can create effective messages. Know the pains you need to eliminate, and you have the script of your best selling arguments!

Indentifying the Top Pains

We have conducted thousands of surveys and interviews of which the sole purpose was to unveil customers' top pains. Although the products and services for which we did these interviews vary greatly, from *f*MRI equipment to cosmetic products, we have consistently been able to categorize pain insights in three categories.

The Three Sources of Pain. Pain always falls into three main categories: financial, strategic, or personal.

1. *Financial pain* pertains to economic factors such as the loss of revenue, low profitability, or bad ROI. Financial pain is typically highly visible and easy to measure.

2. *Strategic pain* includes issues that affect key business risks that can compromise the development, manufacturing, marketing, or delivery of products and services. Typical types of strategic pains are poor product quality, production inefficiencies, high customer complaints, and poor brand recognition. Strategic pain is not always as visible as financial pain and cannot always be easily measured.

3. *Personal pain* is made up of the negative feelings and emotions affecting those who are involved in the buying decisions. Examples include elevated levels of stress, job insecurity, or working longer hours.

Table 5.1 should help you quickly understand how to recognize and label the pains you can diagnose.

Conducting Pain Dialogues

There is an effective way to identify the most critical pains. Just create an intimate dialogue with your top customers. Customers, not prospects,

Table 5.1 Pain types.

Source of the Pain	Areas of Pain and Frustration	Methods of Pain Measurement	Fear/Pain Affecting the Primal Brain
Financial	• Lack of funds • Low return on investment	• Data • Stories	• Fear of not having enough • Fear of losing what we have
Strategic	• Quality issues • Long delivery delays • Long product development cycles	• Market benchmarks • Mappings • Surveys • Competitive analysis	• Fear of not knowing enough • Fear of not having control
Personal	• Poor attitudes • High stress • Lack of motivation	• Employee surveys • Leadership assessments • Neurophysiological studies	• Fear of powerlessness • Fear of worthlessness • Fear of extinction

are the best source for this crucial information. Customers have had the benefit of an intimate relationship with your value proposition already, so they can share a unique perspective on what transformation it brought to their lives by your solution. Simply ask them the following questions and be prepared to practice deep listening!

1. What were some of the top challenges, hurdles, or risks you were facing before you found our solution?

2. How much money would you lose by not using our product?

3. How did our product help you eliminate risk or uncertainty? Describe a typical situation where you felt you did not have enough control because you did not have our solution.

4. How did our solution make you feel better about yourself, your job, or your family?

You can adapt these questions to match your situation, but as you can imagine, only a few discussion points can reveal critical areas of pains and frustrations that are at the core of *why* people will choose your solution. Note that if you are selling a product through resellers, you need to do this process twice, once for the end-users and once for the resellers. To the extent that their areas of concerns vary, you will find that you need to change your message to stimulate the primal brains of each target group.

PAIN CASE STUDIES

It is quite remarkable how getting clarity on the top pains that your business or solution can eliminate may be the single most critical issue to solve to find the persuasion code of your messages. Let's consider these examples.

Domino's Pizza

The pizza delivery business seems straightforward and highly commoditized. You would think that to be successful in this activity; you need to focus on making a good pizza. However, very early on, Domino's didn't focus its main claim on the pizza. They focused on solving a critical pain: *the anxiety of not knowing when the pizza will arrive* (Figure 5.4).

This strategic decision is at the center of Domino's success, not just in the United States but outside as well. Today, Domino's Pizza is the first largest pizza restaurant chain in the world (Pizza Hut is the second!), with more than 14,400 locations in over 85 markets. They are like the Federal Express of the pizza industry: the pizza delivery experts! The pizza itself is important but it's not the key differentiator for Domino's Pizza.

For many years their slogan was: "30 minutes or less, or it's free." Notice how it provides a perfect cure to the pain!

Starbucks

Meanwhile, you may think of Starbucks as the company that gives you the drinks you want. However, the success of their mission is because

Figure 5.4   Pizza pain.

they realized that people spend most of their time at home and in the office. Yet people experience the pain of missing a transitional environment that helps them switch mentally from their home mode to their office model. The founder and former CEO of Starbucks, Mr. Schultz positioned the business as an ideal *third place*.

The "third place" is like a decompression chamber, the home away from home, the workplace away from the workplace (Figure 5.5). That positioning has made Starbucks unique and very successful in over 70 countries and over 24,000 locations because it solves a major pain for millions of people every day.

Uber

Meanwhile, another company that did not even exist 10 years ago built an empire by targeting pains many of us share: going from one point to another quickly and cost-effectively without owning a vehicle. How many of us have been frustrated waiting for a cab not knowing exactly when it would arrive? and have you not wondered when you would get to your destination and if you would have enough cash to pay for the ride (Figure 5.6)? Today, Uber operates in 84 countries, has over 160,000 drivers and holds a market value of $70 billion, while not owning one car.

Figure 5.5   Starbucks pain.

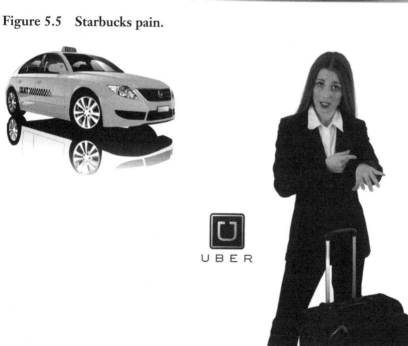

Figure 5.6   Uber pain.

Table 5.2 Marketing to pains.

Wants	Pizza	Coffee	Taxi
Pains	Not knowing	Not having an option between home and office	Lack of control

For the preceding examples, winning market share was not just a function of offering products or solutions, but performing a good diagnosis of the underlying pains. Table 5.2 helps you appreciate the power of making a crucial distinction between marketing what customers *want* and marketing to their *pains*.

Pain Cluster Studies

The process of diagnosing pains typically involves two steps:

1. Qualitative exploration, achieved by conducting pain dialogues

2. Quantitative measurements, done through telephone or online surveys

The best way to organize pain data is to perform a *pain cluster analysis*. The concept is challenging to understand from a mathematical standpoint, but the purpose of the technique is to classify survey respondents (sometimes called segments or clusters) that share common patterns of responses on pain questions that are most predictive of future purchasing behavior. At SalesBrain, we have performed hundreds of such studies and what we have found will not surprise you: pain questions are always the most powerful questions to create segments of customers that have common patterns of consumer behavior.

WHAT TO REMEMBER

- Diagnosing pains helps you unveil the most critical decision drivers out of the many psychological factors that may influence your customer's behavior.

- Humans aspire to eliminate worries to survive and thrive. Our nature is to orient our attention to messages that awaken our fears, which is why a product or solution that can clearly articulate which pains it can eliminate first will receive more consideration and create higher urgency.

- There are three types of pains that can explain how and why people become attracted to a specific value proposition: financial pains, strategic pains, and personal pains. They all point to either material, emotional, and psychological needs we want to satisfy.

- Once you have successfully diagnosed the top pains by conducting pain dialogues, quantify the importance of the pains as well as consider creating segments or clusters of your top customers who share common pains.

The following sections are written by Patrick Renvoisé, the cofounder of SalesBrain, the "other hemisphere" of the SalesBrain team. Before starting SalesBrain with me, Patrick traveled over three million miles around the world to sell sophisticated products and solutions for Silicon Graphics (SGI) and for Linuxcare. As a computer engineer, he is truly passionate about making the complex simple to understand and helping people communicate and deliver memorable messages.

In prior chapters, I helped you understand the why of neuromarketing: Why does it work? Why can we not trust what people say? Why do we need to use new methods to collect invaluable information to decode people's intentions? Why do we no longer have the option to ignore persuasion sciences? I also introduced the first step to prepare your persuasive message based on NeuroMap: Diagnose the pain.

Patrick will now cover the remaining three steps starting with Step 2:

- Differentiate your claims: How to identify the top two or three unique reasons why people should choose your solution – or adopt your ideas – versus buying from your competitors or doing nothing.

CHAPTER **6**

Differentiate Your Claims

DIFFERENTIATE YOUR CLAIMS™

In order to be irreplaceable, one must always be different.
– Coco Chanel, fashion designer

D o you remember the second stimulus: contrastable? If you want your prospects to see the difference between your solution and your competitors' solution, then you need to clearly differentiate by highlighting your claims. The primal brain of your audience seeks a variance in its environment as a prompt for action. If you are not selling something unique, you are selling as much for your competitors as you are selling for yourself.

Most likely, you have many competitors who all offer products or services very similar to yours. Look at your home page; are you saying, "We are a leading provider of…"? Now look at your competitors' homepages; are they using the same "we are the leading provider of…"? If so, how much contrast does this provide? How will that help the primal brain of your audience see, understand, and remember why they should choose your apple in a stack of identical apples unless of course you offer the biggest apple!

To differentiate your claims, you need to use the *Von Restorff effect* to your advantage. First discovered in 1933, and later confirmed by many researchers, this cognitive bias states that an item that sticks out is more likely to be remembered. To make your solution stand out, you need to say: "We are the first/only/best provider of claim 1, claim 2, claim 3." Researcher Erin MacDonald at Stanford wrote: "Generally, product differences prove to attract more attention than commonalities" [143]. Also note that most messages focus on *what* the vendor does rather than *why* the customers should buy. To stand out and construct a message that is friendly to the primal brain you need a clear set of claims, emphasizing *why* they should choose your product. Simply imagine that you are writing a book entitled *Why Buy from Us?* We recommend that the book should have no more than three chapters (see Figure 6.1).

Your claims are the titles of the three chapters in your book (three is the maximum). As discussed in the section on memorable in Chapter 4, researchers have found that working memory can only hold and manipulate between three and five items, hence our recommendation

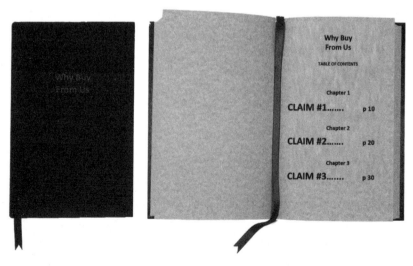

Figure 6.1   Claims book.

to select no more than three claims [144]. Later, we will also insist that you maximize both the *understanding* and the *memorization* of your message by repeating the claims consistently throughout your communication [145].

Claims represent a critical concept at the center of NeuroMap. When companies talk about *who* they are and *what* they do, it creates little or no interest because of the self-centered nature of the primal brain. Therefore, you should translate the *who* you are and *what* you do into a clear, concise, and convincing story about *why* your prospects should choose you. The following are a few examples of well-known companies who have used a strong and consistent claim.

WELL-KNOWN CLAIMS

Consider Volvo. Why would people want to buy a Volvo? Most people will say "safety" in just a few seconds. If we had to write a book titled *"Why Buy a Volvo?"* there would be only one chapter in that book – although we might then see three subchapters under the main chapter on safety.

Think now about Apple. The company started in April 1976, and they have historically used few claims. Why would people choose to buy a Macintosh in the 1980s and 1990s? Back then, you could either buy a PC, notorious for its complexity, or you could buy an Apple. Apple's claim for the first 30 years of its existence was *"easy to use."* More recently, as Apple expanded into the cellular phone business and most computers and phones became easier to use, their main claim became: *"cool to use."* Apple is not sparing any efforts to make their phones aesthetically and technologically pleasing; from the rounded edges, the slimness of the body, to face detection features, and even the shipping boxes, everything is meant to communicate coolness. That includes the price of the Apple X which broke the $1,000 threshold once believed to be the price beyond which a smartphone would never sell, . . . except to people who really want to be cool! In the long list of possible smartphones to choose from, including Samsung, Microsoft, Acer, Alcatel, and many more, notice how Apple stands out as the coolest one to use!

More examples of known brands with strong claims include the following:

- *We're number 1* by Hertz car rental. Nobody else can be number 1, so indeed this is unique, and the suggested value is that since they rent the same cars at the same airport counters for the same price, you will most likely get a better service.

- *We try harder* by Avis car rental: That means they confess to being number 2 – which is unique – but which also implies that you will get better service, even better than if you were renting from the number 1 (Hertz) because, fueled by Avis's ambition to become number one, they will try harder.

- *You got 30 minutes?* by Domino's Pizza. In December 2007 Domino's changed their claim from "30 minutes or less or it's free" to "You got 30 minutes?" Note that the "or it's free" offered a great proof, but Dominos dropped it to avoid the public perception of reckless driving.

- *The ultimate driving machine* by BMW.

How to Select Your Claims

Defining your claims is a rather simple theoretical process, but it can be challenging. Here are three critical steps:

1. Make sure each claim is a TOP claim; TOP is an acronym for:

   - **T**herapeutic: Your claims should provide a cure for a pain experienced by your prospects.

   - **O**riginal: Your claims should provide enough differentiation between you and any of your competitors. To ensure your claims display enough contrast, you need to know intimately the *reason* your prospects would want to buy from your competitors.

   - **P**rovable: You need to support your claims with strong proofs.

2. You should wordsmith your claim(s), so they become mnemonic, that is, they become easily memorable; one of the six stimuli!

3. When they are put together in one sentence, your claims should support your mission statement: "We are the first/best/only company to offer claim 1, claim 2, and claim 3." At SalesBrain, we coach many companies to make sure their mission statement includes their three claims and nothing else!

CLAIMS EXAMPLES FROM SALESBRAIN CUSTOMERS

By using clear claims, you will eliminate the confusion your customers may experience when they need to decide if they should choose you! As shown in the earlier examples, in most business-to-consumers (B2C) businesses, it is often considered more effective to use only one claim. Before going deeper into the science of claims, let's examine a few examples from SalesBrain's B2B customers.

Carothers DiSante & Freudenberger LLP is a labor law firm with multiple offices in California. Traditionally, law firms have focused their message on *who they are* (their list of partners) and *what they do* (the type of law they practice) without a clear indication of *why* you should choose them. By contrast, notice how CDF makes three clear, concise and consistent claims:

Notice how these three claims are

1. Therapeutic to the pain of being exposed to risk.

2. Original to CDF: no other law firm is making the same claims.

3. Provable, and they sound good.

Commenting about her claims (see Figure 6.2), Marie D. DiSante, managing partner said, "Developing and drawing upon this clear set of claims helped us explain why potential clients would want to work with us. We've noticed how these claims centered on protecting our clients are more effective in demonstrating why we are skilled at what we do. We now have a platform to signify to clients that we protect their best interests. This makes it much easier for our attorneys to talk about why companies should choose us!"

Figure 6.2   CDF claims.

CodeBlue is an industry leader in restoration claims management, working alongside a national contractor network to return *insurance* policyholders to pre-loss condition in the fastest, most efficient, and least disruptive manner possible (see Figure 6.3).

Paul Gross, CodeBlue CEO, stated: Nine months after starting to communicate our extraordinary claims to the market, we experienced a 34.87% increase in revenues compared to the nine months prior."

THE CONNECTION BETWEEN BRAND AND CLAIMS

Many marketing experts have attempted to precisely define what a brand is, but the concept remains fuzzy. We suggest the following definition: "A brand is a memory in the brain that connects the name of the product or service with a set of desirable benefits."

EXTRAORDINARY SPEED

Our Elite network of experts commits to the fastest response time in the industry ... anywhere in the United States.

EXTRAORDINARY SCIENCE

Our trained experts use our proprietary methodology to return policyholders to preloss condition in the most efficient manner possible.

EXTRAORDINARY SERVICE

Our active management techniques, and use of technologies like iPads, make a better policyholder experience, which results in improved customer satisfaction scores.

Figure 6.3   CodeBlue claims.

For example, when you heard the name Volvo and retrieved from your memory what you thought about Volvo, most likely the concept of *safety* came to mind. This association between two concepts, Volvo and Safety, is the result of a strategic decision that was made at Volvo headquarters 60 years ago. It is then the consistent repetition of the association of Volvo with safety in most – if not all – Volvo messages that created such a strong memory in your brain. Most likely it took you less than half a second to make that association. It should be noted that this association is driven more by affect than by cognition suggesting a strong connection with the primal brain [146].

Therefore, claims are the explicit expression of a limited set of key brand attributes, carefully worded to facilitate memorization and retrieval.

Meanwhile, there is a significant difference between B2C and B2B brands. For most B2C brands, the claims (or reasons to buy) tend to be implicit. Volvo is indeed an exception. But for a B2B brand, we believe it is critical for the top executives to create clarity, consensus, and commitment on the top three explicit reasons that customers should buy their solution: the claims should be determined once and for all, and they should be the focal point of all communication.

WHY LIMIT YOURSELF TO THREE SHORT CLAIMS?

Please memorize the sentence: "I love the weather in California." Repeat it a few times.

Now without looking at the written words on the page, try to say it backward word by word. Not easy? Why?

Because your brain's working memory can only handle a limited number of concepts at a time – typically three to five. With six words, the memorized sentence will jam your working memory. Try now to memorize the sentence: "I love California" and try to say it backward. It is easier because the message can easily be manipulated by your working memory. As you recall, the primal brain needs your message to be memorable, and organizing it under three claims will ease the processing and recall of critical information needed to make a decision.

Retrieval fluency is the ease with which information can be accessed from memory. To communicate a concept, an idea, or a complete sales/marketing message, our working memory will naturally select three to four chunks of data from a large amount of information, as well as retrieve knowledge about the topic we want to communicate, before it stores relevant information for long-term use [147, 148]. A chunk or package of information can be defined as a thought, feeling, idea, or concept, which, on average, can be held in working memory for about 20 seconds. As soon as working memory requires a new chunk of information, it will need to dump one of the current chunks to make room for the incoming one [149]. According to Smith and Jonides [149], when we hear a message, our brain automatically classifies the complete set of information by breaking it down to three or four chunks. Then it is stored in our working memory where we continue to assign each of the chunks to one simple label or word, even if it involves a very complex concept or experience. So, when you try to communicate your value proposition by giving a detailed description of all the benefits of your solution, the message will be poorly processed and poorly remembered. On the other hand, if you organize your arguments under a maximum of three chapters, whose titles are the claims, you will achieve better understanding and better recall.

Other researchers have shown that the relationship between persuasion and objective information is an asymptotic function. Passed a certain point, providing more information, even if that information is objective, will not increase persuasion [150]. The neural basis of the *verbatim effect*, the phenomenon that the gist of what someone has said is better remembered than the verbatim wording, has been demonstrated and is linked with activity in the hippocampus – part of the primal brain [151].

In conclusion, selecting a maximum of three chunks of information (three claims) upfront and simplifying their expression will make your message more effective with the primal brain: it will be more easily processed, understood, and encoded by your audience!

WHY WORDSMITH YOUR CLAIMS?

Processing fluency describes the ease with which information is handled by the brain, and it has been applied to marketing, to business names, and even to finance for many years. For example, researchers discovered that, during the week following an IPO, stocks that are easier to pronounce tend to perform better than others. For example, their ticker symbols are easy to pronounce such as KAG versus KHG [152]. Moreover, studies have found significant differences in likability, quality, originality, and memorability between rhyming and equivalent but nonrhyming slogans [153]. "Rhyming as a reason" is yet another cognitive bias, a manifestation of how our perception is dominated by our primal brain: it's not so much what you say rather it is the music of what you say that makes an impact!

Processing fluency can also be improved by other means. For instance, by improving font readability. Information provided in an easy-to-read font is typically rated as more familiar and more trustworthy than information provided in a hard-to-read font [154]. Processing fluency can also be raised by using more visible colors compared to colors that are more difficult to read against their background [155]. Even information that is focused versus blurry impacts processing fluency [156].

WHAT TO REMEMBER

You should remember that the primal brain will favor information that

- Claims give your prospects the solution to their top pains

- Uses short and simple words that are easy to pronounce [157].

- Do not use more than 3 claims to not overload the working memory of your prospects

- Reads easily with fonts that are processed with maximum processing fluency and in color, which offer a pleasing contrast with their background. Verdana, Tahoma, Times are always good choices for fonts [158].

- Is pleasing to the ear, so wordsmith your claims using:

  - A repetition of the same word as in "*protect, protect, protect.*" This creates a META-claim, a claim above all claims.

  - An alliteration (the repetition of the same letter or sound at the beginning of adjacent words) as in "Diagnose, differentiate, demonstrate, and deliver."

  - A rhyme as in "Protect your time, protect your dime, protect your peace of mind" (or pain, claim, gain). In the book titled *Pre-Suasion*, Professor Robert Cialdini reports, "The statement *Caution and measure will bring you riches* is seen as truer when changed to *Caution and measure win you treasure.*" There is a lesson here for persuasive success: "To make it climb, make it rhyme" [159].

  - Any other technique that creates a pleasing sound in the expression of your claims.

CHAPTER **7**

Demonstrate the Gain

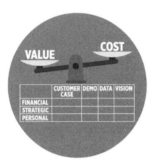

DEMONSTRATE THE GAIN™

Extraordinary claims require extraordinary evidence.
– Carl Sagan, astronomer, author, and science
communicator

A fter you *diagnose the pain* of your customers and *differentiate your claims*, you will now need to *demonstrate the gain* to help trigger a decision. Remember that it is not so much the value that you present that matters, rather it is the value that people believe in. Therefore, you will need to make an effective and convincing demonstration of the value. Your audience should hear or see highly *tangible* proofs, proofs that are simple to process cognitively and easy to believe. You need to lift the curtain of skepticism, and to do so, you need a strong demonstration of the *gain*, defined as the difference between *value* and *cost*.

Researchers at Oxford wrote, "When advertising persuades, the audience can be said, almost definitionally, to have tested and accepted the truth of a claim of value" [160].

THE SCIENCE OF GAIN COMPUTATION IN THE BRAIN

This topic has been the subject of prolific research in neuroeconomics, and we briefly introduced it earlier in the book. It is called *the utility of decision*. *Utility of decision* influences the consumers' willingness to pay different prices for different goods. Utility seeks to explain rationally: why people are willing to buy an expensive four-wheel-drive SUV in Los Angeles when it never snows there!

Brian Knutson, professor of psychology and neuroscience at Stanford University, and George Loewenstein, professor of economics and psychology in social and decision sciences at Carnegie Mellon University investigated what happens in the brain of consumers when they decide to purchase food and entertainment items [41]. The test subjects were given a comfortable sum of shopping money and the items they had to pick or reject ranged from chocolates to a digital voice recorder, to the latest Harry Potter book and more. When the subjects decided to pick an item, its price was deducted from their shopping money. Using an *f*MRI, the researchers visualized the activity of specific brain areas. They discovered that when the subject was first shown the image of an item, the nucleus accumbens (NAcc) was activated. As discussed earlier, this part of the brain plays a key role in the dopamine reward pathway. They noticed that the intensity of the activation of the NAcc correlated with the desire a subject had for an item. If the subject didn't experience an ardent desire for an item (for example, he could already own a copy of the last Harry Potter), his NAcc did not show much activity.

When the subjects were exposed to the cost of the item the *f*MRI data showed that excessive prices activated the insula: an area of the primal brain known to play a role in the processing of pain and negative experiences. Additionally, spending money deactivated the medial prefrontal cortex (MPFC) a brain region involved in complex cognitive functions and in moderation of social behavior. The researchers showed that by independently measuring the activity of these regions they could predict purchase decisions more reliably than the subject's self-reported intentions of purchase. This research confirmed the neural processes involved in weighing the trade-off between the pleasure of receiving the value and the pain of paying for it, that is, the cost, effectively assessing the neural response to the gain.

MEMORY AND GAIN EVALUATION

The encoding of value (or price) in memory is also the subject of intense research because of the complexity of the brain processes involved with numerical data. Numerical data can be represented in different formats:

- Seven: in plain English.
- 7: in Arabic numerals.
- VII: in Roman numerals.
- *******: in symbolic representation.

However, that is not the way people typically memorize the value of a number. Instead, they encode an approximation of the number [161]:

- 7 is "young" when referred to the age of a child.
- 7 is "cold" when referred to the temperature of a day.
- 7 is "cheap" when referred to the price of a bottle of wine.

Furthermore, a number of perceptual biases impact people's ability to process and compare numbers. For example, a bias called the *distance effect* shows that it takes longer to decide that 7 is greater than 2, than that 7 is greater than 6. Another one called the *magnitude effect* makes numbers with equal distance easier to discriminate when they are small, like 2 versus 3 rather than when they are large like 7 versus 8 [162]. From this research, we can conclude that an effective persuader must help the buyer make a simple and direct comparison of the *value* versus the *cost*.

One should note that, in most business-to-consumer (B2C) situations, vendors show or discuss the price only after presenting the value. In most large transactions (B2B), the buyer is informed of the cost only toward the end of the sales cycle. Even for low-cost transactions, such as the ones you may do on Amazon or eBay, notice how the picture of the product is on the left and the price is further to the right, making sure that we see the product first (positive stimulus) and the price second (negative stimulus). In fact, researchers at Stanford studied the impact of price primacy. They looked at the differences in brain response when the consumer is first informed of the price before being informed about the product [163]. They demonstrated that showing the price first promoted evaluations linked to the product's financial worth while showing the product first promoted evaluations related to the products' attractiveness or desirability. The conclusion is that if you are not selling the cheapest solution you should indeed present the product first followed by the price.

Your Value Proposition

Value (often called value proposition) is a favorite topic in the world of marketing. Of the roughly 200,000 books written on marketing about 1,000 focus specifically on the subject of the value proposition. By comparison, less than about 60 books have been written on neuromarketing so far, and over 1,000,000 books have been written on sales!

Fundamentally, when you are trying to sell or market a product or a service (or even an idea) your objective at any given price point should always be to maximize the value your prospects will perceive they receive. In other words, regardless of your price, you should attempt to maximize the value you present, and by doing so, you will maximize the GAIN defined as: value minus cost. Imagine you are selling a car for $50,000. If you can create the perception in the brain of your prospects that the value of your car is comparable to that of a Bentley, a Ferrari or a Tesla, it will become easier to sell than if the perceived value is comparable to a Fiat or a Hyundai. The perception of value is key!

By reviewing the most popular models on value, we identified three sources of value: financial, strategic, and personal. You may remember that we use the same categories to discuss the pain diagnosis. We further believe that the value can be proven with four types

Table 7.1 The value matrix.

Proof VALUE	Social Customer Case	Observable Demo	Analytical Data	Aspirational Vision
Financial				
Strategic				
Personal				

of proofs: social (customer testimonial), observable (demonstration), analytical (data) and aspirational (vision). Therefore, value can be presented as a matrix, shown in Table 7.1.

THE THREE TYPES OF VALUE

Financial Value

The *financial value* refers to the creation of measurable wealth, either by increasing savings or bringing additional revenues. Keep in mind that because of the loss aversion bias, helping your customers save $1 has a greater psychological value – in average about 2.3 times more – than helping them make an additional $1 [164, 165].

In a B2B context, the financial value is often labeled ROI (return on investment) or TCO (total cost of ownership) and it should be carefully quantified. For example, rather than saying "My solution will save you money," you should say, "You will save 12% of your manufacturing cost with my solution." Or even better, "You will save $58,000 annually with my solution." Note how a precise quantification of the value makes it more tangible than a vague and less convincing statement like "we will save you money" [166]. Also quantifying the value with an actual dollar amount as opposed to a percentage will reduce your prospect's cognitive effort. It makes it simpler to compare the value with your cost. If your solution has a price tag of $50,000, then your prospects will instantly understand that they can recoup their investment in less than one year. The gain calculation becomes obvious, even for their primal brains!

Strategic Value

The strategic value refers to a business value your prospect would experience with the understanding that this value cannot be translated into a credible financial quantification but offers nonetheless tangible benefits. For example, imagine you are selling a new type of seat belt to Volvo that offers a higher safety rating than the ones Volvo currently uses. Because safety is central to the value proposition of Volvo (it is, in fact, their main claim!) the increase of safety provided by your solution represents a strategic value. Note that translating this into a financial value would be challenging. Although an overall increase in safety of the Volvo cars is valuable, claiming it would help Volvo sell more cars would be a stretch because it would be difficult if not impossible to make a direct link between higher safety and additional sales.

Similar to the financial value, the strategic value should be quantified with an exact number. In the Volvo example instead of saying, "Our new seat belts will make your cars safer," say, "Your car safety index will increase from 88 to 91 thanks to our new seat belts." Note that in this case quantifying the value makes it more tangible and therefore more appealing to the primal brain.

Other examples of strategic value include less business risk, opportunity to diversify, increased quality, better differentiation, and so forth. All these examples point to a reduction of risk and uncertainty, which are crucial factors for the primal brain.

Personal Value

The personal value refers to the psychological or physical benefits your customers would experience because of your solution. Personal value includes less stress, pride of ownership, reduced work burden, being promoted, becoming a hero, feeling more secure or more empowered in the job, getting a bonus, receiving company or external recognition, etc. Unlike the financial and strategic type of value, personal value is difficult to quantify other than by using psychological constructs. Nevertheless, if your solution allows your customers to work less, you should try to quantify how much less: is it just five minutes per week or one hour per day? Notice that if the benefit of working less implies that your customers could, in turn, decrease the cost of their solution, it would then be wise to quantify that financial component of the value. Instead of saying "Our solution will save you time," say, "You will save five minutes on the assembly time of each of your machines, which means you will no longer have to do extra hours on Fridays (personal value) and it will result in production cost savings of $27 per machine (financial value)." Even in large B2B transactions, the personal value should not be underestimated. For example, for years when IBM was selling large computers, their motto was "Nobody ever got fired from choosing IBM."

The objective of an effective persuader should always be to maximize the amount of value presented and not to leave it open to the imagination of the audience.

THE FOUR TYPES OF PROOF

Please note that the value matrix presents the proofs in decreasing order of strength: the first type of proof, a customer testimonial, represents the strongest possible proof, whereas an aspirational proof, a vision, is the weakest type because it requires an act of faith from your audience: people have to believe your word.

Social Proof: Customer Testimonial

In his book *Influence: The Psychology of Persuasion*, Robert Cialdini identifies six laws of influence [167]:

- Social proof: The more people behave one way, the more it will incent others to match that behavior.

- Consistency and commitment: Once people make a statement in one direction in the future they will be psychologically motivated to remain consistent with the original statement.

- Reciprocity: When you do something nice to people, they will want to reciprocate.

- Liking: The more you have a positive rapport with people the more chances you have to influence them.

- Authority: People perceived as expert or in charge are more influential.

- Scarcity: The rarer an item, the more valuable it becomes.

A simple example of the impact of the law of social proof – which we want to use here to strongly demonstrate your value – is "canned laugher," which has proven to cause the audience to laugh longer and more often and to rate the comedy as funnier [168]. Cialdini states that we define as correct behavior what we see other people do. Other manifestations of this phenomenon can be seen when bartenders prime their tip jar with a few dollars, when car manufacturers claim "the number 1 selling truck in America" or when companies are eager to communicate the long list of customers who use their solution. Remember, our primal brain will make us behave like sheeps. The more we believe people behave one way, the more we will want to conform. In a business setting, how can you use this law to your advantage? The answer is by using one or more customer testimonials.

Customer testimonials or customer stories represent the best type of proof because not only do they come from a third party, as opposed to coming from the vendor, but they give an example of what the social norm could be. Furthermore, when carefully scripted and properly delivered, customer testimonials can transport viewers into a different world, a phenomenon described in detail in the section on persuasion catalysts: stories in Chapter 8. Imagine you are trying to sell seatbelts to BMW, and you have already sold your products to Volvo. You could use the following testimonial:

> By using the seatbelts from our new vendor, we saved $7 per car resulting in an annual saving of $3.5 M (financial value), while increasing the safety index of our cars by three points (strategic value). As a result, our entire purchasing department received the Best Department Contribution award directly from our CEO (personal value). – Johann Swenson, Purchasing Director, Volvo

Notice how difficult it would be for the prospects at BMW to argue with such a proof. Knowing the similarities between their business case and Volvo, most likely the buyers at BMW will start to imagine that they too would experience the same benefits!

Cialdini insisted that the law of social proofs works even better when we are observing the behavior of people with a high degree of similarity to us [169]. In the story, the obvious similarity between BMW and Volvo would make the social proof work stronger than if the prospect was a tractor manufacturer like John Deer or an airplane manufacturer like Boeing. Here again, note the link with the primal brain and the importance of similarity!

Finally, a customer testimonial represents the past. There is nothing speculative about it. It is factual, which is why it has such impact on the primal brain!

Example of the use of a customer testimonial to support the value of a claim. Tovar is the largest snow removal company in the United States, and their clients include large institutions like banks, hospitals, and big shopping malls. The pain of their customers is all about speed: How long will it take after a major snowstorm for their parking lots to become accessible again? For a hospital, lives are at stake when the ambulances cannot reach their facilities, and for shopping malls revenue loss is immediate when shoppers cannot enter the parking lot. Guided by SalesBrain, Tovar endorsed a set of claims centered on the swiftness of their intervention: Instant Communication, Instant Action, and Instant Relaxation. They also asked SalesBrain to develop a set of slides to help sell their services. To prove the value of instant relaxation we recommended that they use customer testimonials such as the one presented in Figure 7.1. In this example, notice that the customer uses the word "relaxed" to support the wording of one of their claims.

In conclusion, the best way to prove your value is to use the right customer stories. Testimonials are social proofs that have a strong persuading effect on the primal brain of your audience. Make them into videos to augment their visual and emotional impact.

Observable Proof: Demo

A demonstration (or demo) uses a prop, a visual, or a sequence of logical steps to prove a value statement in the present. Think about Domino's Pizza slogan: "30 minutes or less or it's free." The "or it's free" is a strong demonstration that the pizza will arrive on time.

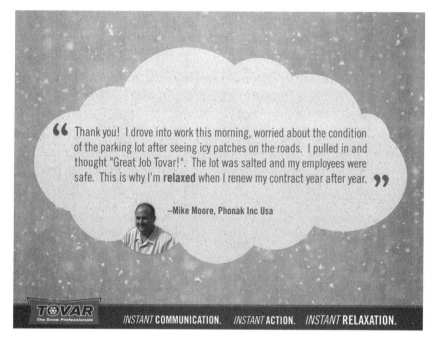

Figure 7.1   Tovar testimonial.

Table 7.2   Domino value matrix.

Proof VALUE	Social *Customer* *Case*	Observable *Demo*	Analytical *Data*	Aspirational *Vision*
Financial				
Strategic				
Personal		☑		

In Figure 7.2, notice how Sony highlighted the personal value of a small projector: it is difficult to tell which one is the laptop, and which one is the projector! At the time this ad was used, nearly 20 years ago, most projectors were bulky and heavy.

Figure 7.3 shows another example of a great demo, which uses the natural curiosity of the readers to deliver their value proposition!

VALUE Matrix of Sony Projector				
Proof VALUE	Social *Customer* *Case*	Observable *Demo*	Analytical *Data*	Aspirational *Vision*
Financial				
Strategic				
Personal		☑		

Figure 7.2   Sony value matrix.

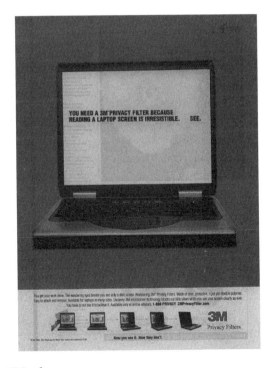

Figure 7.3   3M ad.

Table 7.3   3M value matrix.

Proof VALUE	Social Customer Case	Observable Demo	Analytical Data	Aspirational Vision
Financial		☑		
Strategic		☑		
Personal		☑		

Although the value is not clearly stated or quantified, note that the value of privacy is communicated on three types of value (see Table 7.3):

- Financial: You could lose a significant amount of money if your confidential information was seen by the wrong eyes.

- Strategic: Losing confidential information could be detrimental to your business.

- Personal: Having to deal with identity theft or the loss of your credit card and other sensitive financial or health information could bring stress for years.

Although each of those examples speak to radically different value points, note the space the demonstration of the value occupies: for instance, in the case of 3M, the visual highlighting the value proposition (the *why* you should buy) is 8 to 10 times bigger than the series of five images at the bottom that explains the *what* the product does. Now contrast this with what most advertisers do. They give a long explanation of the *what* with few or no reason for the *why*!

An observable proof such as a demo or a demonstration is second to a customer testimonial in providing an irrefutable type of proof.

Analytical Proof: Data

"In god we trust…all other please bring data!" is the motto of the skeptics. Despite that skeptic opinion, data are abstract and provide weaker proof than a customer testimonial or a demo. However, you can still prove your *value* using data.

When using data as a proof, research shows that the credibility of the source of the data impacts the persuasion effect [170]. Furthermore, studies have shown that quantification of the data always brings some persuasion benefit. The exception to this rule states that quantification might put more reliance on the fact that the source of information needs to be perceived as an expert for the persuasion effect to occur [171]. Note that the diagnostic phase of NeuroMap serves to unveil the pain of your customers and provides an opportunity to establish your expertise in the domain.

Imagine you are selling manufacturing equipment. To prove your value, you could say, "Our new machines would save you $240,000 per year on your manufacturing cost." Note that such a statement is not using data to prove the value, it's just a quantification of the value but the proof is aspirational, it's your hope that you would save them that amount.

Now imagine if you were saying, "Our machines will shorten your manufacturing time by 10%. Your plant is running 2,400 hours a year, so as a result you will save 240 hours per year. Since you mentioned that your production cost is $1,000 per hour, you will save $240,000."

Notice that although the savings presented in the two examples above are identical, the first one requires a total act of faith in what the vendor says (the $240,000), whereas the second requires two assumptions:

1. Your prospect believes you will shorten the manufacturing time by 10%. The rest of the numbers will be easily accepted because they came from them.

2. Your prospect understands the logic of your argument. For that, he needs to comprehend how you came up with the $240,000 savings.

The current example is obvious but in most B2B situations these calculations can be very complex, and they will inevitably lead to a major cognitive load on the brain of your audience, a task that is energetically taxing and is often conducive to confusion, not persuasion.

Therefore, your objective is to arrive at quantification of the value – financial, strategic, or personal – by using the simplest possible formula compatible with your audience's level of comprehension of mathematical or abstract concepts. For example, if you sell a complex solution that will be reviewed by a CFO, it would be relevant to use a sophisticated ROI model. But if you are in a B2C situation, the use of data to build your proof should be simple to understand. Remember, even the simplest data are not appealing to the primal brain!

Figure 7.4 and Table 7.4 are great examples of data to prove the value.

Notice how the ad in Figure 7.4 uses data: the percentage of times the judges have agreed with them. However, they provided the proof but didn't translate it – most likely a difficult task – into either a financial value, how much money you would save on average by winning your lawsuit, and/or a personal value, not spending many sleepless nights under the stress of a lawsuit.

Monarch Medical Technologies has developed innovative software to better manage glucose for diabetic patients. In the first slide,

Figure 7.4   Quinn law firm data example.

Table 7.4   Quinn value matrix.

Proof / VALUE	Social Customer Case	Observable Demo	Analytical Data	Aspirational Vision
Financial			☑	
Strategic				
Personal				

shown in Figure 7.5, note how they used data to emphasize the pain of the nurse who is caring for her patients.

Then in the following slide (Figure 7.6) see how they used data to prove the value of their solution and how these numbers contrast with the numbers associated with the pain.

To further strengthen the proof, note that they could present the original data they used to come up with the numbers:

- 0.7% of deviation versus 93.3%

- 46% of reduction of checks

- 75% increase in nurse satisfaction

In conclusion, data could be used when stronger types of proof (social or observable) are not available. An effective persuader should make the data easy to process and believe.

Aspirational Proof: Vision

When no other proofs are available, there is still a way to persuade: by using the power of your vision or belief. You surely have heard this kind of proof when a seller says: "Trust me, we'll save you $1,000!" Because of the absence of actual proof, the seller needs to make the vision bold and impressive. Such an aspirational proof typically requires telling a story, an analogy or using a metaphor to get your prospects to trust the value they will receive.

The ad shown in Figure 7.7 received multiple advertising awards.

156

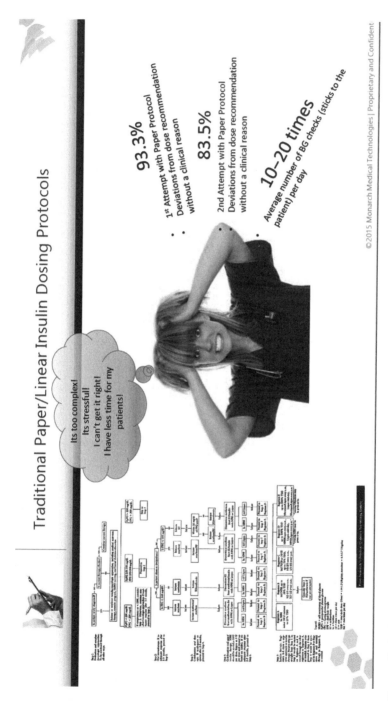

Figure 7.5   Monarch pain visual.

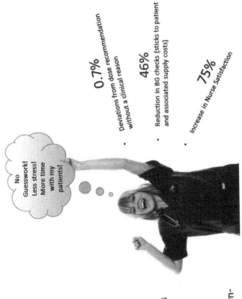

Figure 7.6   Monarch gain visual.

Figure 7.7   Sanders ad.

Note that it is not a customer case because most readers are not naïve enough to believe that this license plate really exists as opposed to having been created by the ad agency. It would have been a customer case if a famous divorced woman like Ivana Trump (divorced Donald Trump in 1991) or Angelina Jolie (divorced Billy Bob Thornton in 2003) was standing by the car. It is also not a demo because the ad doesn't prove that indeed the woman would be able to get the car out of a settlement. Therefore, this is using a vision: "Trust us, we'll be able to get you the car." The value has a financial component: the worth of that vehicle, say $50,000, and it also has a personal component: revenge! The value matrix for this ad is shown in Table 7.5.

One should note that although the type of proof used is quite weak, the ad still has a great impact because the message is delivered emotionally to your primal brain!

Another splendid example of the use of a vision to close a deal, and revolutionize the world in the process, is the story of how

Table 7.5   Sanders value matrix.

Proof / VALUE	Social Customer Case	Observable Demo	Analytical Data	Aspirational Vision
Financial				$50,000
Strategic				
Personal				Revenge

Jim Clark started Netscape – Jim, the only entrepreneur who ever started three companies that were worth more than $1 billion, first founded SGI (Silicon Graphics Inc). I met Jim when I opened the first Branch of Silicon Graphics in Toulouse France and later when SGI offered me a job at their headquarters in Mountain View, California. Jim left SGI in 1993 and invested $3 million of his own money to start Netscape, the company that invented the first browser and spearheaded the revolution that became known as the Internet era. In 1994, and before its world-record-breaking IPO (initial public offering) in August 1995, Jim was desperately trying to raise money, so he pitched his ideas to the top venture capital (VC) firms in Silicon Valley. The value of a browser, which made accessing the web easy through its graphical interface, could not be proven by using any other proofs of value than the vision of Jim Clark and he couldn't use:

- A customer case by saying that Bill Gates made a fortune with Microsoft Internet Explorer. It took several years after Netscape for Microsoft to develop its first browser.

- A demo. In fact, much of the money Jim needed was to develop a first running demonstration of Navigator, the first Netscape browser.

- Data, because there was no reliable data that could predict how many people would use a browser to access the Internet. There was no consensus on what people would do with the Internet besides what the research community had done –that is, exchange scientific data over the Internet!

Between 1993 and 1995 Jim was trying to keep Netscape alive because the company was losing a lot of money. Yet, on the IPO day of August 15, 1995, many people started to buy Jim's vision; the IPO raised over $300 million on a valuation of $2 billion with revenues of only $16 million for the six months preceding the IPO, with no prospect of making a profit for at least two years. That's the value of a good vision!

However, before this incredible success, Jim had a tough time selling his vision. In fact, New Enterprise Associates, one of the tier 1 VCs in Silicon Valley, turned down Jim's offer to join as an early investor. It was not obvious then that a browser would be worth anything. And betting investment money on the vision of an entrepreneur is a risky proposition.

The moral of this story is that even if you are Jim Clark and even if you're holding a piece of software that will change the world, you should try to present a better proof of value than your vision to influence the primal brain of your audience. Yes, it's possible to persuade using a vision, but it represents the weakest type of proof!

Note that the border between the four kinds of proofs we are suggesting are not definitive. For example, if you were selling toothbrushes you could use the following statement: "Our new toothbrush is recommended by 80% of dentists." Note that this proof is a combination of data and a social validation, so its strength should be considered greater than a proof that uses only data as in the earlier manufacturing example.

THE COST

Just as for the value, the cost can be categorized into three components, discussed next.

Financial Cost

Financial cost is always the most well-defined element of cost. In B2C, the price is usually on the tag attached to the item. And in B2B, the cost typically appears prominently on the first or last page of the proposal.

Table 7.6 Cost matrix.

Cost Matrix	Cost
Financial	
Strategic	
Personal	

Strategic Cost

Strategic cost is most relevant when selling a B2B solution. This includes the business cost of acquiring your solution such as increased risk, less flexibility, diverting critical resources to the deployment of your solution, and so forth.

Personal Cost

It covers how your solution could impact negatively the personal lives of buyers. This may include the risk of a switching to a new vendor, the pain of learning a new system such as what would happen if you went from a Google phone to an iPhone or vice versa, having to work overtime, dealing with a new and stressful process, and so forth. The cost can also be represented in the form of the following matrix.

THE GAIN EQUATION

The gain equation can be represented by:

$$\boxed{\text{Gain}} = \boxed{\text{Value claim 1}} + \boxed{\text{Value claim 2}} + \boxed{\text{value claim 3}} - \boxed{\text{Cost}}$$

We recommend that you calculate the total value by adding only the value brought by the unique benefits presented by your solution – those offered under your claims, as opposed to simply adding the value presented by the difference between the existing solution versus the new solution. This is to emphasize that to compare and contrast the primal brain needs first and foremost to understand the unique value offered by your solution. In that case, the gain calculated doesn't represent the difference the client would experience between their existing solution and your solution, but the difference between what they would get between you and any of your competitors' solutions. To account for the loss aversion bias, a more psychologically accurate representation of the gain equation is:

$$\boxed{\text{Gain}} = \boxed{\text{Value claim 1}} + \boxed{\text{Value claim 2}} + \boxed{\text{Value claim 3}} - 2.3 * \boxed{\text{Cost}}$$

Furthermore, it should be noted that the customers' brain will experience the pain of the cost immediately after the purchasing decision. And, it is expected to be counterbalanced by the hope of receiving the value at an uncertain point in the future. Thus the equation becomes:

$$\boxed{\text{Gain}} = -2.3 * \boxed{\text{Cost}}$$

[experienced immediately at time of purchase with 100% probability]

$$+ \boxed{\text{Value claim 1}} + \boxed{\text{Value claim 2}} + \boxed{\text{Value claim 3}}$$

[experienced at an unknown future time, with a probability linked to the strength of the proof]

As you now understand, presenting this complex equation to the no less complex intricacies of the brain remains a challenge. At SalesBrain, we believe the vendor is responsible for making that demonstration primal brain friendly. This means, achieving cognitive fluency with a gain demonstration that is well laid out, so it can be easily understood and easily remembered.

WHAT TO REMEMBER

- Gain is the difference between value and cost.

- Gain proofing is critical to make sure your value proposition is not only clear but credible.

- It is your burden to prove that the gain is believable.

- Break down your gain in terms of financial value, strategic value, and personal value.

- There are four ways to prove the gain. The most effective way is to use customer testimonials, then a demo, then data, and finally a vision.

Now you have

- Diagnosed the pain
- Differentiated your claims
- Demonstrated the gain

Now that the content of your message is defined, it is time to work on the delivery of your message, and you need to

- Deliver to the primal brain.

CHAPTER **8**

Deliver to the Primal Brain

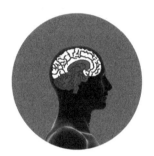

DELIVER TO THE PRIMAL BRAIN™

The answers to the first three steps of pain, claims, and gain will define the content of your message i.e *what* you should communicate to maximize the probability that your targets' brains, both their rational brains and more importantly their primal brains, will support a *yes* decision. Now you need to work on *how* to communicate those concepts of pain, claims, and gain, so their brains truly understand, believe, and remember what you are saying. You need to make the delivery of your message brain-friendly! NeuroMap gives you the blueprint of the best delivery to achieve the maximum persuasive effect. There are two critical concepts we will discuss next: persuasion elements and persuasion catalysts. We recommend that you look up the poster illustrating NeuroMap printed on the back of the book cover, or go to www.salesbrain.com to download it for free!

Six Persuasion Elements

The persuasion elements are the building blocks or fundamental ingredients of the content you need to communicate to your customers (Figure 8.1).

Figure 8.1   Six persuasion elements.

To use a chemistry analogy, if the persuasion elements are the various components of your messages, the persuasion catalysts (Figure 8.2) represent the Bunsen burners, that will turn up the heat on your elements and accelerate and amplify their persuasive effect.

Figure 8.2   Seven persuasion catalysts.

Let's now review the appetizer of your message, the first persuasion element that will whet their appetite to learn more about you and your value proposition.

Grabbers

"If you grab attention in the first frame with a visual surprise you stand a better chance of holding the viewer."

                       – David Ogilvy, advertising expert

Most people cannot easily capture attention. Let's face it, your prospects are not typically eager to receive another sales message embedded in a piece of advertising, an email, voicemail, a presentation, a website, or a brochure. Undoubtedly, they are focused on something else, and your objective is to divert their attention so they can start to orient their mental energy to process your message.

As our discussion on the neuroscience of attention established, attention is a complicated neurological process that cognitive neuroscientists have studied for many years. The human body sends about 11 million bits of information per second to the brain yet, the conscious mind can only process about 50 bits per second [172]. So how do we decide to focus our attention, or how does our brain decide to select 50 bits per second out of 11 million?

Consider the experiment conducted by Darren Brown, a British mentalist and illusionist. How much attention do you think a wallet with $300 in cash would receive when left unattended on a busy sidewalk in London? How long would it take for people to notice it and pick it up? Check the video at https://tinyurl.com/kku4raj.

Surprisingly, if a yellow circle is drawn around it, the wallet goes unnoticed for hours and many passersby simply miss it. Of course, without the circle, the wallet is picked up in seconds. This experiment suggests that the circle signals to our primal brain something abnormal, and therefore the presence of the wallet is denied to our conscious awareness. The experiment was later repeated in other cities around the world and generated identical results: it's not just about how British minds work!

Likewise, Chabris (Harvard University) and Simons (Illinois University), psychologists and cognitive scientists, revealed the surprising effect of change blindness and inattentional blindness [173]. In a famous experiment, which won them the Ig Nobel Prize – a prize similar to the Nobel Prize to reward ten unusual achievements in scientific research – Chabris and Simons demonstrated that humans often fail to recognize an unexpected stimulus in plain sight. See it for yourself at https://tinyurl.com/8fuake8.

Consider what this means for a stimulus like your website, your marketing campaigns, your brochures, your trade show booth or your PowerPoint presentations. How can you capture your audience's attention every single time you have a message to deliver? Maybe you think you are offering your customers a wallet full of cash. But how do you make sure that your message is noticeable? How do you ensure that its complexity or lack of self-relevance does not trigger attentional blindness? Its length, the use of too much text or simply the lack of an emotional cocktail are all conditions that would make it ignored. Too often, messages do not capture the attention of your audience simply because they are not primal brain friendly!

Also, consider what Wolf Singer, neurobiologist and director of the Max Planck Institute for Brain Research, said: "Preliminary attention ensures a fast treatment of the information and a good transmission of the computational results, it means an effective programming in the entire cortical network" [174, 175]. That's what a grabber does: it creates the preliminary attention that will make the rest of your message easier to understand.

Even if you were able to initially divert the attention of your prospects, are you holding it long enough? Researchers actually discovered specific neurons in the nucleus accumbens – a brain section associated with motivation, pleasure and positive reinforcement – that trigger sleep when the subject is bored [176].

Additionally, researchers Richard Anderson and James Pichert demonstrated that what is remembered depends upon early information received. In a classic experiment, subjects were asked to read a story about a residential home either from the perspective of a burglar or that of a homebuyer. Their memories about the story were not an accurate recording. Instead, it was a filtered version impacted by instructions they had received [177, 178].

Before your targets decide to open your email, read your brochure, or pay attention to your PowerPoint presentation, you need to motivate them to change the object of their attention. You also need to prepare their minds for remembering what is important for them in your message. Think of a grabber as a short, highly condensed, yet exciting way of telling your audience why they should stop doing what they are doing, stop thinking what they are thinking about, and why, instead, they should focus their mental energy on your message right away.

Imagine if you were selling a gold mine. Your best grabber could be to lay your largest nuggets on a table just in front of their eyes. The effect of your grabber would be to create an instant understanding of your value proposition, capturing attention in the immediate experience or the forever present in which the primal brain lives.

Often, print ads are just grabbers. The advertiser tries to get you to stop flipping the pages, so you invest a few seconds of your precious attention to notice it. It's the visual as opposed to the text that will make you stop. To explore the concept of a grabber, consider the familiar exercise of giving a presentation using PowerPoint, Keynote, or similar tools. Keep in mind however that the concept of grabber applies to any form of communication.

Think about the last time you gave a sales presentation using slides? Did you start with

1. Your corporate overview?

2. Your agenda?

3. Your personal background?

4. A description of your product or services?

Do you think this information was compelling enough to stop the current train of thoughts of your audience's brain so that they give you their undivided attention? Do you realize now that you were drawing a circle around a wallet full of cash? Instead, learn to throw a nugget right in front of them!

How do you create a powerful first impression? How do you immediately capture attention and give your audience an instant understanding of what your solution, product or idea could do for them? Remember the stimulus of memorable, which discussed how important it is to hijack attention at the beginning: the primacy effect? The first minutes of your presentation, the first line of your email – its subject line – your website landing page, or the first words of your voicemails all require special attention. That is why you need a grabber! With a grabber, you recruit their attention and get your audience to focus their limited – 50 bits per second – of conscious perception on *your message*.

We will discuss five different types of grabbers. Note that by combining them and using your creativity, you can certainly come up with more ideas. You will notice that all grabbers can be used in face-to-face presentations, and some of them can also be used in videos, web pages, emails, voicemails, printed ads, and even direct mail.

1. Prop: using an actual object representing a metaphorical symbol of your value proposition.

2. Minidrama: making your prospects' brains re-experience pains or frustrations when they don't use your product, solution, or idea. Then, contrasting this negative experience with how painless their life would be if only they could use your product or solution.

3. Word plays: finding the right words to express your value proposition compellingly and surprisingly.

4. Rhetorical questions: asking questions that will force the brain of the audience to imagine what benefits you can provide with your product or solution.

5. Stories: making your value proposition alive by turning one or several of your benefits into a narrative your audience's brain will believe.

Props

Meet Health and Safety Institute (HSI) a company based in Eugene, Oregon. HSI delivers high-quality training materials, courses and programs in CPR, first aid, and advanced emergency care to health professionals, first responders, and employees (Figure 8.3). In 2011, Bill Clendenen, HSI CEO and president, asked SalesBrain to solidify its claims. During a two-day NeuroMap workshop, the executive team was able to quickly identify the best claims that would appeal to the thousands of instructors who buy their products. The real benefits were that they made their life easier. Bill and his top 12 managers agreed on the following wording for their claims: Easy for your people, easy for your business, easy for you.

Then in 2015, during their two-day annual user conference called Summit Connect, Bill gave his opening keynote to a crowd of over

EASY FOR
YOUR PEOPLE

EASY FOR
YOUR BUSINESS

EASY FOR
YOU

Figure 8.3   HSI claims.

300 instructors, all eager to learn more about HSI. A terrific presenter, Bill first thanked the audience for taking time out of their busy schedules, then he dived in the topic. Bill said: *"In the next two days you will see how much easier your lives will be by using our courses. Our objective will be to demonstrate how: easy for your people, easy for your business, and easy for you it will be to work with HSI. As you now understand our goal is really to make it easier for you. You should get prepared to hear the word **easy** a million times in the coming 48 hours."* Then Bill continued: *"In fact, I'd like you to reach under your seats."* Puzzled attendees leaned down and discovered that a curious object had been taped under their seats. While people were opening their package, the large conference hall became filled with a metallic voice that said: "That was easy!" Everybody had received the famous "easy button" from Staples (Figure 8.4), and 300 people were frantically pushing it!

Figure 8.4   Easy button.

As you can imagine, the easy button became the hit of the conference, and all the attendees heard the easy message a thousand times!

Later Bill reported: *"Aligning our executive team on a set of consistent EASY claims, was a turning moment in our company's history. It brought us vision and clarity of purpose. After endorsing these claims and making them more tangible with the help of the easy button, we have grown consistently at over 21% per year for the last four years. In an otherwise flat industry, gaining market share brings a big smile on my face!"*

Clearly, Bill's results are not only attributable to the use of that prop, but it certainly contributed to the growth of HSI and to the success of that conference.

Other examples of the powerful use of a prop include when Bill Gates released a flock of mosquitoes in the auditorium where he was delivering a TED talk on eradicating malaria [179].

Or when Steve Jobs introduced the MacBook Air. His objective was to demonstrate the claim that the new computer was super thin and Jobs used an envelope as a prop in which he unveiled the MacBook Air (https://tinyurl.com/y9dw2q5w at 1:20).

How can props produce such an effect? Why do they have such a positive, strong, and memorable impact on the primal brain of your audience? NeuroMap predicts they do because they trigger the visual and tangible stimuli. However, there is more evidence proving the remarkable power of props.

The Science of Props. Todd Rogers, a behavioral scientist at Harvard School of Development, ran a series of experiments to test what makes people remember more easily. Rogers showed that a physical object is a more effective way to spark your memory than written or electronic reminders. For example, tying a knot on your handkerchief will be more effective than writing a note on your smartphone [180]. Marie Stadler from the University of Wisconsin also demonstrated the effects of props on how well kids remember a story [181]. Her findings suggest that the manipulation of physical props assisted the children in better remembering the story leading to the inclusion of more descriptors in their narrative retells.

Dr. Todd C. Handy, a neuroscientist at Dartmouth University, said, "Screwdrivers, steering wheels and coffee mugs could soon join food, flashing lights and sexy bodies as neurological *attention-getters*. They are so important they can automatically draw our attention to them" [182]. Handy's team hooked up groups of college students to electroencephalograms (EEGs) to measure brain activity in neurological areas responsible for attention. They asked students to quickly look at pictures featuring both a graspable object (such as a screwdriver or mug) and a less-graspable object (the sun, a sailboat), arranged side by side. After a split-second, flashing lights would appear over one of the two objects presented. From the EEG readings, Handy's team found that brain activity was always higher when the flashes occurred over the tool versus the nontool, suggesting that the viewer had automatically been focusing on the tool, even before the flashing began. In other words, the screwdriver or the mug was already in the "spotlight of attention," he said. Handy proposed that the findings tell us "that grabbable objects can, in fact, grab our attention" in ways that mimic our brain's response to sexual triggers, danger signals, food and other important stimuli."

Examples of the Use of Props. With over 20,000 CEO members, Vistage is the world's largest membership organization of CEOs worldwide. Since 2003, Christophe and I have delivered well over 1,000 talks on the topic of neuromarketing to Vistage members around the world. Because of the enthusiasm for our topic and the value CEOs receive from NeuroMap, we both received the 2008 "Above and Beyond" speaker award. Vistage CEOs meet monthly in groups of about 15 members, and they are coached by a chair (typically a former CEO or senior executive). The role of Vistage chairs is to help CEOs become *Better Leaders* who make *Better Decisions* and achieve *Better Results* – claims that SalesBrain helped develop. Did you also notice the acronym of LDR for *Leaders, Decisions, Results*? Vistage is indeed an organization of leaders helping other leaders. Prospective CEO members do not always understand the value of joining Vistage so we recommended that Vistage chairs use a prop to describe the value proposition. The prop includes several critical instruments: A whistle symbolizes the nature of their unique role as

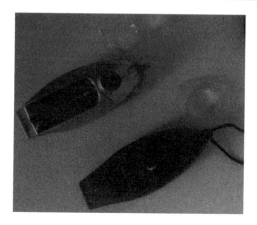

Figure 8.5   Vistage prop.

executive coaches and strategic facilitators. It also includes a small thermometer, a compass, and a magnifier. It became easy for the chairs to explain that once a CEO has established his heading (compass), his group of peers can help him find which tactics he should be focusing on (magnifier) and what could prevent him from reaching his goals (mirror). The thermometer represented the metrics the CEO would share with the group each month to track his business, and the whistle was used by the chair to remind the CEO they would be held accountable for the commitments they would make to them and the group members.

Dan Barnett, Vistage COO at the time, said: *"Using a common, clear, and consistent set of claims really helped our large community of chairs, speakers, and members understand the unique value proposition of Vistage. Then, when we started to use props, the concepts of better leaders, better decisions, better results came to life. Aspiring chairs and prospective members quickly understood why they should invest some time, money, and energy with our organization and we saw a significant growth."*

If your value proposition is linked to money, for instance, if you can demonstrate a financial gain, using real cash (or shredded money) can be very effective. After attending one of our Vistage workshops and learning about the impact of using a prop, Mary C.

(a Vistage Member and CEO of a collection agency) sent this email to her fellow group members:

From: Mary C.

Sent: Wednesday, November 02, 2005

Subject: Y'all are going to think I'm crazy – but it worked!

FYI – I had a meeting with a client this morning that I lost to a competitor about 2 years ago when the CFO changed. This was a very profitable client that we did a great job for and only lost because we did not have a relationship with the new CFO. We finally got an appointment after calling for over 18 months. We had one shot at this because the guy was tired of hearing from us so I decided to step out on Patrick Renvoisé's ledge and I brought $111,476 in cash with me – this was the dollar amount that we collected for them in 2004. (I was not 100% sure that I was going to take the money out cause I personally thought the cash all over the place approach was a little in your face – possibly even obnoxious.) The beginning of the meeting went well but I was not going to be walking out the door with anything more than a thank you so when it came time to tell him how important his account was to us. I opened the briefcase . . . his eyes were huge (I felt like a drug dealer). The contract was signed 15 minutes later and we will get accounts from him in 2 weeks. "No one has ever done something like that to get my attention." He believes that he is very important to us because we made the effort to bring the cash to him to literally "show him the money." I was not mugged and the money is back at the bank.

Unbelievable!

I had to share that with you guys 'cause I never thought it would have worked!

– Mary

Do you remember CodeBlue presented in the claim section in Chapter 6? They use the claims of

- Extraordinary speed
- Extraordinary science
- Extraordinary service

Working with SalesBrain, Paul Gross, CEO, became convinced that using a prop would create an effective grabber. Later Paul said *"One of the most effective campaigns that we ever deployed used a prop:*

Figure 8.6   CodeBlue prop.

a box of crap! It was sent to the top insurance executive in America, showing water-damaged construction materials like wallboard, carpet, and wood. It got the attention of many of the senior claims officers, and our business has prospered as a result" (see Figure 8.6).

What to Remember About the Use of Props

- Your audience might not remember much of what you tell them, but they will remember your prop. Using a bottle of wine at a conference on addiction might bring you boos or a standing ovation. It all depends on the pain of the people in your audience and the relevance and originality of your prop. Test it before you use it!

- You should plan on learning how to manipulate the prop. Don't just hold it without a purpose. Learn to tell a story where the main character is the prop. Notice how Steve Jobs carefully held the envelope and slowly retrieved the notebook out of it!

- The best props are the ones that become a metaphor for your value proposition. For Steve Jobs, the envelope symbolized super thin.

Minidrama

"When you sell fire extinguishers, open with the fire!"
– David Ogilvy, advertising expert

In 2003, when Stratex (now part of Aviat Networks), a telecom-munication company in Silicon Valley, contacted SalesBrain, they had been a global supplier to one of the largest Telecom Operators in the world. But that year, their client decided to create a single purchas-ing center and launched a worldwide process to decrease their number of hardware suppliers from 12 to 3, with the ultimate goal to get bet-ter prices for 25 of their subsidiaries. Back then, Aviat was a relatively small player in this industry, and this opportunity was both exciting because they could gain more sales, but also risky because they could lose the revenue they were already making with a handful of interna-tional subsidiaries. Also, Stratex would need to invest a large amount of time, money, energy, and resources to respond to a complex request for proposal, and, given their size compared to other bidders, they believed they had a very low probability of winning one of the three vendor seats. The competition was made of large telecom generalists companies like Ericsson, Alcatel, NEC, Siemens, Lucent, Marconi, and more.

Patrick Martini, director of European business, tells the story of how SalesBrain helped Stratex use minidramas to impact the primal brain of their audience and win a spot in the limelight.

The first thing we did was to gather a huge amount of information on the pains of all the decision influencers. After submitting our response to a preliminary eval-uation, we learned that we ranked 8 out of 12 suppliers; still very far from being in the top 3 to be awarded one of the coveted global procurement contracts! At that point, we evaluated our probability to win at about 5%. Since a critical event in the selection process was to deliver a formal presentation in front of the buying committee – 30 members strong from 24 different nationalities – we decided that our best chance to grab the attention of the buying committee and sway the odds in our favor was to deliver a minidrama. The buying committee had reserved 2 full days at their headquarters when each of the eight pre-selected vendors would give 2 hours to present their proposal. Our presentation was set just after lunch on the second day when the committee had already heard the six previous ven-dors. Needless to say, they were tired and bored of hearing some very technical and not-so-exciting presentations. We really needed to recapture their attention and a series of short minidramas aligned with their top pains provided the best option to do that. Here is what we did: for the first 2 minutes, we started to deliver what promised to be a long, boring, and very technical presentation. Several of the committee members were so disconnected that they yawned uncontrollably. Then our VP of marketing abruptly and loudly interrupted the presentation. It created an uneasy moment which helped us regain their attention and prepare them to receive our well-crafted message. This is when we recapped their top pains which were based on the diagnostic we had conducted in prior months and we asked them to confirm that:

1. *They couldn't choose a partner that is not focused on providing top notch customer service in the wireless space.*

2. *They couldn't take any risk with a supplier that is not 100% focused on serving the wireless technology market.*

3. *They needed to reduce cost without compromising technology and customer service.*

Our punch line was to ask them if they wanted to hear how Aviat was better positioned than any of the other vendors to help them: Delight (as in customer satisfaction), Derisk, and Decost the network operator. These were our carefully crafted claims for which we even had created icons [see Figure 8.7].

Our presentation on these three chapters lasted only 1 hour and 15 minutes and one of our minidramas served to illustrate that we offered the best option to mitigate all their risks: financial strength, constant innovation, multiple sites of production, excellent installation services, even in the most dangerous countries. To further grab their attention and demonstrate that we were their only risk-free partner, we decided to use the skills of Heinz Stumpe, our VP of sales. Heinz was a former karate champion and he had competed with the German team in the World Championship! Heinz told the following story to the buying panel:

Figure 8.7   Stratex claims.

"A couple of years back, I was asked by a very famous karate school in the US to award black belts. After the ceremony, one of the freshly awarded new black belts said: We have a black belt, like you . . . so we have the same level!" Feeling a little teased I asked them to break a brick as it is a standard practice when you reach the black belt level in karate . . . but I added a twist: I asked him to do it with a "2-inch punch" where he had to place his hand only 2 inches above the brick. "The young black belt attempted to break the brick that way but hurt his fist trying. In the end, he protested that it was impossible," added Heinz.

This is when Heinz took a real brick out of his briefcase, placed it on the table in front of the committee of buyers and with a loud BANG he broke the brick with that 2-inch punch. His punch made such a big noise that all the meeting participants jumped out of their seat. Heinz had their attention and he delivered his punch line: "It is not because you have a black belt that you will perform the same way a champion black belt would. It takes complete focus to not hurt yourself in this exercise: similarly, our 100% focus on microwave radio is the best insurance for your business. We are your best option to: Delight, Derisk, Decost."

When we finished, the committee concluded that we understood their pain even better than they did and that out of all the presentations they had seen so far, this one was the only one they wished had lasted longer! Bottom line: after a few more months of arduous negotiations the operator announced that we had won one of the three agreements which generated $150 MM in revenue for our company over the next five years. They still remember our presentation today and these minidramas did help us close the deal!"

Most people think that a B2B sales message *must* be delivered in a rational, traditional, PowerPoint format. So, the basic element of a presentation is a slide. Yet, most PowerPoint slides fail to capture the attention of an audience. Why? Because they are rarely addressing pains that are the most relevant to the audience. They do not state clear claims and typically they do not prove enough gain. By contrast, researchers have shown: "When an argument is successful the audience weighs the evidence and then yields to it. When a drama is successful, the audience becomes lost in the story and experiences the concerns and feelings of the character," [160].

Other Examples of Minidramas. On June 29, 2007, when Steve Jobs introduced the first iPhone he used a minidrama to demonstrate how the device could perform actions which, before, would be complex and would require multiple steps and lots of clicks. Jobs showed how easily the new iPhone could perform these complicated tasks, including doing a three-way conference call with just a simple click.

To see the video, go to https://tinyurl.com/lhtbg66. At 26:47 notice how Steve Jobs pretended to be surprised by a second caller when of course it was all scripted! Notice also the reaction of the audience: they loved it!

Let me tell you story of mini-dramas delivered in 2001 when I got invited to give a keynote at the Linux users conference in Seoul Korea.

With over 3,000 IT executive attendees the objective of the event was to show the benefits of Linux and its open source approach to developing software. In a world driven by Microsoft, Linux promised to offer relief from the shackles of dependencies from a single provider. In an unusual and concert like fashion, the conference started in complete darkness with loud music playing the song "The Wall" from Pink Floyd. When the lights came up, the audience discovered that a huge wall was occupying most of the stage. The wall was made of wooden bricks, and the middle of the wall had been painted with four large squares in the colors of orange, green, yellow and blue. Although the name Microsoft was not printed or even mentioned the reference to the Microsoft logo was obvious to all the attendees.

This is when the first minidrama took place!

U-Jin Kim, the CEO of Linux One, walked on stage with 20 or so of his employees. All of them were wearing a uniform and walked in a military parade fashion in unison with the music, strangely reminding us of the video that accompanied the music "The Wall." They were carrying a big hammer on their shoulders when suddenly U-Jin started to hit the wall. Instantly he was joined by the rest of his crew happily destroying the wall. The punch line of this intro act came when the 20 people on stage removed their jacket to reveal a t-shirt that read: "Linux: Break the wall"... of the dependency on Microsoft.

About 15 minutes later after the welcome introduction by U-Jin, I was invited to come on stage to deliver a speech on behalf of LinuxCare. Using a deck of slides, I started to present in a traditional way, which wasn't going to win me the attention of the thousands of prospects in the room. Suddenly, when I clicked for the next slide, the blue screen of death appeared: my laptop had crashed displaying the message "Fatal Error Detected." It was doubly embarrassing because not only was my presentation going to be interrupted by this computer issue, but it revealed that I was using PowerPoint, running on a Windows operating system: a mortal sin at a Linux conference!

Looking embarrassed and panicked I spent a few seconds talking to an assistant who was trying to fix my laptop. These seconds felt like an eternity and finally I asked: "Next slide." But how could my computer display the next slide when it had just crashed. Everybody knew that it would require several minutes to reboot? To the total surprise of the audience, the laptop instantly displayed the next slide which read: "It didn't crash: I run Linux on my computer." I had created a fake slide that flashed the famous Microsoft crash error message of the time: "Fatal Error Detected." So, when I asked for the next slide, the display jumped to it with no delay! This was highlighting a major benefit of the Linux Operating system: its stability versus Windows. Instantly, the audience understood the point and a sigh of relief could be felt in the entire hall. As a result, over 300 people were waiting in line to grab my business card: a sure indication that my message had hit home.

What to Remember About Minidramas

- Of the different types of grabbers, minidramas are certainly the most effective, yet the most difficult to deliver.

- Minidramas help the audience experience an emotion; they have a direct impact on the primal brain, far stronger than any PowerPoint slide!

- Creating a minidrama requires attention to details and rehearsal because it can easily fail. Imagine if, when Jobs tried to merge his two conversations into a three-way call, it had failed to work properly. The history of new product launches is filled with minidramas or demos that failed. Did you ever see the announcement of Windows 98 when Bill Gates witnessed his own application crash (Figure 8.8)? [Notice the blue screen of death at 0:10! a screen similar to the one I used in South Korea]

To see the video, go to https://tinyurl.com/zkuwugy.

- You should rehearse your minidramas until you have 100% confidence it will work properly. This means your minidrama should be scripted just like a play or a movie. When you deliver your minidrama, think that you are delivering an acting performance: it is no longer a business presentation, it is a theater play! Your objective is to get your audience to experience an emotion, and this can only be achieved if you put your soul into it. You cannot afford to fake it. Your words,

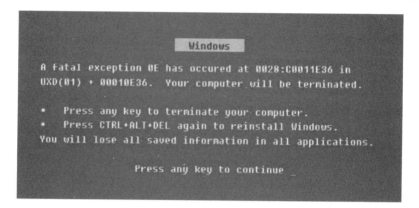

Figure 8.8   Gates blue screen of death.

your tone of voice, your facial expressions, all need to help your audience re-experience the painful state they live in (negative emotion) when they don't enjoy your solution, and then later you will help their brain feel the positive emotion your solution would provide.

- Minidramas can have only one act. In that case, the one act is typically centered around the pain of the customers. Or they can include a second act that would demonstrate the relief of the pain. Contrasted minidramas are often seen on QVC infomercials: think of the presenter who is trying to sell you a knife sharpener. First, they show you how a dull knife won't easily cut a ripe tomato without squishing it [Act 1: the pain], then they sharpen the knife and it now makes a perfect cut on the same tomato [Act 2: the relief of the pain].

- The best minidramas will be acted live in front of your audience. They can involve only one presenter who would deliver a monologue, or they can include several people as in the case of Steve Jobs and the iPhone. If you are not comfortable acting in a minidrama live, you could film it and play it as a short video clip.

- Sometimes, even just a picture can represent a minidrama, such as the ad for a campaign to deter people from drinking and driving (shown in Figure 8.9).

Figure 8.9   Drink-and-drive ad.

Stories

"...in the end, it's the story that matters. Be unpredictable, be real, be interesting. Tell a good story."

– James Dashner, American author

At an empirical level, stories are described in every sales manual as an effective technique to create a stronger rapport and to help persuade people. On a more scientific level, stories constitute a prolific topic of discussion among psychologists, philosophers, educators, historians and more recently neuroscientists. Their effect is described in the research literature as "narrative transportation," a phenomenon in which the listener is mentally *transported* in the world of the story.

Antonio Damasio, director of the neuroscience department at University of Southern California, said it best when he wrote: "The problem of how to make all this wisdom understandable, transmissible, persuasive, enforceable – in a word, of how to make it stick – was faced and a solution found. Storytelling was the solution; storytelling is something brains do, naturally, and implicitly. It should be no surprise that it pervades the entire fabric of human societies and cultures" [183].

Drawing on neuroscience, psychology, and evolutionary biology, author Jonathan Gottschall in *The Storytelling Animal* explains how stories serve the biological function to encourage prosocial behavior, a critical component of survival [184]. The stories we hear growing up teach us the working principles of the world and they simulate possible outcomes in the service of decision making; our brains can play out several scenarios without the risk and expense of attempting them physically.

Think back to who told you stories: your parents, grandparents, educators, and friends. What do all these people have in common? They all cared for you. We rarely if ever tell stories to people we don't like. So fundamentally when you say: "Let me tell you a story . . . " the subliminal message you are communicating is "I care for you."

Stories are very effective because they transport the listener's primal brain into a pseudoworld where he or she is made to believe that the story is happening. Have you ever noticed how easy it is to frighten little kids with a scary story? Why do stories have such an impact on kids? Because when the story is properly told it makes their primal brain believe it is real. Their rational brain has not yet learned to fact-check a story. The immediate reaction of their primal brain drives their experience and makes them live the story as if it was truly unfolding.

Try this:

Tell one of your friends or relatives the following story: Have them picture in their mind a bright, yellow, juicy lemon just in front of them. Then ask them to close their eyes and to imagine taking a sharp knife to cut that lemon in half. With their eyes closed, ask them to cut a ¼-inch slice of that lemon. Dropping the knife, they now should bring the slice under their noses to enjoy the zesty fragrance of that sweet lemon. Ask them next to hold that slice between their lips and to take a firm bite into the lemon meat. The sweet-and-sour lemon juice is reaching the tip of their tongues and the back of their front teeth, creating a pleasant sensory impression that inundates their whole palate and nose. At that point, stop and ask them what is happening in their mouths. Inevitably, if they properly focused on your lemon story their mouths started to water. Why? Because their primal brain believed they had some lemon in their mouths and needed to mix the lemon juice with predigestive saliva! It didn't matter if their rational brain knew it was imaginary, the narrative transportation made it all too real to deny the actual presence of lemon juice. In fact because of your own mirror neurons, reading that story might be enough to trigger your own salivation!

The Science of Stories. There is a huge body of academic research on the effect of stories on the brain. So much so that some researchers have found it valuable to perform meta studies: research on the existing research. The conclusion on stories is clear: stories can help you persuade. In the paper entitled "The Extended Transportation-Imagery Model (ETIM): A Meta-Analysis of the Antecedents and Consequences of Consumers' Narrative Transportation," the authors analyzed 76 published articles on narrative transportation [185]. They coined the term "narrative persuasion" to describe how story listeners experience a mental transformation whose effect can be strong and long-lasting to the point of changing their opinions or beliefs. They concluded:

- "Storytellers' narrative transportation leads to emotional contagion on story receiver."

- "The more stories are noncommercial, the more narrative transportation increases."

- "Young children (under the age of 8) are more affected by narrative transportation because they haven't yet developed deception detection abilities."

A straightforward way to summarize the complexity of this research is to remember that stories have the power to reshape the beliefs and behaviors of the listeners because they fool the story receiver's primal brain in believing the story is real. Stories typically put the listener in the middle of the action.

Winston Churchill was trying to influence the British Parliament to increase the budget for the development of new weapons during WWII. At that time, the economic situation in the UK was critical and Churchill was facing great opposition to his request for a military budget increase. After using all logical arguments to make the members of Parliament realize the importance of his proposition, Churchill decided to use a story.

I would like to tell you the story of the battle of Omdurman. This battle took place on the bank of the Sudan River on September 2, 1898. This war against the Mahdist – also called the Dervishes, a fearless tribe of Muslim fighters – had started in 1881. It opposed 8,000 of our troops supported by 17,000 Sudanese to 52,000 warriors on the Dervishes' side. The Dervishes had been fighting with great determination and courage, and the outcome of the most recent battles was a casualty ratio of about 1 to 1: for every Dervish who perished, one British soldier had to lose his life. Now, imagine if you had been one of our soldiers. You were far outnumbered, and you knew it. You had been on the campaign for a long time and had not enjoyed a good cup of tea for many months, sometimes years. Inevitably on this day of September 1898, the temperature would climb again in the 100's, not a comfortable place for a Brit. The air was so dry that your mouth felt you had swallowed sand and the clean desert air you breathed was soon to be replaced with the burning smell of powder and blood. Then, suddenly, over the dunes as the sun barely reached the sandy ridge, you see the first wave of Dervishes charging. They are coming down on horses, on camels, and by foot, yelling their frightening war cry. And so was the situation of our soldiers until that day of September 1898. However, everything changed that day! We introduced a new weapon called the Maxim gun, a much-improved version of the Gatlin gun that delivered 600 rounds per minutes. The outcome of the battle was devastating for the Dervishes. 12,000 were killed, 13,000 were wounded and 5,000 were captured for only 50 killed and 400 wounded on our side. The Dervishes capitulated shortly after the battle was raging.

Churchill concluded his story by saying, *"And that was the difference between keeping up with technology and thinking it would always be the same."* A few days later the parliament accepted his proposal to increase the budget for developing new weapons.

Now, if you had been a British soldier during the battle of Omdurman, would you be supportive of new weapon technology? Of course, you would because it most certainly saved your life! If the story was properly told, your primal brain wouldn't make the difference between having been at Omdurman and hearing the story of Omdurman.

Stories work because they transport the mind of the audience and create a pseudo-real experience. A story is like telling your audience they have a slice of lemon in their mouth: their primal brain will believe it!

What is the secret of good storytelling? The storyteller needs to create visual, auditory, kinesthetic (movement), and possibly taste and smell clues that will make the primal brain of her audience believe that the story is actually happening to them.

The Dos of Stories

- It's all about the punch line: a story without one will have no persuasive power; worse, it will make you appear as a poor presenter with bad charisma. Start with the end in mind: clearly, define what your communication objective is and what will be your punch line. Then look for a story that best leads to that climax.

- Learn how to tell stories effectively. You need to paint a picture with enough details to make it believable. These details become most transporting when they are communicated using different senses:

  - "As the sun barely reached the sandy ridge you see": the word *see* and the concept *sun* implies using the visual sense.

  - "Yelling their frightening war cry" is using the auditory sense.

  - "The temperature would climb again in the 100's": the word *temperature* is triggering the sense of touch.

  - "Your mouth felt you had swallowed sand" suggests the sense of taste.

  - "With the burning smell of power and blood" is about the olfactory sense.

- Make sure you hold 100% of the attention of your audience. Remember it is about creating narrative transportation, so make sure the environment is conducive to deep listening: no disturbing noise or interruption, nothing should draw the story receiver's attention away. Notice how in movie theaters they filter the noise and light from the outside and remind the audience to turn their phones off: nothing can inhibit narrative transportation as effectively as a ringing phone.

- Project bold confidence and passion with your words, with your tone of voice and with your body language. Don't hesitate to use a prop to make the story even more visual. In the earlier

Churchill story, note also the use and repetition of the word *you*, to help transport the listener in the story. Remember that effective stories are communicating emotions, not just facts: make your audience cry or make them laugh but make sure they experience a strong emotion. Just don't only tell a story: act your story!

- If you don't have acting talent, stick to a true story you have lived personally. It will increase the effectiveness of your storyteller antecedents because your subconscious (primal brain) will not have to perform any translation, distortion, or lie.

- Customer stories constitute the best proof of value and should be used when the objective is to demonstrate the gain. However, using a story not related to your business to convince will be even more effective when true narrative transportation is needed. Notice for example how you could use the Churchill story to persuade a prospect who doesn't believe in investing in new technology even though he might believe in the proofs of value you already presented. Again, note that persuasion works better when the persuadee is not aware of the persuader's intentions or as the previous researchers stated: "The more stories are noncommercial, the more narrative transportation increases" [185].

- Practice telling your story. It will confirm if your punch line is effective and if the details you are painting make the story believable. Get a few people to confirm that your story is appropriate for your audience: a story about cigarettes at a cancer conference might get you a standing ovation or boos; it all depends! The more you practice the story, the more you can include valuable details that draw a vivid and believable picture. Note the use of visual clues in these words…to remind you that the primal brain is highly visual!

- Look for good stories in books that present a collection of stories specifically for business. There is even a book entitled: *Business Storytelling For Dummies!*

- Use a story for your own introduction. Instead of presenting a conventional – and often boring – script about who you are, tell your audience a good story about you. It will incent people to pay attention because you'll be bringing something unique. Even better, have somebody else tell that story for you; it will further increase your credibility.

The Don'ts of Stories

- Don't make the story too long, or worse, without a punch line!
- Don't use stories that oppose too abruptly the general social opinions of your group of story receivers: it impacts the narrative transportation.

What to Remember About Stories. Stories represent such an effective persuasion tool that we consider that they are not optional. The effective persuader will always tell one or more stories in her presentation. Stories can be used as a grabber at the beginning of your presentation or anywhere later when you need to recapture the attention of your audience. Good stories require research to find the proper narrative and practice to sharpen the delivery so that when the punch line is delivered, it is with the expected persuasive effect. Later, in the section on persuasion catalysts, we will describe how your *charisma* – the science of what makes somebody believable – makes you a good storyteller.

Word Plays

"The writer has to take the most used, most familiar objects—nouns, pronouns, verbs, adverbs—ball them together and make them bounce."
– Maya Angelou, American poet, writer, and educator

Researchers like Albert Mehrabian [186] have long established that *what* we say is potentially less impactful than *how we say it.* The primal brain is by nature not sensitive to the ephemeral, intangible nature of words. Yet, we would like to suggest a few techniques centered specifically around words. After all, as Russell Baker, an American journalist said, "When you write you make a sound in the reader's head. It can be a dull mumble – that's why so much government prose makes you sleepy – or it can be a joyful noise, a sly whisper, a throb of passion."

Alexander Huth, a Berkeley neuroscientist, established a semantic atlas of the human brain. He and his colleagues mapped which brain areas respond to 985 common English words according to the semantic (meaning) of the words [187]. They found that these maps are highly similar across humans. For example, on the left-hand side of the brain, above the ear, is a tiny region that represents the word *victim*. The same region responds to *killed, convicted, murdered* and *confessed*. On the brain's right-hand side, near the top of the head, is one of the brain spots activated by family terms: *wife, husband, children, parents*. This suggests that some words have a different but rather consistent impact on people.

The first technique we recommend grabbing attention using words is to list four to five words or expressions and link them together. For example, imagine you sell a security software and imagine that your targets are CIO (chief information officer). Here is how you could grab the attention of your audience with a word play.

Start by listing the following five concepts on paperboard or bring them up on a PowerPoint slide. Then ask: "What do the following have in common?"

- A neurosurgeon
- The central bank
- An airline pilot
- A nuclear scientist
- A CIO

After letting your audience search for possible answers for 20 to 30 seconds, deliver your punch line: "They all rely on safe and secure solutions to deliver their services."

Notice that after you deliver the punch line, your audience will experience a brief eureka moment and make the connection between why security is important and why it's important for CIOs like them!

Researchers have established that such eureka moments, also called aha moments, insights, or epiphanies, require four defining attributes:

- They need to appear suddenly.
- The solution to the problem should be processed fluently.
- It triggers a positive affect.
- The subject is convinced that the solution is true.

Stellan Ohlsson, professor of psychology, believes that the initial difficulty of a question drives unconscious processes (the realm of the primal brain) which changes the mental representation of the problem, thus causes a novel solution to appear [188]. Such a cascade of events produces a pleasurable moment. Auble and Franks, from Vanderbilt University, studied the effect of "effort toward comprehension" and established that the experience of "aha" resulted in an increased recall [189].

The second technique in using words to grab an audience's attention is to create a combination of words that produce unusual or multiple meanings. Here are some good examples:

- "More bank for your buck" by Wells Fargo
- "Why Weight?" by Weight Watchers
- "If we break the news: blame us!" by ABC News

Notice that when you read these slogans, your brain becomes engaged, maybe even intrigued for a few seconds. The dual meaning (also called *double entendre*) of the sentences produces a brief "aha" moment.

The third way to deliver a word play is to ask one or more rhetorical questions that start with, "What if you...?"

After consulting with Bill.com, the number-one software to simplify online payments, the company adopted the following claims to convince CPAs to use their solution: real growth, real control, real advantage. To grab their attention, SalesBrain recommended they use a series of "What if you..." questions. When they present to CPA prospects immediately after the cover slide they ask:

- "What if you could increase your billings by three to four X?" (four-second pause)

- "What if you could eliminate the conditions for fraud?" (four-second pause)

- "What if you could make payments for a global customer base from an airplane?" (four-second pause)

First, notice how each of the questions points to its claims in the same order they present them. If you use the rhetorical questions in an oral format (as opposed to displaying them on a screen), the four-second pause is critical to the effectiveness of grabbing people's attention. The pause provides the listener with some time to process the question. A good persuader will recognize that it is not the question that is important but what the listener's brain does while answering it. Without that lengthy pause, the listener will not have enough time to think about the question and imagine the benefits suggested by the technique.

The Dos of Word Plays

- Give enough time to your audience to understand the word play or if you ask a question, don't be afraid to let the audience experience the difficulty of the question: people need to actively look for the answer. Even if they don't find the answer, they will still experience an "aha" moment.

- Make sure that the question can be processed promptly, that is, that the "aha" happens without hesitation. The audience shouldn't need a calculator to get it!

The Don'ts of Word Plays

- Don't use your word plays without testing them first. Often, people think that they have an effective use of words to grab attention, but the expression does not generate any response.

What to Remember About Grabbers

Regardless of the nature of your message, you will need to distract the current attention of your audience so that people start to spend cognitive energy on your product or service. To do this, you need more than just pure rational information: you need a short but strong stimulus with emotional content, self-relevance, and appeal. In short, you need a good grabber. Most likely at the exact moment, your message reaches the brain of your prospects, their focus is on something else:

- They are driving on the highway thinking about the bad day they had in the office, and you would like them to read your billboard.

- They have 127 emails in their inbox, and you want an answer to your question.

- They are sorting their snail mail, and you want them to open your envelope even though it's 8 p.m. and they haven't yet fed their kids.

In all these situations consider that:

- You need to interrupt their current trains of thought.

- Immediately after you have created that interruption, they should hear why they should pay attention to your message: they need to understand what's in it for them. You need to find an effective way to prove what they will gain in a matter of seconds.

And that's what a good grabber can do for you!

Consider that every communication needs a grabber:

- With emails, recipients often only use the title or the first few words to decide if they want to read it. When you are limited to a short subject line with only text, no color and the same font and font size, think about how you can grab their attention to avoid being ignored.

- With PowerPoints, most presenters lead with the history of their company, their technology, their products, their services, their customers. Remember that the primal brain favors personal stimuli; therefore communicate your value prop in a few seconds so your audience will be motivated to invest their full attention on your presentation.

- With a voicemail, are you starting with: "Hi my name is John Smith…Many people will erase the voicemail of those they don't know…without listening to the entire message! Instead, consider starting with "what if you…"

So, change the order, break the status quo of the way most people communicate, eliminate information that has no value for them. Deliver a grabber that focuses on their pain and presents a strong proof of gain. Making sure it fits your audience style and culture use a prop, a minidrama, a story, a wordplay or any other creative ways you can think of to get their attention!

Your Claims

"Tell them what you're going to tell them, tell them, then tell them what you told them."
– Aristotle, Greek philosopher and scientist

In Chapter 6, Differentiate Your Claims, we described how identifying the top three reasons why your customers should buy from you satisfies the primal brain's need for a *constrastable* stimulus. As you build a persuasive message, you will need to make sure that your argument is built within a maximum of three chapter(s) titled *"Your Claims"* and you will need to repeat those claims throughout your message. The repetition of your claims will signal to your audience's brain how important and urgent they are to solve a critical pain.

When an audience is presented with a message, the primal brain has one priority: to quickly understand its relevance and importance. Yet, when a presenter communicates a message, her objective is double: to be understood *and* to be remembered. These objectives are sometimes conflicting, and we believe that claims maximize both understanding and memorization [145, 190]. Although finding good claims is challenging, communicating them visually is also an important step few companies take as seriously as SalesBrain does. Our clients understand that claims have not reached their full potential until they are paired with what we call *NeuroIcons*. NeuroIcons are to the claims what logos are to a brand. They add a visual and emotional stamp to the expression of unique benefits. Erin MacDonald, a Stanford researcher, wrote: "In text-only an attribute repetition cancels it's importance in decisions, while in image repetition of a feature reinforces its importance" [143].

Let's review a few more examples of effective claims and their associated NeuroIcons.

Example of Claims: ShotSpotter

ShotSpotter is a Silicon Valley-based company that provides police departments with a real-time detection of gunshots – detection includes the number of shots fired, type of weapon used, and location accuracy within a few yards (Figure 8.10). Using an array of microphones spread over a city or a campus, StopSpotter detects gunshots in real time. When nearly 80% of gunfire events go unreported to emergency services, ShotSpotter:

- **Detects** outdoor gunshots and alerts law enforcement to the precise location within 30 to 40 seconds, giving them greater chances to engage perpetrators or assist victims and retrieve physical evidence (gun shell casings) and interview witnesses.

⌐●⌐ Shotspotter

DETECT **PROTECT** **CONNECT**

Figure 8.10   ShotSpotter claims.

- **Protects** law enforcement officers as they can now enter an active shooting event better prepared for a given threat. This, in turn, better *protects* the residents in underserved communities.

- **Connects** the law enforcement departments to their local communities. Before, because 80% of all gun activities were not reported and therefore had no law enforcement response, the local communities had grown distrust of their police department. Now, because of ShotSpotter, they see better, faster, and more effective interventions of the law enforcement agencies. ShotSpotter *connects* communities to police departments.

"I had been looking for an effective way to upgrade our messaging to reflect our new services business model pivot. Because of our technical culture we were more focused on the what we were doing – the technology is both awesome and complex! – than the why police departments should consider ShotSpotter. But after working with SalesBrain we quickly aligned our executive team on a set of three Claims: Detect, Protect, Connect. It was an eye-opener as immediately our prospects started to understand our value proposition. The NeuroIcons are extremely effective because these three simple yet meaningful visuals communicate the whole story about why law enforcement agencies should consider our gunfire detection solution."

– Ralph Clark, CEO

Example of Claims: Mann's Packing

Mann Packing is a large, Monterey County, California–based producer of vegetables including sugar snap peas, fresh-cut vegetables, vegetable platters, veggie bowls, and more. They even introduced the world to a new vegetable: Broccolini (a cross between broccoli and Chinese broccoli). Before working with SalesBrain, and similar to all their competitors, they claimed to offer fresh vegetables and to work diligently with all their customers: large groceries, club stores, and food-service distributors. After brainstorming about their value proposition, the executives zeroed-in on their claims: Fresher Ideas, Fresher Experience, Fresher Results.

Notice in Figure 8.11, the three subclaims under each claim.

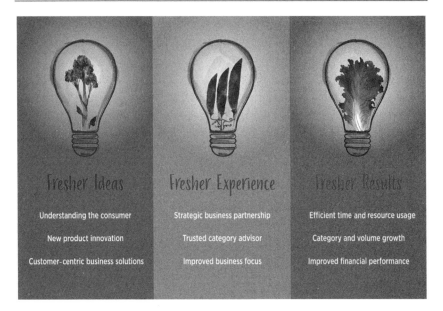

Figure 8.11 Mann's Packing claims

Note that these claims are not for the consumers: they are relevant only to the purchasing managers of food distributors. Nevertheless, the sheer repetition of the word *fresher* sends a strong signal about Mann's commitment to providing the freshest produce. The word *fresher* can still be used with any consumer campaign. About her claims, Lorri Koster Chairman and CEO of Mann Packing Company, stated,

> *We work in a very traditional industry, in a sea of producers offering the same items at similar prices. Many of us are multi-generational, family-owned business with the best quality and best service. Finding a differentiation had always been a challenge. So before working with SalesBrain our presentations to the buyers were boring and we were not getting much more margin than our competitors. But by starting to consistently and repeatedly use our set of three fresher claims, we were able to help our buyers understand how committed we were to deliver the freshest produce with the best quality and service. We are not just in the fresh produce business—we are in the "fresher" produce business. Not only was it useful externally but the "fresher" mantra also became effective to help our own employees understand that we are not so much in the produce business but that it is all about speed and accuracy: we are the experts at delivering freshness!*

Example of Claims: ClearLight Partners

ClearLight Partners LLC is a private equity firm located in Orange County, CA. A few years ago they contacted SalesBrain to help them communicate their competitive differentiation to business owners thinking about bringing on a partner. After a thorough reflection on what made them unique, the team categorized their benefits under the three chapters of

- Clear principles
- Clear journeys
- Clear outcomes

Notice how these claims nicely tie in with the name of the company to create a strong branding image. Michael Kaye, Founder of ClearLight Partners said, *"SalesBrain was helpful in guiding us towards a concise presentation of our key points of differentiation and unique offerings as a firm. They were important contributors to the aesthetic of our website and*

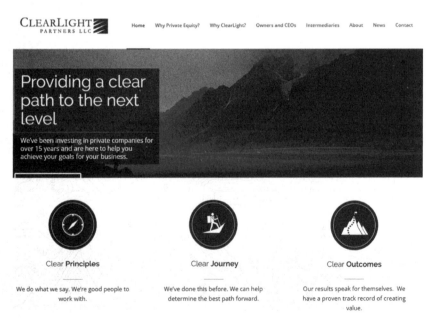

Figure 8.12   ClearLight claims.

other marketing materials. We have received positive feedback on these revised materials from all constituents in our network – business owners, intermediaries and executives."

Example of Claims: Eemax

Eemax is the number 1 supplier of tankless water heater solutions in the United States. For over 25 years, they've offered energy efficient, on-demand hot water heaters for commercial applications, residential homes, industrial and safety applications. Their green, environmentally friendly water heaters offer the largest selection in the industry.

Jens Bolleyer who runs marketing at Eemax reported: *"As soon as we integrated claims and visuals in our website we saw a 54% bounce rate reduction"* (Figure 8.13).

Figure 8.13   EEMAX claims on home page.

Example of Claims: Digitech Systems

Through software and services that deliver any document, anywhere, anytime, Digitech Systems bring all the benefits of enterprise content management to small, medium, and large organizations. H. K. Bain, the CEO of Digitech Systems, said: *"Having claims has completely changed the way we sell our solution. It makes selling especially easier with our network of resellers who no longer have to wonder what the three unique compelling reasons are why companies should choose the Digitech Systems solution"* (Figure 8.14).

Figure 8.14   Digitech Systems claims.

Example of Claims: Shepherd Chemical and Shepherd Color

Headquartered in Cincinnati, OH, Shepherd Chemical manufactures high-quality compounds. One of their divisions called Shepherd Color specializes in color pigments such as the ones used in paints. A few years ago, they contacted SalesBrain to help solidify the claims of a new type of pigment called dynamics.

Notice how they present dynamics under the three chapters of pure convenience, pure consistency, and pure profitability (Figure 8.15). Further notice that each of these chapters is segmented into three subclaims or subchapters.

Shepherd Color also endorsed the claims of more expertise, better performance, and best value as their corporate claims (Figure 8.16).

Figure 8.15   Shepherd Color claims.

Figure 8.16   Shepherd Color corporate claims.

Notice how they wisely created a tab labeled Why Shepherd? on their website, where those three claims are prominently displayed (Figure 8.17).

Tom Shepherd, the Shepherd Companies' owner and CEO, said: *"We come from a very technical culture with lots of chemists and engineers on the team. Using a consistent set of claims helped us come up with a better story to explain 'Why Shepherd?' That story is really centered on the unique value we bring to our customers. We are still material science experts, but the difference is that our claims now help our customers and prospects understand why they should choose us rather than someone else. It helped us move from a technology-driven sales effort to a more customer VALUE sales effort. As a result our business has grown more than 25% in the past five years."*

Chris Manning, sales and marketing manager, also said: *"When we present in the SalesBrain style in conferences and public presentations, everyone listens, and we have received several recognitions for best presentations. This has been an exciting journey and has certainly had an impact. Giving up words and details entrenched in our style for so long and moving into claims and graphics is hard but well worth it."*

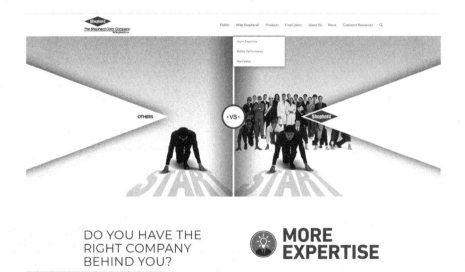

Figure 8.17   Shepherd more expertise.

Example of Claims: IBA Dosimetry

Headquartered in Nuremberg Germany, IBA Dosimetry manufactures sophisticated medical devices used to calibrate radiation devices for cancer treatment. They started to work with SalesBrain 14 years ago and, since then, whenever they introduce a new product, they never fail to apply NeuroMap. In 2015 they introduced a revolutionary new product called Dolphin. Dolphin allows for the real-time measurement of the amount of radiation received by a patient. After a two-day brainstorming session the marketing team selected the claims of

- Care
- Control
- Confidence (Figure 8.19)

In their presentations they often highlight the contrast between the existing solutions and theirs as illustrated in the big picture (Figure 8.19).

Ralf Schira, vice president of marketing, IBA Dosimetry, said, *"We have been using our corporate claims of Fastest, Most Accurate, Most Reliable for over 12 years and these have been instrumental to our growth. When we launched Dolphin it was obvious that we needed to organize its VALUE proposition under three chapters and we chose the claims of: Care, Control, Confidence. Lead by the SalesBrain Team, the in-depth customer pain analysis and claim workshop – helped us define the best claims and better understand the needs of our customers. I can't say for sure that our business success came*

Figure 8.18   IBA claims.

| Limited Care | Limited Control | Limited Confidence | OnLine Care | OnLine Control | OnLine Confidence |

Figure 8.19   IBA Dolphin claims.

just from communicating these clear, consistent, and compelling messages but the discipline we created around these sets of claims certainly helped. Since we started to work with SalesBrain back in 2004 our business grew between 5% and 15% every year, year after year; and I don't think it's a coincidence."

Example of Claims: Mountz

Based in the heart of Silicon Valley, Mountz Inc. provides torque tools to industries such as aerospace, automotive, medical, electronics, and more. Chances are very high that the tiny screws in your cellular phone were fastened with the right amount of force (torque) using a tool from Mountz.

Although Mountz enjoys a leadership position in their market, they do have competitors, and when they reached out to SalesBrain a few years ago, their objective was to solidify a clear set of claims that could become their mantra and help them emphasize their differentiators. During a constructive two-day claim session, the executive team reached consensus on their claims:

- Guaranteed quality
- Guaranteed expertise
- Guaranteed support

Brad Mountz, CEO and president, reported, *"It was not easy for us to align our message on 3 simple reasons why our customers should choose us. But in the end, our commitment to delivering on our promise is really what sets us apart: our people know more about torqueing than anybody else in the industry, and we can guarantee our quality, our expertise and our support. Creating that level of clarity on what makes us unique and guaranteeing it helped our business grow nicely in the last years. In the competitive world we live in, I am proud and happy with those results."*

Example of Claims: Talking Rain

Based in Seattle, Washington, Talking Rain Beverage Company is an industry leader that creates brands using innovative ingredients and ideas. A few years ago, the vice president of marketing reached out to SalesBrain to help them improve their sales message. The Sparkling Ice brand had always been strong at a consumer level, but they had a tough time linking it to business value for the resellers – big retailer chains. SalesBrain showed them how they could unify benefits under three claims (Figure 8.20). Here's a testimonial from Chris Hall, COO:

A few years ago, we reached out to SalesBrain to improve our sales message. Our branding had always been strong, but we were looking to link that strength to actual value for our resellers. SalesBrain showed us how to unify our benefits under three claims. As a result our business presentations have gotten shorter, clearer and more effective. We have trained our entire sales and marketing team and we now share the same way of presenting our unique value proposition.

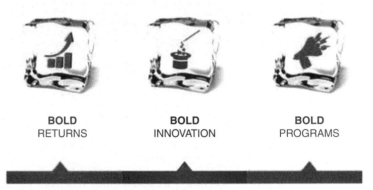

| BOLD | BOLD | BOLD |
| RETURNS | INNOVATION | PROGRAMS |

Figure 8.20   Talking Rain business claims.

Our distributors hear a consistent and differentiated message about why they should put our products on their shelves . . . this has been a critical component to our rapid growth!

What to Remember About Your Claims

- Use up to three claims. Note that at SalesBrain we do not recommend using just two claims: just like a painter would draw one apple or three apples or many apples, the obvious symmetry of two is not appealing to our brains [191].

- If necessary, create subclaims – the subchapters in your book. These should follow the same rules of simplicity and tangibility as the main claims.

In the case of HSI presented earlier in this chapter, notice how they also present subclaims (Figure 8.21).

- The music behind the words is more important than the words themselves. Make your claims rhyme – like pain, claim, gain, brain! Repeat the same word three times or use any

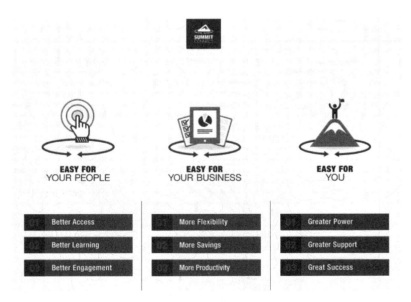

Figure 8.21   HSI subclaims.

other creative technique to make them sound better and more mnemonic.

- Use simple and tangible words and don't use more than three words per claims. The shorter the claims, the better: avoid words that have more than three syllables. Note that pain, claim, gain, brain are monosyllabic words.

- Look for the possibility of using various forms of abbreviations of your claims. For example:

  - Diagnose the pain

  - Differentiate your claims

  - Demonstrate the gain

  - Deliver to the primal brain

Can become pain, claim, gain, brain or diagnose, differentiate, demonstrate, deliver.

- Once you have solidified your claims, make them even more primal brain friendly by creating NeuroIcons. It will further accelerate your audience understanding of why they should buy from you or adopt your ideas.

BIG PICTURES

"Of all our inventions for mass communication, pictures will speak the most universally understood language."
– Walt Disney, cartoonist

You learned earlier that the primal brain has a visual bias! There is ample proof that using visual cues to influence people is effective. We start to think in pictures and as our brain matures, we later acquire the capability to think in more abstract ways. Although the four items shown in Figure 8.22 represent the same concept, our brains gradually learn to decode the meaning of the concept with a stimulus that is more and more dissimilar to the original concept we want to communicate, in this case, a real cat.

Picture   Drawing   Icon   Word

Figure 8.22   Communication options.

The Science of Pictures

Visual information is processed in the back of the brain (occipital lobe) but reading a word recruits multiple brain regions including the auditory cortex and the frontal lobes. Reading text is far from being a visual task, except for the very first step, which consists in recognizing the shapes of the letters.

Outside of the world of advertising where professional communicators understand the power of using images, the average business executive typically uses words – not images – to communicate and influence. We have all attended agonizing presentations using dreadful Power-Point slides. Every day, we receive emails, proposals, legal documents and surf web pages with a ton of text and little or no images. Likewise, we are regularly exposed to messages that include images that are not related to the topic at hand: like the ubiquitous smiling person on the phone in her office!

A revealing research study on visual cues demonstrated the potency of visual information. Brian Wansink of Cornell University conducted a test with 54 participants who were asked to eat soup from a bowl [192]. Half of the participants had a normal bowl that provided for an accurate visual cue of the quantity of soup they would eat. The other half ate from a self-refilling bowl (biased visual cue). The self-refilling bowls were strictly identical to the normal ones, and the refilling process was made slowly and imperceptibly to ensure the participants were not aware they were eating from a self-refilling bowl.

Measurements included participants' soup intake volume, their intake estimation, self-perceived consumption monitoring, and satiety. The researchers found that participants eating from self-refilling bowls ate 78% more soup than those eating from regular bowls. Yet, those eating from the self-refilling devices didn't believe they consumed more nor did they report being more satiated than those eating from normal bowls. The visual cue dominated their perception and overrode other sensory impressions! The researchers concluded that the amount of food on a plate or in a bowl provides for a visual cue or norm that influences how much one will eventually consume. They further recommended that to eat less: people should simply eat from small containers!

If eating from a small plate can help a person eat less, what visual information do you need to present to your audience to help them understand why they should buy from you? The answer is a big picture.

Before we go further into this concept, grab your phone, call one of your best friends and ask him or her to draw the shapes shown in Figure 8.23 on a letter-size piece of paper in landscape format:

Of course, you cannot send them the image of that page; you can only use words to guide their drawing.

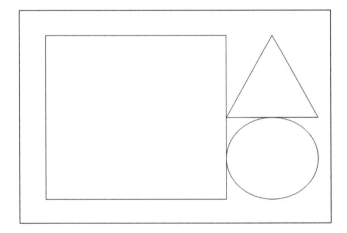

Figure 8.23   Geometric shapes.

How long did it take both of you to complete the task? Did either of you experience some frustration in the process? How similar is the final drawing from the original?

Did you notice how difficult it is to perform this task (fundamentally a visual exercise) by using a different modality, in this case, words? Since your audience's primal brains are strongly biased toward visual stimuli, you need a good picture: a big picture.

Let's start with a precise definition of a big picture: **A visual or graphical representation of how your product or service will impact the world of your prospects.**

Figures 8.24 and 8.25 show two examples of big pictures, the first one (Figure 8.24) for a hair regrowth product.

And Figure 8.25 is a twist on another familiar one: the value of joining a weight loss program!

Notice in both examples the use of contrast to further appeal to your primal brain. Notice also that in these ads the before is on the left and the after is on the right (or if written vertically the after should be located under the before). This is because, in the western world, we read from left to right and, conventionally, the future flows to the right. In other cultures where it is the opposite, the picture should be modified accordingly to avoid creating cognitive dissonance.

Before   After

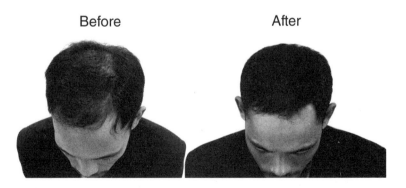

Figure 8.24   Before and after hair visuals.

Figure 8.25   Weight Watchers ad.

A good big picture helps your audience understand "visually," that is, with little or no text, in one simple concept, what you can do for them!

You should notice that any image that represents your world, as opposed to the world of the prospect, cannot, according to our definition, be called a big picture. All too often, marketers who use images fail to provide the proper brain's response, because they are

- Self-centered: The image provides a picture of the vendor's world, not the customer's world.

- Not related to the value proposition of the product. You often see pictures of smiling people, but it is not clear how the smiles are linked to the value proposition.

- Too complex to be assimilated by the primal brain. Pictures that include too much text, or complex hierarchical representations like an organigram do not qualify as a big picture, because their complexity will require a lengthy cognitive analysis.

Other Examples of Big Pictures

Figures 8.26 and 8.27 are examples of big pictures developed by SalesBrain.

Remember HSI (Figure 8.26) and their "easy" claims. Notice how the concept of easy is now conveyed with a contrasted visual!

Remember Tovar, the snow removal company (Figure 8.27)? Notice how their big picture focuses on the pain with the assumption that, if you choose Tovar, a "slip and fall" will not happen in your parking lot. Meanwhile, the big picture for Bill.com (Figure 8.28) shows the sharp contrast of continuing to handle bills the old way versus the new way. And Talking Rain (Figure 8.29) shows through their big picture that retailers who reference their brands will receive bold merchandising programs.

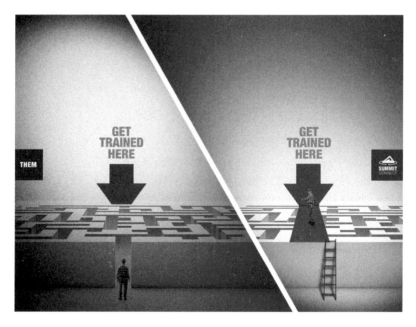

Figure 8.26   HSI big picture.

Figure 8.27 Tovar big picture.

Figure 8.28 Bill.com big picture.

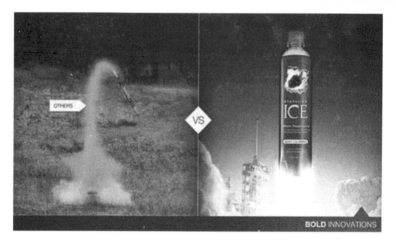

Figure 8.29   Talking Rain big picture.

PROOFS OF GAIN

"Raise the roof, that I might see the stars to gain wisdom and see things for what they are. Please I need proofs."

– Barry Privett, musician

We have already discussed the topic of demonstrating the gain in the third step of NeuroMap. Yet, it needs to be reviewed again here. Now that you are building your message, your proofs of gain represent another persuasion element. In fact, these proofs represent the core of your message.

Remember:

- Your grabber is a high-level snapshot of the pain of your customers typically followed by a brief inspirational representation of the relief of the pain reinforced by a prop, a minidrama, or a story. It appeals to the *personal* nature of the primal brain and its desire for *memorable* information

- Then, your claims communicate through *contrastable* benefits the top three unique reasons why your prospects should decide to buy from you.

- Then, your big picture represents *visually* how your solution will impact the world of your prospect.

- Now, you finally need to present your proofs of value to demonstrate what the prospect will gain. This needs to be done *tangibly* and simply to appeal to the primal brain.

The Dos About Your Proofs of Gain

- Because they offer so much persuading power, customer testimonials are not optional; they are mandatory. Please note however that they should not be presented as a long list typically displayed on a web page called "Our Customers." If you use all your customers' names under a single tab, your communication appears to use the law of social proof to convince them. This is not effective, because persuasion works better when the persuadee is not aware he/she is being persuaded. Instead, your customer stories should be used as a visual and emotional medium to demonstrate the value of your claim.

- Because videos provide the strongest narrative transportation the best medium to communicate these customer testimonials is to make them like short movies. At SalesBrain, we call these videos NeuroTestimonials. Check this example from the CEO of HSI: http://youtube/UMNEg5z6BKw.

- The second-best would be short-written testimonials of the customers including their names and pictures. Provided there is no confidentiality issue; you should avoid using anonymous customer cases: it is too difficult for the primal brain to believe these are real.

- These customer cases need to appear as genuine as possible, and even in their shortest expression, which could be only two or three sentences, they need to tell a story that sounds, looks, and feel real. Nothing pushes back a prospect as much as the fake sounding corporate voice that claims that a customer is *"delighted* by the *extraordinary* solution" of their vendor.

It should be short and to the point. Ideally, the customer should use the same words used in your claims. In fact, a well-structured customer testimonial would start with a sentence that specifies the pain, shortly followed by the delivery of the punch line where the customer state that her pain was eliminated by your solution. Sometimes, to build theatrical tension, you can also include a sentence that demonstrates that there were one or more obstacles before the value could be experienced. Yet in the end, you the vendor still delivered. For example, assuming you were selling seat belts, here is a good testimonial given by Johann Swenson, purchasing director at Volvo:

> I had been looking at procuring new seat belts for years [the pain]. Our research showed that drivers were looking for more comfortable seat belts without sacrificing anything to safety, not to mention that we have drastic cost reduction objectives, so it was not an easy problem [the *obstacle* to build narrative tension]. Yet, when we switched to ABC seat belts, we saved $7 per car resulting in an annual saving of $3.5 M [financial value], while increasing the safety index of our cars by 3 points [strategic value]. As a result, our entire purchasing department received the "Best Department Contribution" award directly from our CEO [personal value].

- Your value needs to be quantified, and the demonstration of the value needs to be done simply, logically, and fully. For example, note the progression in this example:

  1. "My solution will save you money."

  2. "You will work 10% faster with my solution." Now it's quantified.

  3. "Because you will work 10% faster, you will save 8% on your manufacturing cost, and you will be able to launch new products 5% faster." Now both a financial and a strategic value have been quantified.

  4. "Because you will work 10% faster, you will save $80,000 yearly on your manufacturing cost, and you will be able to shorten your time to market of new products from 18 months to 12 months giving you an advantage over your competitors current 18 months." Now, both the financial and strategic values have been fully quantified and

translated into a tangible number. Note the strategic value has also been contrasted with that of the competition.

5. "After purchasing ABC Systems, we saved $80,000 yearly on our manufacturing cost, and we were able to shorten our time to market of new products from 18 months to 12 months giving us a competitive advantage." – John Smith, ACME Manufacturing. Now you have proven it with a customer case.

- With the preceding example in mind, notice how most companies fall short on their demonstration of the gain. For instance, they only provide a long list of past customers without quantifying the value or using a strong proof.

- Many companies confuse the concept of value with the concept of proof. For example, you will often see law firms, accounting firms, financial advisers, or real estate brokers claim: "We have 150 years of combined experience." In this case, maybe the strategic risk of choosing them is lower because they bring much experience, so the statement can serve as a proof, but this is not a value, rather a feature. In fact, the primal brain will probably associate all these years of experience with a higher sticker price!

- Lastly, your gain should be so obvious that the whole gain equation should fit on one page. Although this is often done in B2C sometimes with just one image with little or no words, like in this example, in complex B2B transactions, it is almost never done.

At SalesBrain, we have helped countless corporations improve the demonstration of their gain by presenting the value and the cost on one page... And the following testomonial from Olivier Legrain, CEO, IBA, is the proof!!!

With SalesBrain, we learned the impact of eliminating the guesswork from our customers on the value they will receive from us. With highly complex medical solutions costing $50MM and more, being able to synthesize the value is an excruciatingly difficult exercise. At the end of a "salesbrained" presentation, when many of our customers tell us "I get it now" and you win the deal, the effort was well invested.

Objection Reframe

"Logic will never change emotion or perception."
                                          – Edward de Bono, psychologist

Most salespeople are uneasy when their prospects object: they feel it is a sign of rejection when it should be considered a request for more information. As the prospect gets closer to deciding, the fear of regret – of making a wrong move – will impact their decision and prompt for additional information [193].

Consider the most frequent objections: "Yes I like your solution, but you're too expensive." Even if you are indeed more expensive than your competitors, is this a valid reason for your prospect not to buy from you? Are they comparing apples to apples? Often, with a price objection, the customer is only comparing the cost of each solution without comparing the value of the respective offers. Have you properly demonstrated all the gain or is some of your value still unveiled, unquantified, or unproven? Before deciding if you need to implement an objection reframe, be sure that you have fully demonstrated the gain.

Objections come in two forms: objections that arise from a *misunderstanding* and objections that come from *perceptions*. Misunderstandings can be addressed by using logic and by providing additional information. Imagine your prospects said you're too expensive, but they hadn't seen that your price includes a 12 months warranty. Realizing that none of your competitors offer that warranty might be enough to change their opinion on the price difference.

By contrast, objections based on perceptions cannot be dissolved using logic. If your customers believes – rightly or wrongly – that your solution is too expensive, no amount of rational information will change their minds. The objection is simply the expression of the fear of potential regret. NeuroMap proposes that the best way to handle such an objection is to reframe it using a story, an analogy, or a metaphor. Doing so will produce a positive emotion to counteract the negative emotion associated with the fear of regret.

Do you remember the story Wilson Churchill told to convince the Parliament to increase the budget for new weapons development?

(See the Stories subsection in the Grabbers section.) Now imagine if the objection of your customer had been: "Your solution is interesting, but we are concerned about this modern technology: it might be too *bleeding edge* for us." You could use the Churchill story and simply change the punch line: "The outcome of the battle was devastating for the Dervishes. 12,000 were killed, 13,000 were wounded, and 5,000 were captured compared to only 50 killed and 400 wounded on the British side. The Dervishes capitulated shortly after the battle was raging . . . and this is what our modern technology could do for you: it will help you give a major blow to your competitors!"

How should you handle the objection?

1. Agree or respectfully disagree with the objection.

2. Step into the objection.

3. Highlight a positive side of the objection using a story, an analogy, or a metaphor.

Agree or Disagree with the Objection

Although many sales books recommend never disagreeing with a customer, we believe your persuasive effectiveness is higher if you state your own opinion because (1) the customer is not always right and (2) their primal brain will quickly detect any sign of manipulation or dishonesty, and do so often unconsciously [194]. Stating your opinion demonstrates that you stand by your own truth and are not afraid to disagree with your customer, a form of fearlessness that works well on their primal brains.

Robert Cialdini also established that whenever you mention something negative about you or your solution (hopefully lightly negative) whatever you will mention just after that will be more believed by your audience [195]. Imagine for example that you disagree with your prospect about the fact that your solution is too expensive. You might first say something negative like, "Although, as you pointed out, our customer service is not operating 24/7." You can then follow with, "I believe we are not more expensive than our competitors," which will more effectively help your customer let your statement on price influence her. Go for the truth even if in the immediate moment you feel that a small lie would serve you better.

Step into the Objection

Assume you are selling face-to-face to your prospect and they start raising an objection. We recommend that you step into the objection, which means that you need to move closer to the person you are trying to persuade. By doing so, you will show that you are not afraid of the objection. The absence of fear will confirm to his primal brain that the objection is not relevant, and this happens below their level of awareness. On the other hand, a physical retreat movement would be the surest way to confirm that the objection is supported by truth. Using Pr. Mehrabian's approximation, you can dissolve 55% of the objection subconsciously by just using your body language [195].

The amount of forward movement should be proportional to the distance between you and the prospect. If you are sitting close to him, then lightly leaning forward is enough but if you're standing on a large stage, you should be making several steps in the direction of the person who worded the objection.

Highlight a Positive Side of the Objection Using a Story, an Analogy, or a Metaphor

When an objection is expressed, regardless of the force of the reframing counterargument, the prospect will rarely surrender and admit: "You're right, your solution is not too complex, or you're not too expensive." Your objective here is to eliminate or at least decrease the negative emotion at the origin of the objection. To do this, logic is not effective. Instead, you need to find a source for a positive counteracting emotion, and we recommend using a story, an analogy, or a metaphor to communicate that emotion.

Some Common Objections with Their Positive Side and Some Story Tracks

Objection: You Are Too Expensive. To reframe this common objection, you need first to find a positive aspect of being expensive.

Typically, expensive products offer better quality and last longer. Then, you need to find a story, analogy, or metaphor that can communicate the value of better quality and a longer lasting product. Here is an example: before you launch into the reframe, agree or disagree based on your own conviction. For instance, if you agree, just say: "You're right, we are a few points more expensive than our competitors. But I do not believe that this is not a reason for you to turn us down."

Then introduce your reframe. You could say: "This reminds me of the last time I bought new tennis shoes. As a tennis player, I have always played with a pair of Adidas that cost $100. I was always happy with the grip, stability, weight, and looks of their shoes. I also loved that their soles lasted at least for 25 games before being worn out. Then recently I bought another brand [name withdrawn] because they looked quite similar to the one I was regularly buying, and they were discounted at $50...a good deal indeed. Or so I thought! Although at first, my new shoes felt as good as the one I was accustomed to, after only a couple of games it became obvious that they were wearing out faster, much faster. In fact only after five games a hole appeared at the toe and they needed replacement...So, 25 games on, my $100 shoes turned out to be much better than five games on the $50 shoes. We might be a bit more expensive than some of our competitors, but our solution will give you much greater mileage!"

Notice the punch line and how it matches the story on shoe qualities.

Objection: You Are Late to Market. A positive side of this objection is that solutions that are late to market are often more robust because the vendor had time to work out the early bugs and provide a more robust solution. Here is how you could reframe the objection using the story of Tesla: "Yes, it's true we've been delayed in our product introduction. That reminds me the story of Tesla: Their first model, the Roadster, was delayed numerous times, as was the model S, and more recently the model X also launched with a delay of over two years. Despite all these delays, Tesla users report one of the highest satisfaction ratings. Similarly, if you choose us, once the solution is deployed, you can expect to experience the highest level of satisfaction." Notice that if the objector is a Tesla driver this story will resonate even more with him!

The more you know about your prospect, the better because it will help you choose the best possible reframing story: the story that will produce the strongest positive emotion needed to counterbalance the negative emotion attached to the fear of regret.

Objection: Your Solution Is Too Complex. You could use the analogy with a car automatic gearbox: indeed, from the inside it looks complicated, but its usage is simple: park, reverse, neutral, and drive, and a gearbox is very reliable. So, you could say: "You're right when you look under the hood, our solution is quite complex."

Notice that by starting to agree with the objection – a negative trait for you – they will be more open to letting the positive emotion generated by your upcoming story dissolve the negative fear of regret.

"It's a bit like an automatic gearbox. These devices found on all modern cars are quite complex. Yet for the users they are very simple: just select drive or reverse and off you go. Notice that most modern gearbox now provide 250,000 or even 300,000 trouble-free miles: these devices are very reliable and long lasting. And so will be our solution if you choose to work with us: complex on the inside but simple and reliable to use."

The Dos of Objection Reframes

- Consider the objection as a gift: it's a signal the prospect is getting closer to deciding, and it shows they are afraid of making the wrong decision. By considering it a gift, you will minimize the amount of unconscious fear you are displaying through your words, your tone of voice and body language.

- Remember if you are standing in front of your prospect, step forward; that movement alone could dissolve 55% of the objection. If you are sitting at their desk, simply lean forward to shorten the distance between the two of you. The amount of forward motion should be proportional to the distance between you.

- Coming up with the perfect story, analogy, or metaphor that will generate a strong positive emotion in their brain is challenging. And coming with those on the fly is almost impossible, *even for the best sales and marketing people*. It means that you should prepare a list of the most common objections you hear together with a list of possible stories to use. Then, using your knowledge of the personality, behavior, activities, and passion of your objector, you should select from your list of possible reframing stories, the one you believe will generate the best positive emotion. If you know he plays tennis, the tennis-shoe story will most likely have a good impact.

- Because emotional responses can vary greatly from the same stimulus, testing the stories on others and practicing your delivery is key. What you think can create a positive response might not have the desired effect on a given prospect.

Now that you have reframed their objections, it's time to close!

CLOSING

"One doesn't leave a convivial party before closing time."
– Winston Churchill, former British Prime Minister

The subject of closing remains one of the favorite topics of sales methodologies. However, none of them suggests a simple yet scientific and effective way to help the brain of your audience progress on the persuasion continuum: from suspect to prospect, to hot prospect, to becoming a customer!

In a face-to-face situation, to achieve that outcome systematically, we believe the most effective way is to close by

1. Repeating your claims

2. Asking "What do you think?" and waiting

3. Asking "Where do we go from here?" and waiting

Notice that in all other elements of NeuroMap, we encourage you to be creative and add bells and whistles to increase the saliency of your message. But closing is where a more standardized, scripted process that consists of three simple steps including two short questions will bring the best results.

Repeat Your Claims

Your claims represent the top three *reasons* why your prospects should buy from you and the best way to clearly highlight their importance is to consistently repeat them. Because the closing happens toward the end of your message, the recency bias will help them remember those words more than what you presented in the middle of your message. As you near the end of your communication, we recommend that you state your claims one last time:

"In conclusion, today we discussed how only our company can help you protect your time, protect your dime, protect your peace of mind."

Ask, "What Do You Think?" and Wait

Do you remember the six laws of influence as demonstrated by Robert Cialdini?

Notice that all these are promoted by NeuroMap. For example, the law of scarcity applies when you state your claims: "Only with our solution will you be able to: claim 1, claim 2, claim 3." Or the law of social proof will work in your favor when you use strong customer cases to prove your value.

So, after you've repeated your claims, you will trigger people's *law of consistency* by asking, "What do you think?" and by waiting for their answer. This will reduce your audience's resistance to later change their mind and increase cognitive fluency.

The Law of Consistency

Inconsistency is simply not a desirable personality trait. People find it positive to be consistent. The law of consistency can be witnessed in many situations and the simplest demonstration was made by psychologist Thomas Moriarty [196]. Moriarty staged a test on a beach in New York. It involved two research accomplices:

- The first one laid down a beach blanket and a portable radio a few yards away from a randomly selected subject. After laying down for a few minutes, the researcher stood up and went for a walk on the beach, leaving his blanket and radio unattended.
- A few minutes later the second researcher, acting as a thief, picked up the blanket and the radio.

The test consisted of observing the behavior of the selected subject who stood close to the blanket and radio and had obviously witnessed the thief misdeed. In the first test conditions out of 20 trials, only four subjects tried to stop the thief. Understandably, few people are willing to intervene, risking being aggressed for protecting the valuables of a stranger. How could the law of consistency be used to reverse the odds and have 19 subjects out of 20 try to stop the thief? The researchers found the solution by asking a simple question. Before leaving his belongings for his walk, the first researcher just asked the neighboring subject: "Could I ask you a favor: would you mind watching my blanket and radio?" and for waiting for the subject to provide a verbal and public approval. Because people want to be consistent, those who responded positively will later feel obliged to act resulting in 19 subjects out of 20 trying to stop the thief.

Social psychologist Steven Sherman was able to increase the number of volunteers who would go door to door to collect donations for a charity by 700%. How? Instead of asking people to commit right away to volunteer, they introduced a step before. They called people and asked them to guess how many including them would agree to spend three hours collecting donations for the American Cancer Society to which question, the clear majority respond: a large majority would. When a few days later the same people received a call from the American Cancer Society asking them to volunteer, wanting to remain consistent with their earlier prediction (and implicit commitment), the number of volunteers was seven times higher than before because most said they would agree to serve as a volunteer on a prior call [197].

In Dallas, Texas Daniel Howard, a consumer researcher, helped the Hunger Relief Committee recruit more volunteers to host sessions at their home where cookies would be sold, the proceeds from which would be used to feed those in need. The standard direct approach of asking to volunteer returned an 18% success rate. However, by simply adding a question at the beginning of their standard request like "How are you feeling this evening?" the researcher found that of the 120 people called, 108 replied the expected response of "Well," "Fine," or "Real good." Of these 108 individuals, 35 agreed to host the cookie party almost doubling the initial closing ratio from 18% to 29% [198].

In a California residential area, psychologists Jon Freedman and Scott Fraser asked residents if they would agree to display a large and ugly billboard in their garden. The sign simply read "Drive carefully" [199]. Unsurprisingly, only 17% agreed. That percentage jumped to 76% when two weeks before being ask for the permission to put the large billboard; residents were asked to display in their window a post card sign that read: "Be a safe driver."

So how do you use the law of consistency to perform a persuasive close?

After you have asked, "What do you think?," you should wait. At that point, if they don't say anything, you might be tempted to suggest a few positive comments about your solution but remember that they must make that first positive statement without pressure or incentive. Your objective is to sit quietly and wait until what they say creates a positive momentum in your direction. By pronouncing a few positive statements, regardless of how insignificant these may seem at first, you are on track to close successfully. To further strengthen the law of consistency, make sure you are not the only one in the room to hear the positive feedback: you may want to have your prospect state it in a public forum with many of their own employees witnessing the moment.

The Power of Public Commitments

Notice that most people finish their presentation by asking, "Do you have any questions?" Yet, asking "What do you think?" is more effective, because although they may not have any questions, they will undoubtedly have opinions and most people are eager to share their opinions publicly.

Social psychologists Morton Deutsch and Harold Gerald asked students to evaluate the length of lines drawn on a piece of paper [200]. The students were organized into three groups:

1. The first group had to publicly commit themselves to their initial estimates by signing their name and turning their estimates to the experimenter.

2. The second group committed themselves privately by simply writing their estimates on erasable pads and erasing it before turning the pad to the experimenter.

3. The third group was just asked to keep the numbers in mind.

Later, the students were presented with additional information about the lines' length and were asked if they wanted to revise their estimates. Students of group 3 were the most likely to be influenced by the additional information and they changed their estimates. Students of group 2 were more resistant to change. Students of group 1 most strongly refused to change their minds even in the presence of the new evidence; the fact that they had committed publicly to their first estimates made them stick to it!

When you ask people publicly what they think of your presentation, they will feel compelled to provide their opinion to illustrate their understanding and eventually showcase their mastery of the subject. Remember, your objective is to make them say a lot of positive comments – even if small – and to make these comments publicly.

Often, people object to this type of closing arguing: "But what if they say something negative about my solution?" Most likely the objection would have surfaced anyway, and it is better if you are in the room when they express it because you'll have a chance to respond. If the feedback is:

• Negative, treat it as an objection.

• Positive, congratulate yourself because using their law of consistency you have helped them build positive momentum toward buying your solution. In the future, it will become harder for them to diverge from this initial direction.

Ask, "Where Do We Go from Here?" and Wait

Similar to the question, "What do you think?" this last question is designed to trigger their law of consistency and have *them* suggest or confirm the next step: not *you*. Notice also that, in this sentence, we have now switched from using the word *you* instead of the word *we*. Although the difference is subtle, it implies that after hearing their response to the question "What do you think?" they now agree to a next step regardless of how far they are from buying. Yet, because they expressed enough positive interest, the *you* has become a *we* because you earned their trust and you allow them to think of you as an extension of their team. The objective of that question is to start a dialogue in which you will want your prospect to state publicly what they see as the next steps. You should be ambitious but realistic in how far you can push them to bring them closer to a final decision. If you are selling a complex solution costing millions with a typical sales cycle of one year or more, and this is only your second visit, trying to close the deal would be premature. By contrast, if you're selling a car, and both husband and wife have been with you driving the car and discussing it for two hours when you ask: "Where do we go from here?", you should stop at nothing short of "Where do I sign the contract?"

What to Remember About Closing

- Start by repeating your claims: it's your last chance to tell them *why* they should choose you. Most people feel uncomfortable repeating their claims, yet persuasive communicators do it naturally to help their audience understand the relevance and importance of their claims.

- Ask, "What do you think?" and wait. Encourage them to talk. Let your prospect freely express her opinion. Do not interrupt her; instead, demonstrate a genuine interest in her comments. Ask for clarification and drive the discussion to encourage her to state as many positive points as possible.

- Ask, "Where do we go from here?" and wait. If at first their initial responses are not moving fast enough toward a final decision, you may want to suggest a next step yourself. Then re-ask: "What do you think?"

Let's now review the persuasion catalysts.

SEVEN PERSUASION CATALYSTS

Remember that if the persuasion elements are the basic building blocks of what you need to communicate, the persuasion catalysts represent a way to amplify their impact on their primal brain. They represent different communication techniques to further increase the persuasive effect of each persuasion element. Each of the persuasion catalysts can and should be used on any of the persuasion elements. Persuasion catalysts turn up the heat on the impact of your message.

WORD WITH "YOU"

"A gossip is one who talks to you about others; a bore is one who talks to you about himself and a brilliant conversationalist is one who talks to you about yourself."
– Lisa Kirk, American book publicist

Of the long list of word choices, you can make at any point in time when you communicate, there is a simple yet effective communication strategy that will help you create and deliver your message with the strongest influencing power. The strategy is called "Wording with you," a simplified version of what communication experts call "self-referencing." Using the word *you* is an easy way to address the primal brain with a personal stimulus!

Researchers showed that on average, people spend 60% of conversations talking about themselves [201], and this jumps to 80% on social media platforms like Twitter and Facebook. The reason is simple: talking about themselves makes people feel good as demonstrated by the Harvard Social Cognitive and Affective Neuroscience lab [202]. In an *f*MRI experiment, 195 participants were asked to discuss their opinions and those of others, showing that talking about them triggered the nucleus accumbens and the ventral tegmental area, two regions associated with rewards and pleasurable feelings such as sex and tasty food!

Further, out of the 188 cognitive biases presented earlier, about 40 can be logically explained by the stimulus of personal such as the blind spot bias, the choice-supportive bias, the confirmation bias, the conservatism bias, the curse of knowledge bias, the illusion of control, the law of the instrument, naïve cynicism, the overconfidence effect, the self-relevance effect, the spotlight effect, and so forth. Since people are so consumed by their own lives, an effective way to get the attention of their primal brain is to use the word *you*.

Consider the following statements:

- "The new process is 40% faster than the current one" versus "You will save 40% of your time thanks to the new process."

- "This copier includes a sorter and a stapler" versus "You will no longer waste time sorting and stapling."

- "We are the leading provider of . . ." versus "You can minimize your risk by choosing the leading provider of . . . "

Or even in a shorter format consider these slogans:

- "Do you Yahoo?" – Yahoo

- "I want you" – Uncle Sam

- "Obey your thirst" – Sprite

- "Because you're worth it" – L'Oréal

- "You have 30 minutes" – Domino's Pizza

Or the new mantra of IBM: "you IBM."

Or even these slogans:

- "Got milk?" from the California Milk Board

- "Just do it!" from Nike

- "Think different" from Apple

Notice in the preceding slogans that, although the word *you* is not explicitly written, it is implicit as in "You got milk?" or "You just do it!"

When you use the word *you* (or *your*), you create instant rapport between the writer and the reader because you put the reader at the center of your story!

The Science of Using You

Burnkrant and Unnava, from Ohio State University, showed that increasing self-referencing (processing information by relating it to oneself or our personal experiences) can lead to increased persuasion [203]. Later, Jennifer Escalas proposed that *even* when an ad uses a weak argument, the narrative self-referencing will have a persuasive effect through transportation: people will be moved by the story [204].

When you hear "You have 30 minutes," your brain engages in a story of all the things you could do before eating your pizza. Notice how this conveys a positive concept, rather than having to suggest that you may have to wait 30 minutes!

The Use of You in Claims

Do you remember the company HSI and their "easy" claims? *Easy for Your People, Easy for Your Business, Easy for You*. Do you also remember the "protect" claims of the law firm Carothers, DiSante and Freudenberger: *Protect Your Time, Protect Your Dime, Protect Your Peace of Mind*. These claims are effective not only because they emphasize the single concept of protection – a critical value for a law firm – or because they rhyme, but also because there is an emphasis on the word *you*!

The next time you write an email, a brochure, a web page, or any other communication just reread it one more time and see how you can use the word *you*. Make a point of minimizing the use of *I, we, our, the company* and replace them with sentences that use the words *you* and *your*. You will also notice that forcing your thinking around the notion of *you* will naturally de-emphasize the message from the functions and features of your solution. Instead, it will anchor your message in the benefits for your audience!

TELL STORIES

"The one who tells the story rules the world."
– Hopi Native American Tribe proverb

Earlier we described stories as a type of grabber. Because stories are highly effective on the primal brain, they can also enhance the persuasive effect of any of your ideas, arguments, concepts, or persuasion elements. Therefore, in the NeuroMap model, stories represent not only a form of grabber, but they can also augment the persuasive effect of any of your persuasive elements such as your big pictures, your proofs of gain, or your objection reframe. Stories work as a persuasion catalyst.

BE CREDIBLE

"The reason we're successful, darling? My charisma, of course."
– Freddie Mercury, lead singer, Queen

Imagine two different people delivering the same message: Will they have the same impact on the audience? Will both generate the same persuasive energy to move the audience to act? Of course not: it's a matter of credibility or charisma!

Most people think that "you have it or you don't but you can't do much about your charisma." However, we believe learning the science of charisma can help increase your persuasive power. We will attempt to define it scientifically and remove as much of its mystical aspect as possible. More important, we will show that it's all about the primal brain! You will note that this section is the longest in the book. Why? Because even with an inferior product or solution, the more charismatic salesperson win most deals!

We believe that your charisma or the level of credibility you have with an audience is a function of six attributes:

1. Similarity: the common traits or beliefs you share with your audience.

2. Expression: what you communicate through your *words*, your *tone* of voice, and your *body language*.

3. Creativity: the imagination you use to deliver many "aha" moments that helps your audience grasp what you say with less cognitive effort.

4. Passion: the love and enthusiasm you display for your topic or expertise.

5. Fearlessness: the confidence you exude when you are not attached to the outcome.

6. Integrity: the evidence that creates solid trust with your audience.

Your Similarity

"If you wish to persuade me you must think my thoughts, feel my feelings and speak my words."
— *Cicero, Roman statesman*

For decades, empirical sales models have recommended looking for similarities with your prospects. Many sales executives quickly jump on an opportunity to talk about golf if they discover their prospect is a golfer. John Bargh, an expert on the unconscious mind, reported: "Baby animals in general have evolved a predisposition to stay close to those who are similar to them," [205]. We look for similarities with our prospects to build rapport more effectively. Rapport is defined as "a positive emotional connection" [206]. It is about building relationships through a sense of mutual trust and confidence, establishing effective communication and identifying common beliefs and knowledge. Rapport can simply be described as a feeling you experience when you are with someone you intuitively like.

Researchers have coined the term in-group, out-group bias. They showed that people in groups – even totally artificially created groups, such as when the groups were defined by the fact that people had randomly drawn either a blue versus a red ball out of an urn – who were given the opportunity to share money, would give more to those who had drawn the same color ball as them [207].

Multiple types of research showed that a powerful way to build rapport and to start an effective communication is to "mirror" or match the behavior of the other. This includes body postures and gestures, dress code, energy level, speaking habits including vocabulary and tone of voice, and even breathing synchronously. When two individuals are in good rapport they will naturally and unconsciously adopt the same attitudes [208–210]!

Essentially, the conclusion is this: the more similar you sound, look, and feel to your customers, the faster and stronger the rapport will be and as result, the more charismatic you will appear to them. This will shorten the sales cycle because rapport and credibility are the basis of trust. We tend to trust members of our own tribe we respect.

What to remember about similarity:

- The concept of similarity applies to everything: if your customers dress conservatively, so should you. Remember the days when the employees at IBM wore a three-piece suit with a tie? By contrast, if today you are trying to sell to a young start-up south of Market Street – the digital center of San Francisco – wearing casual dress will surely lead to a better connection with your audience than a three-piece suit.

- You should speak the same language as your customers. Remember every industry uses its own vocabulary, so it is your job to learn their language: they shouldn't have to adapt to your expression style. If your customers use long pauses, so should you.

- Mirroring: In his book titled *Mirroring People: The New Science of How We Connect*, Marco Iacoboni [211], professor at UCLA, made a great case for the science of empathy.

He recommends mirroring (not mimicking) the person you are trying to build rapport with. Neuroscientist Antonio Damasio and colleagues showed that when we act like our listener, it helps us live an experience from the standpoint of the other party and this mirroring behavior triggers the neural mechanism of authentic empathy [212].

• If your customers notice that you are mirroring their behavior, it may produce the opposite effect, because persuasion works better when the persuadee is not aware she is being persuaded. So, make sure your audience doesn't notice that you are making a deliberate attempt to dress like them, speak like them, or move like them! The more genuine you are in your practice of similarity, the stronger the rapport will be.

For the primal brain, seeing or hearing another individual with great similarity provides a safe environment from which trust can be built.

Your Expression

"He who wants to persuade should put his trust not in the right argument but in the right word. The power of sound has always been greater than the power of sense."

– Joseph Conrad, novelist

Logic commands that, if we were rational decision-making machines, we would only consider the meaning of the words of people on a mission to influence us. We wouldn't be influenced by other factors such as the tone of their voice, the style of what they wear or their facial expressions. Unfortunately, because our primal brain plays a dominant role in our decisions, the music, tone and rhythm we hear from the presenters' voice, what we see (i.e., what they wear and their body language) all matter more than the words they use.

Because there is no record of spoken languages, evolution experts use a large spread of estimates to describe when homo sapiens first started to use words, how language evolved, and what impact this had on the brain. Studying the changes in the hyoid bone – the only bone not connected to other bones, which is only found in Neanderthals and humans and is the foundation of speech ability – researchers hypothesized that words appeared about 300,000 years ago together with the development of tools. One will note that the first forms of written words appeared only about 10,000 years ago and, for most humans, reading became a necessity only a few hundred years ago. Although the brain demonstrates a capacity to reorganize its pathways – a phenomenon called brain plasticity – this rewiring does not operate at the same level of performance as the dedicated circuits resulting from the long-term effects of evolution. Written words and even spoken words haven't had enough time on the evolutionary scale to make an impact on the brain. Therefore, in order to read, the brain had to recruit regions genetically programmed for other tasks. Reading requires three distinct steps [213]:

- The *visual* processing of text, which recruits the occipital lobe and specifically the ventral visual pathway in the back of your brain. For example, while reading the word *CAT*, you would decode the visual shapes of the three letters C-A-T. After training, this process of recognizing letters becomes highly automatic and the brain can decode a letter in less than 150 milliseconds.

- The *auditory* processing of sound to extract phonemes (smallest unit of sound which when assembled constitutes syllables). For example, the phonemes from the letters C-A-T form the sound "CAT." This task is associated with the superior temporal sulcus on the left side of the brain.

- The *semantic decoding* of words to retrieve from the mental lexicon the concept associated with them. The sound "CAT" now needs to be associated with a furry animal. This system accesses several areas of the brain but is believed to be mainly in the temporal lobe, also on the left side of the brain.

In summary, reading and other language-related activities such as listening/talking/writing recruit complex brain circuits generally not associated with the primal brain. Therefore, persuading with words is less effective than with nonverbal cues. This is what communication researcher Albert Mehrabian [186] demonstrated by performing a series of experiments, from which he concluded:

- In a face-to-face situation, there are three elements of communication:

  1. Words
  2. Tone of voice

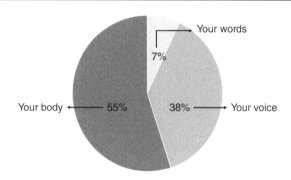

Figure 8.30   Mehrabian research.

3. Facial expressions (body language)
   He quantified the importance of those factors and proposed the now-famous and *often misinterpreted* rule of 7-38-55. According to Mehrabian, the effect of the communication is for

- 7% from your words
- 38% from your tone of voice
- 55% from your body language

- When the three elements of communication are not congruent, people tend to believe the tonality and body language more than the words.

In addition, researchers at Emory University in Atlanta, Georgia, confirmed that your tone of voice – pitch, loudness, tempo, rhythm – often conveys more information than the words you pronounce [214].

Since the primal brain is mostly visual, it is no surprise that what your audience sees has more impact than what it hears. In fact, studies suggest that when you are on the phone and there is no visual communication between the two communicants, words now account for 14% of the impact, while 86% comes from the tone of voice [215].

Let's now review the importance of key elements that influence the quality of your expression: your words, your voice, and your body language.

Using the Right Words

"The difference between the almost-right word and the right word is really a large matter—it's the difference between the lightning bug and the lightning."
– Mark Twain, American author

In the claim section in Chapter 6, we already saw that using claims with carefully chosen words will greatly improve how much your customers will remember and how much they will be convinced by your pitch. Let's further investigate the impact of words.

There are about 170,000 common words in English in the Oxford dictionary (about 100,000 in French and 370,000 in Chinese), and it takes only about 7,000 words to be considered fluent in any language. Now the question is: Do certain words or expressions produce a greater persuasive effect?

The answer is a resounding yes.

The Dos of Using Words

- Use simple, short, and concrete words. Since the primal brain does not perform language processing, which resides in the cortex, use words a four to five-year-old child would understand. Avoid complex words that require evolved cognitive functions to comprehend [216]. Shorter words (monosyllabic) are typically easier to grasp and remember than longer words [217]. Aim for simplicity and familiarity to minimize the demand on the brains of your audience [218].

- Use short sentences. Initiated by the work of George Miller [97], researchers have hypothesized that our working memory can typically hold seven digits, six letters, or three to five words.

- Limit your usage of negations. Psychologists Nieuwland and Kuperberg showed that most statements that use a negation generate greater brain activity and are processed more slowly [219]. Notice that, if you are instructed to *"not think* of a pink elephant," you cannot *"not think"* about the animal! Notice the cognitive load necessary to process double negatives like "you cannot not think!"

- Speak in positive terms, but don't overdo it. The use of positive words will, by association, set a positive mood to your communication. However, the overuse of overly positive words such as fantastic, excellent, fabulous, or phenomenal can be interpreted as a deceptive tactic [220] and will decrease persuasiveness.

- Speak in the specialized language of your audience: to an audience of doctors, use medical terms, to an audience of engineers, use technical expressions.

In *Words Can Change Your Brain*, authors Newberg and Waldman [221] suggest 12 speaking strategies that will stimulate deep empathy and trust in the listeners' brain:

- Relax.
- Stay present.
- Cultivate inner silence.
- Increase positivity.
- Reflect on your deepest values.
- Access a pleasant memory.
- Observe nonverbal cues.
- Express appreciation.
- Speak warmly.
- Speak slowly.
- Speak briefly.
- Listen deeply.

Furthermore, and applying the rule of similarity, if you know or can infer the emotional state of your audience, using words that are most likely to appeal to that emotional state will surely generate greater interest. For example, if your audience feels

- Curious, you can use: *confidential, secret, confession, hidden, unbelievable, insider, hidden,* and so forth.
- Confused, you can use: *hesitant, perplexed, manipulative, dishonest, disoriented, overwhelmed, anxious,* and so forth.
- Rushed by time, you can use: *instantly, pressed, proven, safe, tremendous, deadline, urgent,* and so forth.
- The only exception to the rule of mirroring of emotion would be anger. If you mirror anger it may trigger a fight-or-flight reaction from your listeners, which is not an effective way of building rapport.

The Don'ts of Using Words

- Don't use words your audience may not understand. Avoid obscure acronyms or jargon that could confuse your audience.
- Don't insert fillers like: "Eh," "I think," "I believe," "hopefully," "you know." They dilute your message, distract your audience, and decrease your charisma.
- If you are using PowerPoint, Keynote, or any other presentation software, do not read or repeat what is written on your slides. People read two to three times faster than you can talk (the average speaking rate is 120 words per minute when average reading rate is around 250 words per minute), so if you have text on your slides and typically read or repeat what you have on those slides, your audience will be reading the last sentence when you are still pronouncing the words of the first sentence. It desynchronizes what your audience reads and what they hear, raising the cognitive load in their brains.

Using The Right Voice

"Surely whoever speaks to me in the right voice him or her I shall follow."
– Walt Whitman, American poet

We have all experienced this: a close friend or relative calls you and as soon as they pronounce the word "Hello" you instantly can tell if something is wrong. The tone of the voice conveys so much meaning that you immediately suspect something unusual.

The human voice is a complex combination of sound waves generated by the vocal cords, which vibrate at different frequencies. Voice is further modulated by the laryngeal muscles (the muscles in and around the voice box) and the shape and size of the tongue, palate, cheeks, lips, throat, and nasal passages. Researcher Christy Ludlow demonstrated the complexity of the brain processes involved in the generation of sounds. Ludlow revealed the critical role played by subcortical structures in the production and control of human sounds – such as the nucleus accumbens – a group of cells located in the primal brain [222]. Claire Tang from UCSF also revealed the existence of neurons, located in the superior temporal gyrus, that respond specifically to pitch changes [223]. Linguists call these pitch changes prosody. These pitch changes can alter the meaning of a sentence. For example, "John loves fruits," said with a descending pitch indicates that John rather than another person loves fruits. With a flat pitch, "John loves fruit" would indicate that John loves fruits rather than other types of food. Moreover, a rising tone toward the end of the sentence would indicate a question, "John loves fruits?"

Although it was long assumed that the brain used a complex mechanism to add a layer of meaning based on prosody, Tang confirmed that specific neurons respond to pitch changes. Most people are not aware of the existence of neurons dedicated to prosody nor are they aware of their impact on the meaning of their communication. In fact, Annett Schirmer from Singapore University showed that the emotional context created by using various vocal tones actually changes the way words are encoded in memory [224].

A lot of these clues are communicated unconsciously, which is why it often takes a professional actor to sound "true." The truthfulness of your communication will come when all the main constituents of your expression: words, the tone of voice, facial movements, eye contact all communicate a positive message that confirms you are a trustable source.

The human voice is characterized by several parameters you can optimize to increase your persuasive power, including:

- Pitch: high or low frequency
- Intensity: loudness
- Speed: slow or fast
- Rhythm: tempo
- Pauses: short or long

Voice Pitch

Researchers demonstrated that men with lower pitch are perceived as both more attractive and more likely to be respected and followed [225]. For women, higher pitched voices tend to be considered more attractive whereas those with lower voices are perceived more dominant. This may have some evolutionary root as women hormonal changes cause the pitch of their voices to rise during the ovulation period when they are most fertile [226]. For men, lower voices are linked to higher levels of testosterone, which indicate health, good genetics, and the ability to defend from threats, all desirable traits important for survival and all primal traits!

In an experiment involving 121 students who were trying to influence each other, Joey Cheng, a social psychologist from University of Illinois, demonstrated that lowering your pitch increases your influence whether you are a man or a woman [227].

As a result, we recommend that you lower your voice, to the extent that it is possible and does not make you feel awkward when you do.

Voice Intensity

Researchers showed that people of power tend to speak louder and use more variation in the intensity of their voices [228].

We recommend that you speak slightly louder than your audience and vary the volume of your voice.

Speaking Rate

Researchers from the University of Southern California established a correlation between speed of speech and influence [229]. They revealed that faster speech speed functions as a general cue that augments credibility and enhances persuasion. This should be mediated by the research of Gibson, Eberhard, and Bryant [230] which pointed out that, in certain conditions, a slower speech rate can increase listener's comprehension.

We recommend that you speak about 20% faster than normal, but not too fast to avoid sounding pushy.

Pauses

"The right word may be effective but no word was ever as effective as a rightly timed pause."
– Mark Twain, American author

Experts have conducted a significant amount of research just on the effect of pauses in speech. Tyler Kendall, for example, wrote a complete book on the topic: speech rate, pause, and corpus sociophonetics [231].

Pauses are typically used in different contexts:

* After long utterances
* To breathe
* To think
* To offer a chance to let the other person talk

Researchers from Leeds University have confirmed that the insertion of pauses between each phrase increased the listeners' comprehension [232]. Other researchers [233] showed that the use of pauses correlates more with truthful than with deceptive speeches.

Therefore, good persuaders use pauses of various and appropriate length at different points of their discourse.

Variability

The research of Peterson and Cannito [234] confirmed the importance of pitch, speaking rate, and volume. It also showed that *varying* these characteristics further increases the communication effectiveness resulting in increased sales. To persuade, you need to vary the volume of your voice, your speaking rate, the length of pauses, and even your pitch.

Interferences

Researchers at the Air Force Research Lab found that if two people talk at the same time the degradation of understanding is in great part caused by the loss of listener ability to use prosodic and voice characteristic to link together the words expressed in the target phrase [235]. Therefore, any background conversation or outside noise such as traffic noise in the background will impact the listener's ability to learn and comprehend [236, 237]. So make sure your message is properly heard with little or no side conversations and especially no external noise.

Voice Mirroring

Mirroring your listener's voice will always bring benefits, including creating a perception that you are more credible, relatable, and attuned [238].

When there is a discrepancy between the words you communicate and your vocal emotion, it will confuse the listener [239]. Imagine what you would think if one of your relatives was telling you "I love you" in a loud and harsh voice. Therefore, to communicate sadness, make sure your voice becomes monotonous, and to communicate joy, make your voice less flat.

Finally, note that in some cultures like Japan or the Philippines people pay even more attention to the tone versus the words than we do in the United States [240]. Yet people who are not absolutely fluent in the language will not be able to detect these tonal differences.

Using the Right Body Language

"I speak two languages: Body and English."
– Mae West, American actress

According to Dr. David Givens, director of the Center for Non-verbal Studies, "When we speak (or listen) our attention is focused on words rather than body language. But our judgments include both. While we are busy with the conscious content of our communications, the unconscious can be working for or against us."

Consider a common victory sign: raising our arms above our heads. Margaret King, director of the Center for Culture Studies and Analysis in Philadelphia said: *"The arm raised high evokes triumph and it's very ancient. I would bet that comes from a good hunt, from having successfully hunted and killed prey. We still use body language because that's the way our brains worked years ago when we first became humans."* In fact, gesturing is controlled by the primal brain which explains why gesturing is a common form of communication in the animal kingdom.

Your Facial Expressions

"American sign language requires a lot of facial expressions."
– Nyle Dimarco, American actor

Paul Ekman, briefly introduced earlier in the book, is a world expert in human emotions and facial expressions, has identified more than 8,000 human facial expressions [241]. Ekman also devised a system to measure the emotions people experience based on changes of various control points on a human face. For example, the changes coded in Figure 8.31 indicate the emotion of happiness.

Some of our emotions, called micro-emotions, are displayed for only 1/25 of a second. These expresssions are important because no one can hide them, and they reveal the emotional state of your listener, including his or her potential deception tactics. Ekman showed that smiles change the electromagnetic activity of the brain [242]. In fact, the effect of facial expressions are so strong that your brain will respond

Figure 8.31   Facial coding.

similarly to a robot's mechanical movements of the eyebrows, eyelids and jaws, as you would to a real person [243].

Demonstrating how the primal brain is wired for face recognition, researchers Tsao and Le Chang have identified specific clusters of neurons that fire only upon specific facial characteristics. They found that 205 neurons located in two separate areas of the brain are used for facial recognition. In a revealing test, they reconstructed the images of the faces the monkeys were seeing by decoding the firing patterns among these neurons: these images were nearly identical to the original faces the primates were looking at [244].

This explains why primates and humans are so good at distinguishing between millions of faces, and do so without requiring a similar amount of dedicated neurons to perform the task.

The Dos of Facial Expression

- Mirror all expressions to help you create a positive rapport with your audience ... except anger.

- Smile! Use a natural smile: what the experts call a Duchenne smile. According to Ekman, the main difference between a real and a fake smile is in the widening of the orbicularis oculi muscle around the eyes.

- Relax your facial muscles (all 43 of them). First, it takes fewer muscle contractions to smile than to frown, so you'll feel less tired. Second, because of the mirror neurons in your audience's brain, if you smile long enough it will start to make them smile. Strack, Martin, and Stepper (1988), from Mannheim University in Germany, demonstrated that a person's facial activity influences their affective response. In their experiments, they had people watch cartoons and evaluate how funny they were. By asking participants to hold pens in their mouths forcing some of their muscles to simulate a smile, they showed that the participants that were forced to smile rated the cartoon as funnier.

The Don'ts of Facial Expression

- Do not fake a smile, because the primal brain of your listener will detect – often unconsciously – that it is not a real smile and that therefore you are not trustworthy. It will provide an adverse reaction worse than if you were not smiling at all.

To be a good persuader, engage the muscles around your eyes while limiting the contraction of the zygomatic, which, when overcontracted, signals a fake smile, and adopt a Duchenne smile. This may require practice!

Your Handshake

Neurobiologists at Israel's Weizman Institute discovered that human handshakes serve as a means of transferring social chemical signals between the protagonists. People who shake hands tend to bring the shaken hands to the vicinity of their nose and smell them. This may serve as an evolutionary need to learn about the person whose hand was shaken, replacing a more socially awkward sniffing routine [245].

In 2010, for the launch of a new sales campaign in the United Kingdom, Chevrolet asked Geoffrey Beattie, a psychology professor to decode the best handshake: perfect handshake (PH) to "offer peace of mind and reassurance to its customers." Here is the formula Beattie offered:

$$PH = \sqrt{(e^2 + ve^2)(d^2)} + (cg + dr)^2 + \pi\{(4 <s> 2)(4 <p> 2)\}^2$$
$$+ (vi + t + te)^2 + \{(4 <c> 2)(4 <du> 2)\}^2$$

Where:

(e) is eye contact (1 = none; 5 = direct)

(ve) is verbal greeting (1 = totally inappropriate; 5 = totally appropriate)

(d) is Duchenne smile – smiling in eyes and mouth, plus symmetry on both sides of face, and slower offset (1 = totally non-Duchenne smile [false smile]; 5 = totally Duchenne)

(cg) completeness of grip (1 = very incomplete; 5 = full)

(dr) is dryness of hand (1 = damp; 5 = dry)

(s) is strength (1 = weak; 5 = strong)

(p) is position of hand (1 = back toward own body; 5 = other person's bodily zone)

(vi) is vigor (1 = too low/too high; 5 = mid)

(t) is temperature of hands (1 = too cold/too hot; 5 = mid)

(te) is texture of hands (5 = mid; 1 = too rough/too smooth)

(c) is control (1 = low; 5 = high)

(du) is duration (1 = brief; 5 = long)

Although the rules of handshakes vary from country to country, including places such as Japan where bowing is the norm, the evolutionary meaning of the handshake is to prove that neither shaker is carrying a weapon. Because it constitutes the first contact with the prospect, the savvy persuader would be inspired to learn the proper way of shaking hands.

The Dos of Handshakes

- Maintain direct eye contact during the interaction.
- Start with a warm verbal greeting.
- Display a Duchenne smile on your face.
- Engage your hand all the way to the thumb of your shaker to provide for a complete grip.
- Make sure your hand is dry and your hand texture should be average: neither too rough nor too smooth. Your hand temperature should be warm.
- Extend your hand toward the body of your shaker.
- Gauge the strength of your shaker and prepare to match the strength of their grip.
- Give a few up and down movements neither too vigorous nor too weak.
- Make it last for as long as appropriate for the situation: if you're meeting a head of state and the press is present prepare for a lengthy handshake!
- Keep your weight distributed equally between both legs.
- Hold your shoulders parallel to the shoulders of your shaker.

The Don'ts of Handshakes

- Crunch the hand or try to turn the hand over: it's a sign of dominance.
- Give a dual handed handshake: it shows you are too eager to build rapport.
- Offer a sweaty palm: it's a sign of nervousness. Dry your hand first!
- Offer a frozen hand: warm your hand first if you do not want to be perceived as a "cold" person. Remember the primal brain takes things literally: cold hand = cold person!

Your Eye Communication

"As soon as you make eye contact with somebody they become valued and worthy."
— Mary Lambert, American musician

Much has been written on eye contact and it carries so much meaning that some specialists even call it eye communication. Functional imaging studies have revealed that eye contact can modulate social brain network activity [246]. Eye contact is used by all children to attract the attention of adult caretakers and increase their chance of survival by being fed and cared for [247]. In the Western world, too little eye contact is interpreted as distant, cold, and a lack of emotional intelligence. Maintaining eye contact triggers an approach reaction in the brain, a direct invitation for interaction [248]. On the other hand, avoiding eye contact with a person triggers a response of withdraw [249]. This avoidance can be interpreted by your listener as a sign that you are hiding or lying [250], or it can be a sign of social anxiety [251], neither of which are conducive to establishing further social connection.

Yet, too much eye contact, when it turns into staring, can become an act of dominance, a feeling of superiority, or aggressivity. This is a play for the primal brain as fear is mostly communicated through the muscles around the eyes [252]. This explains that if you meet a gorilla or a bear: the advice is to avoid direct eye contact.

Researchers at the University of Newcastle conducted a revealing experiment to highlight the social effect of having eyes look at us. In one of the offices at the university, they set up a coffee and tea station. The price of each item was prominently displayed and an "honor box" was left unattended on the table. The key element of their experiment was the addition of a different image posted just above the coffee and tea station and changed weekly. The images ranged from neutral (such as flowers) to various males and females' *eyes* that were staring directly at the person using the coffee stand. The layout of the coffee room was such that anybody who would not donate would not be detected. On average people paid 2.76 times as much in the weeks with eyes pictures than with flower pictures [253].

Other research showed that eye contact increases trustworthiness and encourages prosocial behavior [254].

Much of the eye communication is below the threshold of awareness. Don't underestimate how much is communicated by your eyes to the primal brain. Consider this: people are shown two identical photos of a woman, the only difference is that on one of the pictures, her pupils have been dilated by software. In that case, 70% of the viewers will rate the women with dilated pupils as more attractive while very few were able to point at the dilated pupil as the source of difference. The study of pupil size known as pupillometrics and pioneered by Eckhard Hess, a biopsychologist at the University of Chicago is now used as an indicator of emotion. Most eye tracking devices also report the size of the pupils and their contraction even on a very short timescale. This allows for the measurement of micro-emotions, which typically escape traditional observations. It should be noted that pupil dilation is not consciously controllable, so there is a scientific truth in the popular saying: "the eye is a window to the soul."

Also, researchers showed that women are more attracted to men with dilated pupils, showing a connection between pupil size and sexual interest [255].

A study conducted by Goldman and Fordyce [256] at the University of Missouri showed the effect of eye contact, touch, and voice expression on the willingness of tested subjects to help a stranger. Greater helping behavior was linked to voice expressiveness, eye contact, and touch but with a unique exception: when both eye contact and touch were combined, the helping behavior decreased. This suggests that combining these two conditions (eye contact and touch) signals too strong of a willingness to influence and as we know; persuasion works better when the persuadee is not aware he is being persuaded!

Here's a side note about the human ability to recognize faces.

Popular belief has long held that the most important feature allowing us to recognize people is their eyes. Yet, research from the Department of Brain and Cognitive Sciences at MIT Sadr, Jarudi [257] demonstrated that it is not so much the eyes but the *eyebrows* that

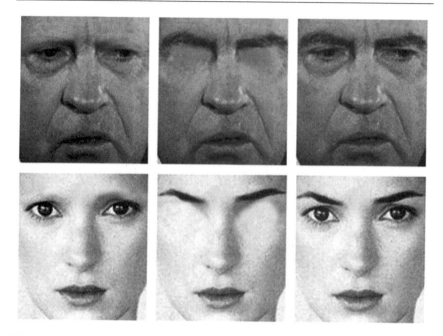

Figure 8.32   Nixon and Ryder facial expressions

play a critical role in recognizing human faces. Notice on the images shown in Figure 8.32 how it is hard to identify President Nixon or Winona Ryder on the first pictures where their eyebrows have been erased compared to the second image where their eyes have been removed.

The Dos of Eye Communication

- Maintain direct eye contact with your communicator for *at least* four seconds.

- Break the eye contact only at the end of a sentence or at the end of the expression of a concept.

- If you are seeking a romantic connection, lower the light: it will dilate your pupils, which will make you appear more attractive.

- Fine-tune these recommendations with the local social norms: In some Asian countries such as Japan or Korea, too strong of an eye contact is considered a sign of aggression and rudeness. This is, in fact, one of the only exceptions to the universal nature of the primal brain where the social norms overrule the primal norms.

The Don'ts of Eye Communication

- If your audience detects your eye contact is not genuine you will invert the benefits. Don't stare; that is, your eye contact needs to be genuinely kind and natural.

Your Expression with the Right Body Posture and Movements.

"Stand tall. The difference between towering and cowering is totally a matter of inner posture. It's got nothing to do with height, it costs nothing, and it's more fun."
— *Malcolm Forbes, American publisher*

Many books on body language suggest that "Our nonverbals govern how people think about us." It turns out that the neural networks that control language are the same ones we use for gesturing [258].

Studies have linked body postures with the presenter's confidence, therefore strengthening the impression she will leave on her audience [259]. Cuddy, at Harvard, even suggested that "Our nonverbal communication govern how people think about themselves." Although Cuddy's research has been the subject of intense controversies, her TED talk remains one of the most watched videos on TED [260]. Cuddy suggests that by adopting a power posture – like when your arms are raised in a winning celebration – for a few minutes, it can change the outcome of many of our interactions. And again, when two people like each other, they will naturally mirror each other's postures, facial expressions, and body movement [261].

The Dos of Body Posture

- If you are standing, adopt what is referred to as the power stance, which signals power from a primal brain perspective.

- Stand tall with a straight back, keeping your head up.

- Distribute your weight equally between both legs with your feet pointing in the direction of your audience and spread at shoulders width.

- Make sure your audience sees the palms of your hands, signaling the absence of weapon.

- If you are sitting, sit straight, don't slouch.

The Dos of Body Movement

- Use as much space as reasonably possible: powerful people own large territories.

- Make your body gesture purposeful and synchronized with your words. For example, if you say: "she entered a very large room" by having your hands go away from each other, you will further highlight the fact that the room was "very large." Make sure the movement happens when you pronounce the words "very large."

- Just like you will want to vary the tone and intensity of your voice, use variation in all aspect of your body language. By creating contrast, it helps your audience stay engaged and focused on you.

You and Your Outfit

Your audience will form an opinion about your style, intelligence, likability, and trustworthiness within a few seconds and with very little awareness, based on the way you look and the way you dress.

In "the beauty bias" Deborah Rhode, Stanford law professor, found that attractive students are considered smarter. Nice looking teachers get better reviews, appealing workers make more money, and good looking politicians get more votes [262].

Researchers in Italy sent 11,000 resumes to 1,500 job postings. They reported that with equivalent qualifications attractive women had a 54% chance of being called back versus 7% for unattractive women. The attractive men had a 47% chance of being called back versus 26% for unattractive men [263]. In the United States, economist Daniel Hamermesh showed that a good-looking man will make $230,000 more over his career than his less attractive counterparts [264]. There is even a name for the economic study of beauty: it's called *pulchronomics*!

This may seem quite unfair but when you consider that good looks (i.e., better genetics) are associated with better health, which in turns leads to better survival chances, it explains why our unconscious primal brain credit those people with an advantage.

To be an effective persuader, stand tall and possibly wear shoes with heels (to appear taller), maintain great physical fitness and grooming, avoid messy hair, wear professional-looking make-up for women, and professional-looking clothing for both genders.

Your Creativity

> *"Making the simple complicated is commonplace; making the complicated awesomely simple: that's creativity."*
> *– Charles Mingus, American musician*

The effect of creativity on the potency of a message has long been established. Some researchers like Robert Smith and Xia Yang from Indiana University have specialized in better defining how creativity contributes to effectiveness of a message.

At its core, the benefit of creativity is about simplification and originality, both of which will appeal to the primal brain. Other persuaders are already trying hard to capture the attention of your audience, and without a bit of creativity, your messages will not provide enough contrast: you will be ignored before you even start.

Chris Watkins, professor of psychology at Abertay University in Scotland demonstrated that people who display creativity are perceived as more attractive, therefore enhancing their charisma.

Figure 8.33   3M billboard.

Figure 8.33 is an example of an ad that could be defined as creative.

The main objection to the use of creativity is that it takes time, energy, and effort to come up with creative ideas: people often spend hours in brainstorming sessions to come up with a simple, yet effective way to communicate their message. The good news is that there is a shortcut to creativity; it's called variety.

Variety as a Short Cut to Creativity

Variety creates a sequence of contrasted events that will help keep the primal brain engaged.

So short of pushing your creativity to invent your own style like Picasso, Ray Charles, or Steve Jobs, here are some ideas to use variety:

- Whenever possible, replace text with a picture or a video: remember the primal brain is visual.

- Use a different medium: for example, in the middle of a PowerPoint presentation, use a paper flip chart or whiteboard to present an idea or discuss a complex concept.

- Change fonts, font size, or color. Readability of text affects retention and intention and some studies have established which fonts on which color background are easier to process either in print, in a PowerPoint, or on web pages. Georgia, Helvetica, Verdana, Gill Sans, and Arial are safe choices in most cases [265–267].

Your Passion

"Nothing great in the world has ever been accomplished without passion."
– Georg Hegel, German philosopher

Question: Besides notoriety, what do the following people have in common?

- Steven Hawking –Theoretical physicist and cosmologist
- Tom Brady – Quarterback of New England Patriot
- Dalai Lama – Buddhist teacher and representative of the Tibetan people
- Meryl Streep – Actress

Answer: They all have an intense passion for what they do.

Building on the theories of emotional contagion, researchers from Munich demonstrated that the perception of an entrepreneur's passion for inventing and developing has a positive effect on the employees [268].

Although intangible by nature, passion is still accurately detected by the primal brain of your audience through your words, your voice, and your body language. Something as hard to notice as a very minor increase in your speaking rate and elevation of pitch at the end of your sentences, or a slight reddening of your skin, or a widening of your pupils at the appropriate moment, all of these changes can be signs of your passion. That might not reach your audience conscious brain, but it will still signal to their primal brain that you are a "passionate" person.

The Dos of Passion

- Learn to gauge your own passion and avoid making important communication when your passion is low such as after an exhausting business trip or an upsetting event.

- Surround yourself with passionate people. Since passion is contagious, choose passionate partners; it will build on itself.

- If you do what you love and love what you do, your audience will naturally feel your passion. Learn to love what you have, not what you want.

- There is no such thing as too much passion, so learn to communicate your passion with a bit of panache and with your own style: it will help your charisma score a few more points. Get your inspiration from some of the greatest communicators like Martin Luther King, Gandhi, Churchill, or Steve Jobs!

The Don'ts of Passion

- Don't fake it. It takes a professional actor to cry on demand and change all his facial muscles, the tone of his voice, and posture to communicate true sadness. So even if you can cry on demand, it takes only a teeny discrepancy from all the other clues to make your audience feel that your passion might not be all that authentic. This would raise a red flag and would make you lose the trust from your audience.

Your Fearlessness

"You always have two choices: your commitment and your fear."
              – *Sammy Davis Jr., American entertainer*

Just like your passion is subconsciously communicated through your words, voice, and body language, so is your fear. Lilianne Parodi research showed that the mere smell of people who had been exposed to a fearful situation triggered an increase of activity in the amygdala – part of the primal brain [269]. Not to mention all the other conscious and unconscious signals your body will inevitably display, your audience will even be able to smell that you are afraid! Any sign of fear in your behavior will be instantly detected by your audience's primal brain and translated into a sign of imminent danger.

According to a now-famous list of the top 14 fears ranked, public speaking is the number one fear of Americans (stated by 41% of respondents) ahead of height, insects, monetary loss, and even death which ranked number 7 with 19% [270].

Stage fright, an extreme form of fear related to presenting or performing in public, activates the sympathetic nervous system by releasing adrenaline into the bloodstream. It triggers a cascade of symptoms: racing heart, dry mouth, increased blood pressure, blushing, sweating, shortness of breath, light headedness, and nausea, a bodily response known as the fight-or-flight syndrome. On the face alone, fear will

- Raise the upper lids
- Tense the lower lids
- Open the eyes wider
- Widen the nostrils
- Widen the lips

All these signs would be quickly detected by the brain of predators and translated into an opportunity to harvest a prey...instead of an opportunity to be influenced by a charismatic presenter! You do not want to display any trace of fear even if limited to your own insecurities related to losing the deal or the trust of your prospect.

Dos and Don'ts About Fear

- If you experience stage fright or noticeable nervousness, you need to de-escalate the loop that creates the fright. Your primal brain goes: my heart is racing so there must be a threat around and I must prepare my body for fight or flight, therefore I need to increase my heart rate even more. As soon as you start to feel your heart accelerating, you should practice deep breathing to increase oxygen intake while keeping a constant heart rate. You should also convince yourself that it's only a presentation . . . even if it's the opportunity of your life and you are on stage in front of two million viewers: it's only a presentation. You're not facing a life threatening tiger: so make sure to breathe deeply; it will limit the biological symptoms of fear.

- A second option to get your stage fright under control requires practice. Several days or weeks before a big event, create a short meditation using a simple technique: visualize yourself entering the stage, getting an introduction, delivering your presentation, and getting a standing ovation at the end. By picturing in your mind as many details as you may know about the person who will introduce you, the aspect, shape, and color of the room, the face of people in the audience, all the elements of your presentation, and so on, you program your primal brain to recognize a familiar, nonthreatening environment. Repeat this routine several times before the event. On the day of the presentation, a small natural nervousness will not escalate into a full-blown stage fright because your primal brain will think: "I recognize this place: I've been here many times, and I have nothing to worry about because I know it will end with a standing ovation." If you experience stage fright or serious nervousness, try it!

- Practice, practice, practice. First, it will help you memorize your content allowing you to better focus on your tone of voice and body language. Second, the mastery you will acquire in your material will help build confidence and decrease the nervousness that will trigger the symptoms of stage fright. You will appear more natural, more relaxed, a trait of charismatic people.

- Act with high intention but low attachment. Do your best and don't worry so much about the immediate outcome: it's just business, not a life-threatening situation!

- Many professional public speakers – including Christophe and I – report that a bit of fear helps them perform better: it sharpens their minds. Yet they transform that nervousness into higher excitement, which their audience interprets as a sign of passion!

As the manifestation of an imminent threat, fear served us well through evolutionary times; however, displaying it in today's business world is counterproductive. Charismatic presenters practice hard to eliminate any sign of it.

Your Integrity

"Whoever is careless with the truth in small matters cannot be trusted with important matters."
– *Albert Einstein*, **Physicist**

Do you realize how we tend to judge a sales clerk right after he asks: "Can I help you"? The question is simple but the attitude behind the question is everything: is the clerk really honest and is he willing to genuinely offer some help? Or he is just asking the question because it's part of his job? In the 400 milliseconds, it took your primal brain to hear these four words you have already decided – unconsciously – if you liked the person enough to take the next steps. Now if the clerk is a good communicator, he would have made sure to hold your eye contact and use a friendly tone of voice to ask his initial question, but even beyond all the variables of his charisma described above your brain is asking: Can this person be trusted, is he acting with integrity?

Researchers showed how effective our brains are to detect lies. They also showed that the unconscious detection of deception – a task for the primal brain – is more effective than its conscious counterpart [194, 271].

The Dos of Integrity

- Stick to the truth and nothing but the truth. Don't flex the limits. For many salespeople it's easy to say: "Yes, my product can do this and that" but you can lose all trust immediately if the prospect establishes later that it is not true.

- If you want to emphasize one quality – of you or your product – make that statement just after you confess to a flaw or shortcoming. According to Cialdini [167], people are more willing to trust the truthfulness of your quality if it was preceded by a shortcoming.

- The benefit of telling the truth: it will decrease your cognitive load. Deception researchers in the UK showed that people who were asked to lie convincingly showed signs of cognitive overload like forgetting some details and blinking less than normal [272]. These signs will most likely be picked up by the primal brain of your audience.

To conclude on charisma, the research is revealing. What you say is less important than how you say it. You may consider attending an acting class to sharpen your skills using your voice and body language: it will be the most effective way to improve your persuasive effectiveness! You probably realize that to do this without having to think about it will require lots of practice. Your objective should be to not have to focus your attention on a proper posture, eye contact, or facial expression; instead you want 100% of your brain power focused on the sharpness of your arguments and on reading your audience reaction so you can adapt in real time! The most charismatic people will improvise and give a perfect answer to even the most difficult, unplanned question. If you are not there, practice, practice, practice!

APPLY CONTRAST

"Everything is relative."

– Albert Einstein, physicist

Earlier in this book we described contrastable as one of the six primal stimuli. Contrast is such an important concept that, similar to emotion, it constitutes both a stimulus to the primal brain and a persuasion catalyst. The impact of any persuasion element can be enhanced if you add contrast. For example, notice how some of the grabbers could be improved with contrast: you could use one prop to illustrate a benefit or feature offered by your main competitor and contrast this by using another prop illustrating your superiority. Similarly, you could increase the impact of a minidrama by having a first act about the painful life of your prospect today without your solution, and contrast that by role-playing what their lives would be if only they had your solution.

Contrast can be applied to highlight the benefits of your solution:

- Before and after

- Compared to your competitors

- Now instead of later

Figure 8.34   Dannon Danimals.

Or to avoid or alleviate the pain or cost of

- Complicated versus simple
- Fast versus slow
- Expensive versus affordable

Figure 8.34 is an example for a yogurt ad, where the value prop is clearly communicated with contrast.

The visual contrast helps you understand the value of a yogurt rich in vitamin D to better absorb calcium and build strong bones.

Because of the visual dominance of the primal brain, contrast is most effective when communicated through photography or illustrations. Note how big pictures with contrast are often used to promote products that can regrow hair or help you lose weight. For example, Figure 8.35, you see on the left side an overweight man and on the right side you now have the same man 100 pounds lighter!

Figure 8.35   Gain contrast.

VARY TEACHING MODALITIES

"Tell me and I forget. Teach me and I remember. Involve me and I learn."
– Benjamin Franklin, inventor, scientist, author,
politician, polymath

What else could you do to boost the impact of your persuasion elements? What about using different teaching modalities?

The topic of teaching modalities has been the subject of prolific literature and intense debate among the education community for decades. The stakes are high because

- Governments invest billions of dollars on education.

- Teachers are frustrated at the ever-widening gap between what they know and what their students really learn.

- Many people believe that the web is changing the way younger generations learn.

Furthermore, marketers are continuously looking at more effective ways to capture the attention of their targeted audience and making sure that their messages are understood and remembered!

The Science of Teaching Modalities

There are three teaching modalities that can make your message more brain-friendly:

1. Visual: If you want to teach somebody the concept of a cat you can show them a picture of a cat.

2. Auditory: You can teach people about cats by talking about a four-legged, furry, domesticated, carnivorous mammal who loves mice and weighs about 10 pounds.

3. Kinesthetic-Tactile: To teach people kinesthetically about cats, you can hand them a cat, so they could touch it and play with it.

Notice that using a kinesthetic modality with a blind person, you would achieve a good level of teaching effectiveness, whereas showing a picture of a cat would have zero effect. Similarly, using the auditory experience of talking about a cat to a deaf person would have no effect.

The notion of using preferential teaching modalities to communicate more effectively has long been discussed by experts in neurolinguistic programming (NLP). NLP claims that there is a connection between the neurological processes (neuro), language (linguistic), and behavioral patterns learned through experience (programming). Although the scientific basis of NLP has been overwhelmingly discredited [273], many are still pursuing the framework of NLP today.

Despite the controversy, we do recommend using a mix of all three teaching modalities to communicate your message. Note that most sales messages (emails, brochures, and presentations especially) only use the auditory channel, regardless of the nature of the concept or product advertised. This can explain why so many of them are never processed by the primal brain.

Take an average sales presentation using PowerPoint slides. Although you may find a few pictures in it, 95% of the concepts are typically communicated using words.

Now, let's go back to the three ways to describe a cat and imagine how learning will be limited if you only hear words describing what a cat is. Contrast this with the combined experience of seeing a cat (visual), touching and playing with a cat (kinesthetic), and hearing about a cat (auditory). In fact, researchers have established that the visual presentation of objects (with or without the simultaneous auditory presentation of names) resulted in better learning, better recall, and better retrieval of information than the auditory presentation alone [274]. Knowing the bias of the primal brain for the visual channel, this is not surprising!

Here some other important considerations.

Most Visuals Are Not Visual

Take the example shown in Figure 8.36 from the world of Linux, an open source operating system which people can freely use and contribute to its development.

Because we use our eyes to input the information in our brains (including the text) and because the circles and arrows belong to the realm of visual shapes, most people believe this type of graph uses mostly the visual modality. In reality, the decoding of text involves first and foremost the auditory cortex and the frontal lobe. Furthermore, the circles and arrows provide a well-organized chart but do not convey a strong visual metaphor that could help a viewer quickly understand the concept without spending much cognitive energy. To be understood, such a chart requires a significant cognitive effort that engages many parts of the brain beyond the visual cortex. Contrast this with Figure 8.37, also from the world of Linux.

Note that, although the image contains some text, the amount of text is significantly less than in the previous example (only five words, instead of 12) and more importantly, the central position of the words "Linux Services" and their shape – in the form of a puzzle – visually suggest that these services are central to the value

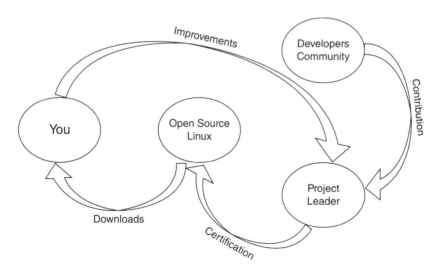

Figure 8.36 Linux visual.

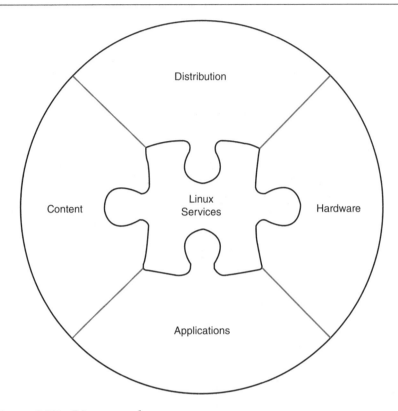

Figure 8.37   Linux puzzle.

of Linux and it helps tie the four concepts of distribution, hardware, applications, and content together. Notice that this chart (even if you are foreign to the world of Linux) requires less cognitive effort than the first example.

The Benefits of NeuroMap

If you start to apply the concepts presented in NeuroMap, your message will undoubtedly be easier for your audience to understand and to remember. Note that Understand + Remember = Learn. Concepts like:

• Using a prop as a grabber will engage your audience visually and kinesthetically.

• Big pictures are, by definition, visual.

- Claims offer an auditory appeal, and their NeuroIcons provide a visual stimulus. The claims' simplicity and brevity do not generate a cognitive overload, which would confuse the primal brain.

Multisensory Selling

The use of multiple senses in marketing – multisensory marketing – has become mainstream [275]. For example, Nike found that introducing scent in their store increased purchase intent by 80% [276]. Diageo who owns multiple brands of alcohol: Tanqueray, Smirnoff, Johnny Walker, J&B, among others, showed that changes to their multisensory environment increased whiskey enjoyment by up to 20% [277].

If you are selling products with a gustative or fragrance quality (food, wine, perfumes, etc.) think about ways to communicate using specifically the sense of taste or smell. That is what many cosmetic companies do by including perfume scratchers in magazines. If your value proposition engages multiple senses, find ways to improve their "holistic" experiences.

Senses Can Distort Perception

Most people believe that our senses provide an accurate representation of the world around us. Yet, our perception of the world is driven by the interpretation made by our brain from the input of the five senses, plus the associated cognitive processes. An easy way to illustrate the difference between reality and our perception is with optical illusions. Figure 8.38 shows one of the oldest.

Regardless of how hard you look at these two horizontal lines of the same length, your brain will keep interpreting the upper one as longer. Or, in the example shown in Figure 8.39, which of the black circles is larger? In fact, they have the same diameter!

One of the most mind-blowing illusions is known as the checker illusion published by Edward Adelson from the MIT (https://tinyurl.com/444xpss) [278]. Meanwhile, a set of 10 remarkable illusions and their explanations can be seen at https://tinyurl.com/yayqtdow [279].

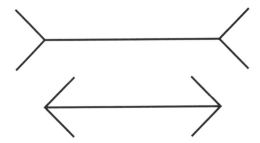

Figure 8.38 Perception.

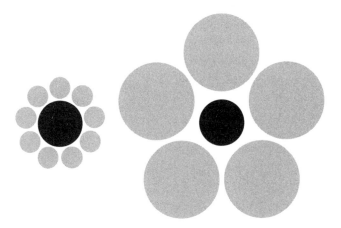

Figure 8.39 Circles.

Because the brain has not evolved to interpret reality as it is, our perception, which is largely controlled by the primal brain, is often flawed. One of the most surprising consequences of this is that the other senses impact our perception of one sense. For instance, what you taste is influenced by what you see, what you see is impacted by what you hear, and so on.

Consider the experiment conducted at the Bordeaux University by Frederic Brochet [280]. Brochet invited 54 wine experts and asked them to give their opinions about two glasses of wine, one white and one red. The experts described each wine with attributes usually associated with either red wines or white ones. But unbeknownst to the experts, they were drinking the same white wine; the red had been simply tinted using a natural, odorless, and tasteless white dye. One of the experts even described the wine as "crushed with red fruit." Brochet ran another experiment in which he poured wine from two different bottles: the first label was a fancy grand cru and the second one was an ordinary table wine. Not surprisingly the grand cru was described as "rounded," "balanced," "complex," and the ordinary wine was noted as "short," "flat," and "faulty." In reality, the experts were drinking the same wine poured from a bottle with a different label! Similarly to the experiment with the self-refilling bowls, our visual channel often overrides other senses! As we saw earlier, visual is one of the six stimuli to the primal brain because it exerts so much dominance on our perception process.

Consider this:

- The higher the sound of potato chips, the crunchier consumers find them, regardless of their actual crunchiness. Similarly, consumers associate higher bubbling sound with more carbonation [281]. This indicates that the sense of hearing along with the touch sensation in the mouth plays a role in food perception.

- Background music impacts perception. A study with 30 volunteers indicated that they perceived oysters to be tastier when listening to the sound of the ocean compared to other sounds.

- Background music impacts purchase. Over a two-week period in a UK store, they alternated playing French music one day with playing German music the next day. It resulted in more French wines being sold when French music was played and vice versa. Meanwhile, the customers wouldn't report being aware of the music being played [282].

The *Harvard Business Review* reported that people invested 43% more money after briefly holding a warm pad, suggesting feeling heat translated into an increased feeling of a being in a safer, and more trusting environment [283].

John Bargh wrote, "The connection between physical and social warmth is hardwired in the human brain. In fact, brain imaging experiments have shown that the same small region of the brain, the insula becomes active to both types of warmth: when touching something like a heating pad and when texting family and friends [205].

In the *HBR* report mentioned earlier, they also noted that during a negotiation over the price of a new car, people who sat on a hard wooden chair offered an average of 28% less than people sitting on softer, padded chairs: hard chairs made people harder negotiators. In those studies, people were not even aware that these tactile sensations had any influence on them.

Once again, think about how you can change your customer's experience to provide positive stimulation of their primal brain.

The Dos of Varying Teaching Modalities

- First and foremost, the effective persuader will match the teaching modality with the concept to be communicated. Don't try to teach tennis or golf, two highly kinesthetic skills, by only talking about golf or showing a video. Your audience needs the kinesthetic experience of playing!

- You cannot overcommunicate visually. Research showed that the presentation of images is advantageous for all learners irrespective of their learning-style preference [274]. Remember, the primal brain is under the dominance of the visual sense, so the more visual your message, the better. In the ad for a yoga center in Figure 8.40, notice how the concept of flexibility is conveyed visually. Further, notice the ad also communicates kinesthetically – you can touch and flex the straw! Even if you can only see the image (as opposed to holding the straw), by creating the perception that this hand is yours your mirror neurons will contribute to stimulating you kinesthetically.

- Short of using an actual visual, use a word that evokes a visual cue. For example, instead of saying: "Do you hear what I say?" say: "Do you see what I mean?" Note the use of the verb "see." Researchers showed that the processing of sentences that evoke visual or abstract information engages not only the left temporal lobe but also the left intraparietal sulcus, a region involved in visiospatial working memory [284].

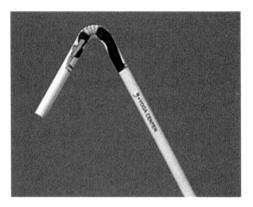

Figure 8.40   Yoga straw.

- Similarly, we could infer that using a kinesthetic cue will activate brain regions responsible for driving kinesthetic functions. Instead of saying: "The new screen technology allows the consumer to...," say, "With the new screen technology the consumer will experience/reach/feel/meet/match/touch..." Note the selection of verbs that imply a kinesthetic connection. Or even better, make sure the consumers have a chance to touch the new device to appeal to their kinesthetic channel.

- When in doubt of the best modality to teach a concept, tell a story! Make sure that your story uses, visual, auditory, and kinesthetic cues. Another benefit of using different teaching modalities is to create variety, a form of contrast that appeals to the primal brain.

The Don'ts of Varying Teaching Modalities

- Don't only use words to persuade!

- Don't ignore what you might consider an unrelated sensory experience. Having your prospects sit on hard chairs, listen to French music or touch a warm cup of coffee will have an impact on their buying experience!

In conclusion, notice how using the primal brain as a reference can explain a lot of these complex often unconscious phenomenon.

TRIGGER EMOTIONS

"The essential difference between reason and emotion is that reason leads to conclusions while emotion leads to action."

– Donald Calne, neurologist

We saw earlier how the primal brain is driven by emotions, one of the six stimuli. Appropriately, emotions can boost the impact of any persuasion element!

Using More Emotions

Remember how Bill Gates increased the impact of his message about the eradication of malaria? He didn't simply talk about the number of death caused by the disease: he released a jar full of mosquitos in the auditorium! This had the inevitable effect of creating a strong emotional cocktail in the brains of his audience, a response that supported Gates's plea to fight the virus.

Researchers have demonstrated that pushing people to use their rational mind to make a decision and therefore discounting the primal brain's influence leads to less satisfying decisions. When people evaluate cognitively multiple product attributes, it can degrade their judgment [285]. In a test, two groups of students were asked to evaluate five types of jam that had been graded on 16 sensory characteristics by tasting experts. The first group of students was simply asked to rank the jam without much thinking. The second group was instructed to use a more rational approach. They were asked to follow a logical process to evaluate the color, texture, sweetness, smell, stickiness, and so forth. In the end, the evaluation of students who were invited to use a more rational approach was further away from the experts' ratings than the evaluation of students who had used only their primal reaction to the jam!

Examples of Emotions in Action

- With over 4,500 injured pedestrians every year, Paris has the highest rate of crossing accidents in Europe. What did the mayor's office do to jolt the jaywalkers with a strong emotion? They launched a campaign called "Impact without impact" on a busy street where people would frequently cross even when the pedestrian light is red. They mounted an elaborate system that would play a startling sound of a tire screeching as if a car was about to hit them. Hearing this, each person would typically freeze, scream, or make facial expressions conveying their terrorized state. At that exact moment, a camera would take their picture. And to elevate the emotional cocktail, that picture would be displayed in front of them on the billboard located on the other side of the street! The video can be seen at: https://youtu.be/vYWmeh6Q-Vk [286].

- The cleaning crew of the toilets at the Schiphol Airport in Amsterdam couldn't keep up with the leakage in the men urinals and they wondered how to help the users be more accurate in their aiming. The decision was made to include the print of a fly inside the bowl. The emotion of the initial surprise of noticing a fly, followed by the ancestral joy of hunting down the insect resulted in a stunning 80% decrease of spillage [287] (Figure 8.41).

- In Hong Kong, advertisers found an emotional way to highlight the danger of using mobile phones while driving. A movie theater played a commercial showing a car driving in the countryside. Then all the people using one of the major phone carriers received a text message: they all quickly reached into their pocket to retrieve their phones. They hadn't yet been reminded to turn off their phones, when suddenly the car on the screen crashed into a tree. The punch line was displayed on the screen: "A reminder to keep your eyes on the road." The video can be seen at https://tinyurl.com/od5m7v4 [288].

In conclusion, remember that decisions are driven by emotions. Once you have decided on the content of your message that is

Figure 8.41   Shiphol Airport urinal.

1. Focused on the main pain of your customers

2. Centered on three claims

3. Demonstrated by convincing evidence of their gain

then, you think about ways to communicate this content that elicit a strong emotional response.

AIM FOR LESS

"A wealth of information creates a poverty of attention."
– Herbert Simon, cognitive psychologist and computer
scientist, 1975 Turing Prize and 1978 Economy Nobel
Prize recipient

When too much information is communicated, the working memory of the listener quickly overloads and the message recipients get confused, not convinced. Consider the research conducted by the University of Missouri which reported that a single sentence of 10 words was difficult to precisely recall by a majority of listeners [148].

Also, researchers established that irrelevant speech disrupts neural coherence patterns, making it more difficult for the listener to understand the real point of what is truly being communicated [289].

In fact, a quarter of all cognitive biases are categorized under "too much information." As an effective persuader, you should only tell what is needed to persuade and avoid adding any information that will add too much complexity or dilute the message.

The three questions that will help you decide if you need to keep a piece of information or if you need to discard it:

1. Is this piece of information linked to a **pain** of your audience?

2. Is this piece of information unique to you; are you telling about your **claims**? If you are not selling something unique, you are selling as much for your competitors as you are selling for yourself.

3. Can you prove what you are saying, and can you attach a financial, strategic, or personal value to your statement? Can you demonstrate some **gain**?

If you responded "no" to any of these questions, you should eliminate the information you were considering.

You should refrain from the desire to communicate all the functions and features of your solution. Instead, and as suggested in NeuroMap, you should focus your message on only one to three claims, which will provide a unique and perfect elimination of the pain, while presenting more value than cost, that is, the gain. In a clever study titled "On the Pursuit and Misuse of Useless Information" Stanford and Princeton researchers Bastardi and Shafir [290] demonstrated that too much information reduces the quality of our decisions.

Behavioral economists also examine the issue of "choice over-load" which most often reduces decision quality [291]. Although these researchers have a hard time separating the concept of "choice over-load" with "information overload" a new field of studies concerning the architecture of choice has quickly emerged.

Choice Architecture: A Counterexample for Making It Short

Researchers study how the numbers of options, the manners in which the attributes are described, and the presence of a default option can all influence people choices. For example, researchers noticed that the percentage of organ donors differed greatly from country to country, even between countries with similar cultures and values like Germany and Austria. They quickly discovered that the discriminant variable was the default value. By simply switching from an opt-out default (such as the United States or Germany) where the percentage of donors is less than 15%, countries like Austria with an opt-in default see 90% of their people donating!

In *Predictably Irrational*, Dan Ariely [70] showed, that in some cases, offering more options can change people's choices. Here is the simple, yet effective experiment, Ariely designed after being struck by noticing the following three options for a yearly subscription of the magazine *The Economist*:

1. Buy Internet only: $59
2. Buy print only: $125
3. Buy print and Internet: $125

The second option seems irrelevant as, for the same price, the prospective subscriber could get the internet version at no additional cost.

Not surprisingly, when Ariely asked his students to choose between those three options, none of them picked option 2: 16% chose option 1, and 84% chose option 3. Should option 2 be eliminated?

No! Because when Ariely asked another group of students to choose from those two options:

1. Buy Internet only: $59
2. Buy print and Internet: $125

Then 68% of them chose option 1 and only 32% chose option 2. Ariely termed option 2 in the first experiment a "decoy," which lures more people to pick both the print and Internet subscription.

The Primal Brain's Narrative Structure

To create an effective narrative structure, simply organize your presentation using four message elements: grabber, claims, gain proofs, and close. The length of each period depends on the format and delivery conditions of your message. For instance, for a face-to-face presentation, we recommend that each period should last no more than two or three minutes. If you are producing a 30-second commercial, each message element should last around 5 seconds. Generally speaking, we tend to be more patient when a message is delivered face-to-face compared to when we process it on a computer or watch it on TV, presumably because human interaction is a stronger stimulus for the primal brain than a digital message delivered by a device.

In fact, research comparing the effectiveness of negotiations conducted face-to-face compared to computer-mediated communication clearly confirms the superiority of face-to-face. For instance, face-to-face requires less brain energy, which, of course, makes face-to-face preferred by the primal brain [292].

To maximize the effectiveness of your messages, we recommend the narrative structure shown in Table 8.1.

The grabber is the fire you need to light under your prospects' chairs to get their attention. Then, you should introduce the top three reasons that they should choose you: your claims. After that, prove your value with credible evidences: your gain proofs. The close should allow you to repeat with force, passion, and urgency that your prospects' pains can be solved by your unique claims. This

Table 8.1 Primal brain narrative structure with timing.

Delivery Format/ Total Length		Grabber	Claims (up to three)	Gain proofs (up to three)	Close
		Reinforce the urgency of solving a personal pain	State unique claim(s) to solve the pain	Use evidence that is credible and easily believable	Repeat pain and claims
Face-to-face presentation	10–12 minutes	2–3 minutes	1–2 minutes for each claim	1 minute for each gain proof	30 seconds
Phone call	5–6 minutes	1 minute	1 minute for each claim	15 second for each gain proof	15 seconds
Corporate video	2 minutes	30 seconds	30–60	15 seconds	15 seconds
Commercial	30 seconds	15–20 seconds	5 seconds	5 seconds	5 seconds
Web page/ print ad	5–7 seconds	2–3 seconds	2 seconds	1 second	1 second

brain-optimized message architecture will make your message easy to understand and easy to remember. Notice that we recommend that all of these messages be brief. So make it short!

What to Remember About Making It Short

- If you need to offer your prospects assorted options, such as in *The Economist* subscription case, you may enjoy learning more about "choice architecture." This field has received much attention and may prove to be valuable for your company [287, 293].

- If you are not dealing with the issue of choice architecture, we recommend that you do not expose your prospects with "information overload." You should thin your messages and use the concepts of pain-claim-gain as a filter to retain only information with persuasive impact.

WHAT TO REMEMBER

To be most effective, your message should be constructed with six persuasion elements:

1. A grabber: a short, but effective way to communicate your value proposition that goes beyond simply using words. It will make it easier for your audience to start focusing their mental energy on your solution because it will trigger an immediate emotional response.

2. Your claims: the top three reasons why they should buy from you or adopt your idea. By nature, these are not only unique benefits of your subject, but they also define the structure of your message: the three chapters under which your selling arguments are organized.

3. Your big picture: a simple graphical representation of how your product, service, or idea will impact the world of your prospect or audience. Visual stimuli are so critical to the primal brain that you need to present a bird's eye view of the result of what you promote.

4. Your proofs of gain: the primal brain is not very evolved and quite skeptical, so you should provide simple, yet strong and effective proofs of your value. Quantify the financial, strategic, and personal value of each of your claims and contrast it with your cost. Make it fit on one page regardless of the complexity of your solution.

5. The reframe of their objections: using logic cannot uproot the negative emotion associated with the fear of regret communicated by your audience. Use a reframe to create a positive emotion.

6. A closing: repeat your claims one more time and ask: "What do you think?" Wait for their feedback and ask: "Where do we go from here?" and wait for their response. Triggering their law of consistency is the most effective way to make your prospect of audience move along the sales or mental continuum to accept your solution or idea.

And to further increase the impact of any of those persuasion elements, use one or more of the seven persuasion catalysts:

1. Tell stories: It will transport your audience in a different world where you control the emotion communicated by the punch line.

2. Use your charisma: Use the words, tone of voice, and body language most conducive to persuasion.

3. Word with *you*: Put your audience in the center of the action by using the most influential word in the English language!

4. Apply contrast: Increase the impact of your persuasion elements by using more contrast: before/after, your competitors/you, their pain/their gain.

5. Vary teaching modalities: Choose the modality most effective to communicate the concept you are presenting. Most people only use the auditory channel. Make *your* message more visual and more kinesthetic.

6. Trigger emotions: People make emotional decisions and rationalize them later. Use more emotions to trigger faster decisions.

7. Make it short: More information leads to confusion not persuasion. Less is more, so focus on pain, claims, and gain and remove the rest!

CONCLUSION

C ongratulations! You have completed your learning journey on the persuasion code. Persuasion is a complex process and our objective was to give you a simple, yet scientific, step-by-step process to help you become much better at convincing others. In the end, we believe that persuasion is a function of how well you understand and communicate to the primal brain. NeuroMap provides a clear path toward getting measurable value from all your messages: emails, website, brochures, PowerPoints, and even commercials.

Let's review the most important teaching moments of your journey:

In the first chapter, you learned the value and power of a brain-based persuasion model. With NeuroMap, you now can avoid the waste of sending ineffective messages to your customers, prospects, friends, family members, and more. You can avoid the pitfalls of A/B testing, and the embarrassment of disastrous campaigns or boring sales presentations. Finally, you learned that traditional marketing research methods fail to capture the subconscious mechanisms that drive persuasion. Fortunately, neuromarketing tools provide new ways to collect brain data that can objectively explain critical neurological processes subjects cannot self-report. The strategic value of using neuromarketing comes from the possibility of answering critical research questions. As a result, the ROI of neuromarketing dollars is measurable in multiple ways. It will drastically reduce money spent in creating and deploying messages that don't work. More importantly, it will allow you and your organization to grow faster.

In the second chapter, you discovered that you do not need to be a neuroscientist to understand the critical importance of measuring more than what people can tell you about your messages. Neuromarketing is about helping you figure out once and for all what a brain-friendly message is. You learned that the brain is a complex organ that has evolved over millions of years. The cognitive functions are relatively young in terms of evolution, whereas the neurological circuitry of our most basic survival-centric responses is ancient. In the past three decades, numerous studies have clarified how attention and emotions affect us and influence our decisions. Neuromarketing can help companies measure neurophysiological responses people experience in front of any marketing stimuli. These responses arise from autonomic and mostly instinctual brain processes, but also cognitive and emotional processes mediated by the central nervous system. A wide variety of tools are now available to produce brain data critical to our understanding of consumer responses to marketing messages. Individually, each method can provide important insights. However, without measuring both the cortical and subcortical activity, the interpretation of brain data is incomplete and ineffective.

In the third chapter, you learned that persuasion has been studied for decades, but old models have long ignored the role played by subconscious brain structures. You also were introduced to the critical path that persuasion takes from the primal brain to the rational brain, a phenomena we call the bottom-up effect. NeuroMap shows that persuasive messages do not work unless they first influence the bottom section of the brain, the primal brain, which reacts to specific stimuli. Once a message has "engaged" the primal brain, persuasion radiates to the upper section of the brain where we tend to process the information more sequentially. Finally, you discovered that 188 known cognitive biases can be explained by NeuroMap.

In the fourth chapter, you discovered that you can use six stimuli to persuade the primal brain. Personal helps you quickly make a frustration or pain relevant to your audience. Constrastable accelerates decisions by comparing two situations that make the best choice obvious. Tangible achieves cognitive fluency and limits the amount of energy or distraction involved in the processing of your message. Memorable creates automatic retention so that the key elements of your message get encoded in the short-term memory of your audience. Visual appeals to the default sensory channel by which the primal brain decides. Emotional creates a cocktail of hormones and neurotransmitters without which your message will not trigger a decision.

Together, the six stimuli propel your message to success, achieving the optimum path of persuasion. Meanwhile, NeuroScoring your message on the six stimuli can help you correct and improve the course of your message on the path of persuasion. Check the Appendix to see how you can quickly NeuroScore your own messages before you deploy them! Finally, NeuroQuadrants also provide a simple tool to optimize the effect of any your messages.

In the fifth chapter, you learned that diagnosing pains helps you unveil the most critical decision drivers that influence your customers' behavior. Our nature is to orient our attention to messages that awaken our fears, which is why a product or solution that can clearly articulate which pains it can eliminate first will receive more consideration and create higher urgency. Once you have successfully diagnosed the top pains by conducting pain dialogues, you can quantify the importance of the pains, as well as consider creating segments or clusters of your top customers who share common pains. Additionally, we recommend that you conduct some neuromarketing research to confirm what your pain dialogues have unveiled.

In the sixth chapter, you discovered that the primal brain will favor information that uses short and simple words that are easy to pronounce and information that is clearly organized under a maximum of three chapters or arguments: your claims. Also, messages that are easy to read, with fonts that are processed with maximum fluency are preferred. Using colors that offer a pleasing contrast with their background will be most brain friendly. Wordsmith your claims to make them more memorable. A repetition of the same word (a meta-claim) is a good technique such as protect XX, protect YY, protect ZZ. An alliteration (the repetition of the same letter or sound at the beginning of adjacent words) is also an effective technique, such as diagnose, differentiate, demonstrate, and deliver. A rhyme provides further auditory appeal – protect your time, protect your dime, protect your peace of mind… or pain, claim, gain are good examples.

In the seventh chapter, your learned that the value you talk about is not as important as the value your prospects believe in. As a result, you need to maximize, not only the amount of value they will receive but also use the best possible proofs of gain. Moreover, your value demonstration needs to be quickly understood by their primal brain. This means that you need to make that demonstration simple enough that even a non-expert would understand it. Use customer testimonials to support your value demonstration, a demo, data or a vision. Lastly, focus your demonstration on what is unique about your solution, that is, what can be categorized under each of your claims.

In the eighth and final chapter, you learned that the most effective messages should include six persuasion elements:

1. A grabber: a short but effective way to communicate your value proposition that goes beyond simply using words and typically re-awakes the pain your customers want to eliminate.

2. Claims: the top three reasons your customers should buy from you.

3. A big picture: a simple graphical representation of how your product, service, or idea will impact the world of your prospect or audience.

4. Undisputable proofs of your gain: the primal brain is not very evolved and quite skeptical, so you should provide simple yet strong and effective proofs of your value.

5. Reframe objections to create positive emotions when your customers express resistance.

6. Close: the repetition of your claims one more time and ask: "What do you think?" Wait for their feedback and ask: "Where do we go from here?" and wait for their response.

You can further increase the impact of any of those persuasion elements by using seven persuasion catalysts:

1. Tell stories that will transport your audience in a different world where you control the emotion communicated by the punch line.

2. Use your charisma.

3. Word with *you*.

4. Apply contrast to increase the impact of any of your persuasion elements.

5. Vary teaching modalities: chose the modality most effective to communicate the concept you are presenting.

6. Trigger emotions to trigger faster decisions.

7. Make it short: more information leads to confusion not more persuasion!

Now the challenging work begins. You have many options when you begin the implementation of NeuroMap.

We recommend that you identify the weakest step in your current sales or advertising narrative. These questions will help:

1. Are you addressing the most relevant and urgent pains?

2. Is your message truly differentiated? Basically, are you selling something unique and using claims?

3. Are you communicating compelling and indisputable proofs of your gain?

4. Is your message easy to understand and impossible to forget? Does it reach the primal brain?

Although focusing on the weakest link of the chain first may appear logical, we recommend that you follow the sequence of the 4 persuasion steps. This means that you should first diagnose the pain and then move on from there. In our experience, skipping steps will compromise the power of NeuroMap, even if you have already done some research on the pains or identified your claims, or completed some work on the demonstration of your value proposition (gain). Rethinking all these concepts around the primal brain will greatly simplify even the most complex messaging strategy.

Second, decide if you can afford researching pains or assessing the neurological effect of your current advertising stimuli based on the cost/benefits of your value proposition. The higher the value, the more you can justify investing in research. Most companies typically invest as much as 10% of the gross margin of researching a product or solution.

Third, confirm who are the stakeholders of this process? Should you do this on your own, or should you involve your executive team? Using NeuroMap to build clarity, consensus, and commitment with your executive team on the concepts of pain, claims, gain, and primal brain will set the foundation of a solid marketing and messaging strategy for years to come.

Fourth, identify who else in your organization would benefit from learning NeuroMap, especially learning to apply effective ways to present your value proposition? The strategic nature of NeuroMap commands that the top-level executives be involved in the process, before it is shared with the rest of the team, including sales and marketing and even R&D executives.

Finally, assess objectively your internal resources and capacity to execute successful neurocreative assets. Although the model is easy to learn, it does require a lot of "unlearning," which some people can't or will not do.

After all the preceding questions have been addressed, you can easily determine to what extent you need external help or support.

Enjoy the journey. You can now persuade anyone, anywhere, anytime!

APPENDIX: NEUROMAP SIMPLIFIED NEUROSCORING TOOL

I f you do not have the time or budget to conduct a full neuro-marketing evaluation, we recommend that you at least score your messages by using 24 questions. Each question has already been tested to assess and improve hundreds of ads. The purpose of this simplified tool is to identify the messages that have little chance of triggering the bottom-up effect. For practical purposes, let's pretend that you are assessing the quality of the home page of your website. Here are the questions you can use to assess how well you are using the six stimuli to communicate your value proposition in ways that make your message optimized for the primal brain.

NEUROSCORING STIMULI

Personal (P)

1. Is your message clearly reawakening the customer's frustrations or threats solved by the product or service you offer?

2. Is the copy focusing on the customer ("you") instead of focusing on the company or product?

3. Are the consequences of not overcoming the pain/frustrations clearly identified (loss of money, higher risk, psychological stress, etc.)?

4. Is the message stressing the urgency of solving the pains?

Contrastable (C)

1. Is the message using claims?
2. Is it clear that each claim is going to eliminate or treat a specific pain?
3. Are the claims helping you create sharp contrast, such as "before and after"?
4. Are the benefits/claims truly unique or original?

Tangible (T)

1. Is the value of each claim/core benefit demonstrated or proven with credible customer stories, demos, data or vision?
2. Are there analogies or metaphors designed to reduce cognitive effort to believe in the benefit of each claim?
3. To which extent is it possible to understand the value of the solution or product in less than five seconds?
4. Overall, is the message designed to be grasped with limited cognitive load (more visuals and less text)?

Memorable (M)

1. Are the claims easy to remember?
2. Is the message using no more than three claims?
3. Are claims repeated more than once?
4. Is there an effort made to simplify and accelerate the decision to choose the product or solution proposed?

Visual (V)

1. Is the page visually salient (using elements with sharp and clear visual definition, limited number of colors and well defined contours)?
2. Is there at least one strong visual presenting the value of the solution from the perspective of a customer?
3. Is the home page more than 70% visual?
4. Overall, can the overall value of the solution be understood without reading any text or thinking a lot?

Emotional (E)

1. Is the message seeking first to attract attention from the primal brain rather than explaining (bottom-up effect)?

2. Is there a clear call to action to move toward closing a transaction?

3. Is there a big emotional lift from the reenactment of the threat/frustration (pain) to the liberation of such pain?

4. Does the final part of the message create anticipation?

Get your NeuroScore by using the following table:

P	Is your message clearly reawakening the customer's frustrations or threats solved by the product or service you offer?	Yes = 10 / No = 0	Report Your Score Below ----------	Circle Your Grade 40 = A 30 = B 20 = C 10 = D 0 = F
P	Is the copy focusing on the customer ("you") or instead focusing on the company or product?	Yes = 10 / No = 0		
P	Are the consequences of not overcoming the pain/frustrations clearly identified (loss of money, higher risk, psychological stress, etc.)?	Yes = 10 / No = 0		
P	Is the message stressing the urgency of solving the pains?	Yes = 10 / No = 0		

C	Is the message using claims?	Yes = 10 / No = 0	Report Your Score Below ----------	Circle Your Grade 40 = A 30 = B 20 = C 10 = D 0 = F
C	Is it clear that each claim is going to eliminate or treat a specific pain?	Yes = 10 / No = 0		
C	Are the claims helping you create sharp contrast as "before and after"?	Yes = 10 / No = 0		
C	Are the benefits/claims truly unique or original?	Yes = 10 / No = 0		
T	Is the value of each claim/ core benefit demonstrated or proven with credible customer stories, demos, data or vision?	Yes = 10 / No = 0	Report Your Score Below ----------	Circle Your Grade 40 = A 30 = B 20 = C 10 = D 0 = F
T	Are there analogies or metaphors designed to reduce cognitive effort to believe in the benefit of each claim?	Yes = 10 / No = 0		
T	Is it possible to understand the value of the solution or product in less than five seconds?	Yes = 10 / No = 0		
T	Overall, is the message designed to be grasped with limited cognitive load (more visuals and less text)?	Yes = 10 / No = 0		
M	Are the claims easy to remember?	Yes = 10 / No = 0	Report Your Score Below ----------	Circle Your Grade 40 = A 30 = B 20 = C 10 = D 0 = F

M	Is the message using no more than three claims?	Yes = 10 / No = 0		
M	Are claims repeated more than once?	Yes = 10 / No = 0		
M	Is there an effort made to simplify and accelerate the decision to choose the product or solution proposed?	Yes = 10 / No = 0		
V	Is the page visually salient (using elements with sharp visual definition, limited number of colors and clear contours)?	Yes = 10 / No = 0	Report Your Score Below ----------	Circle Your Grade 40 = A 30 = B 20 = C 10 = D 0 = F
V	Is there at least one strong visual presenting the value of the solution from the perspective of a customer?	Yes = 10 / No = 0		
V	Is the home page more than 70% visual?	Yes = 10 / No = 0		
V	Overall, can the overall value of the solution be understood without reading any text or thinking too much?	Yes = 10 / No = 0		
E	Is the message seeking first to attract attention from the primal brain rather than explain (bottom-up effect)?	Yes = 10 / No = 0	Report Your Score Below ----------	Circle Your Grade 40 = A 30 = B 20 = C 10 = D 0 = F

E	Is there a clear call to action to move toward closing a transaction?	Yes = 10 / No = 0		
E	Is there a big emotional lift from the re-enactment of the threat/frustration (pain) to the liberation of such pain?	Yes = 10 / No = 0		
E	Does the end of the message create anticipation?	Yes = 10 / No = 0		

Finally, compute your NeuroMap score by using this next table:

NEURO MAP SCORE	Stimulus Points	Persuasive Impact
A	200–240	Your message is very persuasive.
B	160–199	Your message is moderately persuasive.
C	120–159	Your message is neutral.
F	<120	Your message does not persuade.

Once you have scored each stimulus, you can use the following table to summarize your grades.

USING NEUROQUADRANTS

Finally, you can use the NeuroQuadrants map to figure out how you can improve the overall bottom-up effect or your message. To determine in which NeuroQuadrant your message is likely to fall in, use the following table.

	If Your Average Grade For	Then Your Message Is in Neuro-Quadrant	Grade Average is	Grade	Grade	Grade
P and C	P and C is less than B	3 (Neutral)	A/B	C or less	A/B	A/B
C						
T	T and M is less than B	4, 1, or 2	A/B	Any	C or less	A/B
M						
V	V and E is less than B	4, 1, or 2	A/B	Any	Any	C or less
E						
Neuro-Quadrant			1	3	4	2

REFERENCES

1. ESOMAR (2014). *Global Market Research*. ESOMAR. Available from: https://www.esomar.org/uploads/industry/reports/global-market -research-2014/ESOMAR-GMR2014-Preview.pdf.
2. Sloane, G. (2016). Why P&G decided Facebook ad targeting often isn't worth the money. *AdAge* (10 August). Available from: http:// adage.com/article/digital/p-g-decided-facebook-ad-targeting-worth -money/305390/.
3. Vranica, S. and Marshall, J. (2016). Facebook overestimated key video metric for two years. *Wall Street Journal*, 22 September. Available from: https://www.wsj.com/articles/facebook-overestimated-key- video-metric-for-two-years-1474586951.
4. Ariely, D. and Berns, G.S. (2010) Neuromarketing: The hope and hype of neuroimaging in business. *Nature Reviews Neuroscience* 11 (4): 284–292.
5. Fugate, D.L. (2007). Neuromarketing: A layman's look at neuroscience and its potential application to marketing practice. *Journal of Consumer Marketing* 24 (7): 385–394.
6. Hubert, M. (2010). Does neuroeconomics give new impetus to economic and consumer research. *Journal of Economic Psychology* 31 (5): 812–817.
7. Lee, N., Broderick, L., and Chamberlain, L. (2016). What is "neuro-marketing"? A discussion and agenda for future research. *International Journal of Psychophysiology* 63 (2): 199–204.
8. Zurawicki, L. (2010). *Neuromarketing: Exploring the Brain of the Consumer*, 273. New York: Springer.
9. ARF. (2011). *Neurostandard collaboration initiative*. Available from: www .thearf.org/assets/neurostandards-collaboration.
10. Falk, E.B., Berkman, E.T., and Lieberman, M.D. (2012). From neural responses to population behavior: Neural focus group predicts population-level media effects. *Psychological Science* 23 (5): 439–445.
11. Lee, N., Senior, C., Butler, M. et al. (2009). The feasibility of neuroimaging methods in market research. *Nature Precedings*.
12. Kenning, P., Plassmann, H., and Ahlert, D. (2007). Applications of functional magnetic resonance imaging for market research. *Qualitative Market Research: An International Journal*, 10 (2) 135–152.
13. Wilhelm, P., Schoebi, D., and Perrez, M. (2004). Frequency estimates of emotions in everyday life from a diary method's perspective: A comment

on Scherer et al.'s survey-study "Emotions in everyday life." *Social Science Information* 43 (4): 647–665.

14. Morin, C. (2014). The neurophysiological effect of emotional ads on the brains of late adolescents and young adults *Media Psychology*. 104. Santa Barbara: Fielding Graduate University.

15. Ehrlich, B. (2015). Guys: Here's why it's dumb not to give your girl a gift on Valentine's Day. *MTV News*, 9 February. Available from: http://www.mtv.com/news/2074362/valentines-day-presents-chocolates-study/.

16. Dehaene, S. (2014). *Consciousness and the Brain: Deciphering How the Brain Codes Our Thoughts*, 352. New York: Penguin Books.

17. Mendes, W.B. (2009). Assessing autonomic nervous system activity. In: *Methods in Social Neuroscience* (ed. E. Harmon-Jones and J.S. Beer), 118–147. New York: Guilford Press.

18. Bechara, A., Damasio, H., Tranel, D. et al. (1997). Deciding advantageously before knowing the advantageous strategy. *Science*, 275 (5304): 1293–1295.

19. Ravaja, N. (2004). Contributions of psychophysiology to media research: Review and recommendations. *Media Psychology* 6 (2): 193–235.

20. Hebb, D.O. (1949). *The Organization of Behavior*, 423. New York: Wiley.

21. Gazzaniga, M.S., Ivry, R.B., and Mangun, G.R. (2009). *Cognitive Neuroscience: The Biology of the Mind*, 3rd ed., 752. New York: W.W. Norton.

22. DeYoung, C.G. and Gray, J.R. (2009). Personality neuroscience: Explaining individual differences in affect, behavior, and cognition. In: *Cambridge Handbook of Personality* (ed. P.J.C.G. Matthews), 323–346. New York: Cambridge University Press.

23. Lesica, N. and Stanley, B. (2004). Encoding of natural scene movies by tonic and burst spikes in the lateral geniculate nucleus. *Journal of Neuroscience* 24 (47): 10731–10740.

24. Kolb, B. and Whishaw, I.Q. (2009). *Fundamentals of Human Neuropsychology*, 6e, 920. New York: Worth Publishers.

25. Berridge, K.C. (2004). Motivation concepts in behavioral neuroscience. *Physiology & Behavior*, 81 (2): 179–209.

26. Darwin, C. (1872). *The Expression of the Emotions in Man and Animals*. London, England: John Murray.

27. Ekman, P. and Friesen, W.V. (1971). Constants across cultures in the face and emotion. *Journal of Personality and Social Psychology* 17 (2): 124–129.

28. PBS (2002). *The Secret Life of the Brain*. PBS documentary series.

29. McGaugh, J. (2000). Memory: A century of consolidation. *Science* 287 (5451): 248–251.

30. Ornstein, R. (1991). *The Evolution of Consciousness: Of Darwin, Freud, and Cranial Fire: The Origins of the Way We Think*, 326. New York: Simon & Schuster.

31. Panksepp, J. (2004). Affective consciousness: Core emotional feelings in animals and humans. *Consciousness and Cognition* 14 (1): 30–80.

32. Carlson, N.R. (2007). *Physiology of Behavior*, 9e, 768. Boston, MA: Pearson Education.

33. Wallbott, H. G. and Scherer, K. R. (1986). How universal and specific is emotional experience? Evidence from 27 countries on five continents. *Social Science Information* 25 (4): 763–795.

34. DeYoung, C.G., Hirsh, J.B., Shane, M.S. et al. (2010). Testing predictions from personality neuroscience: Brain structure and the Big Five. *Psychological Science* 21(6): 820–828.

35. Glimcher, P.W. (2009). *Neuroeconomics: Decision-Making and the Brain*, 556. London, UK: Elsevier.

36. Langleben, D.D., Loughead, J.W., Ruparel, K. et al. (2009). Reduced prefrontal and temporal processing and recall of high "sensation value" ads. *Neuroimage* 46 (1): 219–225.

37. Tamietto, M., Cauda, F., Corazzini, L.L. et al. (2010). Collicular vision guides nonconscious behavior. *Journal of Cognitive Neuroscience* 22 (5): 888–902.

38. Plutchik, R. (1991). *The Emotions*, 236., Lanham, MD: University Press of America.

39. Panksepp, J. (1998). *The Foundations of Human and Animal Emotions*, 481. New York: Oxford University Press.

40. Hess, U. (2009). Facial EMG. In: *Methods in Social Neuroscience* (ed. E. Harmon-Jones and J.S. Beer), 70–91. New York: Guilford Press.

41. Knutson, B., Rick, S., Wimmer, G.E. et al. (2007). Neural predictors of purchases. *Neuron* 53 (1): 147–156.

42. Hare, T.A., O'Doherty, J., Camerer, C.F. et al. (2008). Dissociating the role of the orbitofrontal cortex and the striatum in the computation of goal values and prediction error. *Journal of Neuroscience* 28 (22): 5623–5630.

43. Rossiter, J.R. and Silberstein, R.B. (2001). Brain-imaging detection of visual scene encoding in long-term memory for TV commercials. *Journal of Advertising Research* 41 (2): 13–21.

44. Tusche, A., Bode, S., and Haynes, J.D. (2010). Neural responses to unattended products predict later consumer choices. *Journal of Neuroscience* 30 (23): 8024–8031.

45. Draganski, B., Gaser, C., Kempermann, G. et al. (2006). Temporal and spatial dynamics of brain structure changes during extensive learning. *Journal of Neuroscience* 26 (23): 6314–6317.

46. Maguire, E.A., Woollett, K., and Spiers, H.J. (2006). London taxi drivers and bus drivers: A structural MRI and neuropsychological analysis. *Hippocampus* 16 (12): 1091–1101.

47. Mercer, A., Deane, C., and McGeeney K. (2016). *Why 2016 election polls missed their mark*. Washington, DC: Pew Research Center.

48. Schneider, J. and Hall, J. (2011). Why most product launches fail. *Harvard Business Review* (April).

49. Morin, C. (2015). Why emotional PSA affect the brains of adolescents differently than the brains of young adults. In: *Digital Citizenship in the 21st Century Monograph* (ed. J. Ohler). Santa Barbara: Fielding Graduate University.

50. Randolph, W. and Viswanath, K. (2004). Lessons learned from public health mass media campaigns: Marketing health in a crowded media world. *Annual Review of Public Health* 25: 419–437.

51. Petty, R.E., Cacioppo, J.T., and Heesacker, M. (1981). Effects of rhethorical questions on persuasion: A cognitive response analysis. *Journal of Personality and Social Psychology* 40 (3): 432–440.

52. Brehm, S. and Brehm, J. (1981). *Psychological Reactance: A Theory of Freedom and Control*, 447. New York: Academic Press.

53. Grandpre, J., Alvaro, E.M., Burgoon, M. et al. (2003). Adolescent reactance and anti-smoking campaigns: A theoretical approach. *Health Communication* 15 (3): 349–366.

54. Farrelly, M.C., Healton, C.G., Davis, K.C. et al. (2002). Getting to the truth: Evaluating national tobacco countermarketing campaigns. *American Journal of Public Health* 92 (6): 901–907.

55. Rothman, A.J., Martino, S.C., Bedell, B.T. et al. (1999). The systematic influence of gain- and loss-framed messages on interest in and use of different types of health behavior. *Personality and Social Psychology Bulletin* 25 (11): 1355–1369.

56. Detweiler, J.B., Bedell, B.T., Salovey, P. et al. (1999). Message framing and sunscreen use: Gain-framed messages motivate beach-goers. *Health Psychology* 18 (2): 189–196.

57. Schneider, T.R., Salovey, P., Pallonen, U. et al. (2001). Visual and auditory message framing effects on tobacco smoking. *Journal of Applied Social Psychology* 31 (4): 667–682.

58. Schneider, T.R., Salovey, P., Apanovitch, A.M. et al. (2001). The effects of message framing and ethnic targeting on mammography use among low-income women. *Health Psychology* 20 (4): 256–266.

59. Lang, A. (2000). The limited capacity model of mediated message processing. *Journal of Communication* 50 (1): 46–70.

60. Lang, A., Zhou, S., Schwartz, N. et al. (2000). The effects of edits on arousal, attention, and memory for television messages: When an edit is an edit can an edit be too much? *Journal of Broadcasting & Electronic Media* 44(1): 94–109.

61. Stanovich, K.E. and West, R.F. (2000). Individual differences in reasoning: *Implications* for the rationality debate? *Behavioral and Brain Sciences* 23 (5): 645–665; discussion 665–726.

62. Kahneman, D. (2011). *Thinking, Fast and Slow*, 511. New York, NY: Farrar, Straus and Giroux.

63. Benson, B. (2016). Cognitive bias cheat sheet, simplified. *Medium*. Available from: https://medium.com/thinking-is-hard/4-conundrums-of-intelligence-2ab78d90740f.

64. Crocker, J. and Park, L.E. (2004). The costly pursuit of self-esteem. *Psychological Bulletin* 130 (3): 392–414.

65. Greenberg, J., Pyszczynski, T., Solomon, S. et al. (1993). Effects of self-esteem on vulnerability-denying defensive distortions: Further evidence of an anxiety-buffering function of self-esteem. *Journal of Experimental Social Psychology* 29 (3): 229–251.

66. Kunda, Z. (1990). The case for motivated reasoning. *Psychological Bulletin* 108 (3): 480–498.

67. Haselton, M.G. and Nettle, D. (2006). The paranoid optimist: An integrative evolutionary model of cognitive biases. *Personality and Social Psychology Review* 10 (1): 47–66.

68. Weinstein, N.D. (1980). Unrealistic optimism about future life events. *Journal of Personality and Social Psychology* 39 (5): 806–820.

69. Gladwell, M. (2005). *Blink: The Power of Thinking Without Thinking*, 296. New York, NY: Little, Brown and Company.

70. Ariely, D. (2008). *Predictably Irrational: The Hidden Forces that Shape Our Decisions*, 310. New York, NY: HarperCollins.

71. Mundell, E.J., (2014). Scientists erase, then restore memories in rats. *HealthDay* (2 June).

72. Cory, G.A., (2002). MacLean's evolutionary neuroscience, the CSN model and Hamilton's rule: Some developmental clinical, and social policy implications. *Brain and Mind* 3 (1): 151–181.

73. McLean, P.D. (1989). *The Triune Brain in Evolution: Role in Paleocerebral Functions*, 718. New York, NY: Plenum Press.

74. Narvaez, D. (2007). Tirune ethics: The neurobiological roots of our multiple moralities. *New Ideas in Psychology* 26: 95–119.

75. Cory, G.A. (2002). McLeans's evolutionary neuroscience, the CSN model and Hamilton's rule: Some developmental, clinical and social policy implications. *Brain and Mind* 3 (1): 151–181.

76. Freud, S. (1915). The Unconscious. In: *General Psychological Theory* (ed. P. Rieff), 116–150. New York: Collier Books.

77. Freud, S. (1930). *Das Unbehagen in der Kulture [Civilization and Its Discontents]*. Wien, Austria: Internationaler Psychoanalytischer Verlag.

78. Freud, S. (1922). *Beyond the Pleasure Principle*. London, Vienna: Intl. Psycho-Analytical.

79. Ayan, S. (2008). Speaking of memory. *Scientific American Mind* (October/November): 16–17.

80. Solms, M. (2006). Freud returns. *Scientific American Mind* 17 (2): 82–88.

81. Dawkins, R. (1976). *The Selfish Gene*, 368. New York, NY: Oxford University Press.

82. Kahneman, D. and Riis, J. (2005). Living and thinking about it: Two perspectives on life. In: *The Science of Well-Being* (ed. F.A.H.N. Baylis and B. Keverne), 285–301. Oxford University Press.

83. Schwartz, B. (2004). *The Paradox of Choice: Why More is Less*, 308. New York: HarperCollins.

84. Iyengar, S.S. and Lepper, M.R. (2000). When choice is demotivating: Can one desire too much of a good thing? *Journal of Personality and Social Psychology* 79 (6): 995–1006.

85. Katz, J. (1984). *The Silent World of Doctor and Patient*, 318. Baltimore, MD: John Hopkins University Press.

86. Beard, F.K. (2013). A history of comparative advertising in the United States. *Journalism and Communication Monographs* 15 (3): 114–216.

87. Singh, M., Balasubramanian, S.K. and Chakraborty, G. (2000). A comparative analysis of three communication formats: Advertising, infomercial, and direct experience. *Journal of Advertising* 29 (4): 59–75.

88. Lindgaard, G., Fernandes, G., Dudek, C. et al. (2006). Attention web designers: You have 50 milliseconds to make a good first impression! *Behaviour & Information Technology* 25 (2): 115–126.

89. Geissler, G., Zinkhan, G., and Watson, R.T. (2001). Web home page complexity and communication effectiveness. *Journal of the Association for Information Systems* 2 (1).

90. Tuch, A.N., Bargas-Avila, J.A., Opwis, K. et al. (2009). Visual complexity of websites: Effects on users' experience, physiology, performance, and memory. *International Journal of Human-Computer Studies*, 67 (9): 703–715.

91. Laham, S.M., Koval, P., and Alter, A.L. (2012). The name-pronunciation effect: Why people like Mr. Smith more than Mr. Colquhoun. *Journal of Experimental Social Psychology* 48 (3): 752–756.

92. Miele, D.B., Finn, B., and Molden, D.C. (2011). Does easily learned mean easily remembered?: It depends on your beliefs about intelligence. *Psychological Science* 22 (3): 320–324.

93. Grabner, R.H., Neubauer, A.C., and Stern, E. (2006). Superior performance and neural efficiency: The impact of intelligence and expertise. *Brain Research Bulletin*, 69 (4): 422–439.

94. Kiesel, A., Kunde, W., Pohl, C. et al. (2009). Playing chess unconsciously. *Journal of Experimental Psychology: Learning, Memory, and Cognition*, 35 (1): 292–298.

95. Shteingart, H., Neiman, T., and Loewenstein, Y. (2013). The role of first impression in operant learning. *Journal of Experimental Psychology* 142 (2): 476–488.

96. Atkinson, R.C. and Shiffrin, R.M. (1968). Human memory: A proposal system and its control processes. In: *The Psychology of Learning and Motivation: II* (ed. K.W. Spence and J.T. Spence), 89–195. London: Academic Press.

97. Miller, G. (1956). The magical number seven, plus-or-minus two: Some limits on our capacity for processing information. *Psychological Revie*, 101 (2): 343–352.

98. Colavita, F.B. (1974). *Human sensory dominance. Perception and Psychophysics* 16 (2): 409–412.

99. Li, Y., Liu, M., Zhang, W. et al. (2017). Neurophysiological correlates of visual dominance: A lateralized readiness potential investigation. *Frontiers in Psychology* 28: 303.

100. Silverstein, D.N. and Ingvar, M. (2015). A multi-pathway hypothesis for human visual fear signaling. *Frontiers in System Neuroscience* 9: 101.

101. Potter, M., Wyble, B., Hagmann, C.E. et al. (2014). Detecting meaning in RSVP at 13 ms per picture. *Attention, Perception, & Psychophysics* 76 (2): 270–279.

102. Ledoux, J.E. and E.A. Phelps. (2004). Emotional networks in the brain. In *Handbook of Emotions*, 2e (ed. M. Lewis and J.M. Haviland-Jones), 157–172. New York: Guilford Press.

103. Todorov, A., & Ballew, C. (2007). Predicting political elections from rapid and unreflective face judgments. *Proceedings of the National Academy of Sciences, USA* 104 (46): 17948–17953.

104. Lorenzo, G.L., Biesanz, J.C., and Human, L.J. (2010). What is beautiful is good and more accurately understood: Physical attractiveness and

accuracy in first impressions of personality. *Psychological Science* 21 (12): 1777–1782.

105. Abrams, R.A. and Christ, S.E. (2003). Motion onset captures attention. *Psychological Science* 14 (5): 427–432.

106. Langton, S.R. et al. (2008). Attention capture by faces. *Cognition* 107 (1): 330–342.

107. Caharel, S., Ramon, M., and Rossion, B. (2014). Face familiarity decisions take 200 msec in the human brain: Electrophysiological evidence from a go/no-go speeded task. *Journal of Cognitive Neuroscience* 26 (1): 81–95.

108. Wolfe, J.M. and Bennett, S.C. (1997). Preattentive object files: Shapeless bundles of basic features. *Vision Research* 37 (1): 25–43.

109. Broyles, S.J. (2006). Subliminal advertising and the perpetual popularity of playing to people's paranoia. *Journal of Consumer Affairs* 40 (2): 392–406.

110. Collin, S.P., Knight, M.A., Davies, W.L. et al. (2003). Ancient colour vision: Multiple opsin genes in the ancestral vertebrates. *Current Biology*, 13 (22): 864–865.

111. Tamietto, M., Cauda, F., Corazzini, L.L., et al. (2010). Collicular vision guides nonconscious behavior. *Journal of Cognitive Neuroscience* 22 (5): 888–902.

112. Guntekin, B. and Basar. E. (2014). A review of brain oscillations in perception of faces and emotional pictures. *Neuropsychologia* 58: 33–51.

113. Changizi, M.A., Zhang, Q., and Shimojo, S. (2006). Bare skin, blood and the evolution of primate colour vision. *Biology Letters*, 2 (2): 217–221.

114. Buechner, V.L., Maier, M.A., Lichtenfeld, S. et al. (2014). Red – Take a closer look. *PLoS One* 9 (9): e108111.

115. Madden, T., Hewett, K., and Roth, M. (2000). Managing images in different cultures: A cross-national study of color meanings and preferences. *Journal of International Marketing* 8 (4): 90–107.

116. Hevner, K. (1935). Experimental studies of the affective value of colors and lines. *Journal of Applied Psychology* 19 (4): 385–398.

117. Grossman, R.P. and Wisenblit, J.Z. (1999). What we know about consumer's color choices. *Journal of Marketing Practices: Applied Marketing Science* 5 (3): 78–88.

118. Kuhbandner, C. and Pekrun, R. (2013). Joint effects of emotion and color on memory. *Emotion* 13 (3): 375–379.

119. Elliot, A.J. and Maier, M.A. (2007). Color and psychological functioning. *Current Directions in Psychological Science* 16 (5): 250–254.

120. Lichtenfeld, S., Maier, M.A., Elliot, A.J. et al. (2009). The semantic red effect: Processing the word red undermines intellectual performance. *Journal of Experimental Social Psychology* 45 (6): 1273–1276.

121. Loeber, S., Vollstädt-Klein, S., Wilden, S. et al. (2011). The effect of pictorial warnings on cigarette packages on attentional bias of smokers. *Pharmacology, Biochemistry, and Behavior* 98 (2): 292–298.

122. Descartes, R. (1637). *Discours de la Méthode.*

123. Bossaerts, P. and Murawski, C. (2015). From behavioural economics to neuroeconomics to decision neuroscience: the ascent of biology in research on human decision making. *Current Opinion in Behavioral Sciences* 5 (Supplement C): 37–42.

124. Bechara, A. (2003). The role of emotion in decision-making: Evidence from neurological patients with orbitofrontal damage. *Brain and Cognition* 55 (1): 30–40.

125. Damasio, A.R. (1994). *Descartes' Error*, 336. New York: Harper Collins.

126. Thaler, R.(2015). *Misbehaving: The Making of Behavioral Economics*, 452. New York: W. W. Norton.

127. Damasio, A.R. (1996). The somatic marker hypothesis and the possible functions of the prefrontal cortex. *Philosophical Transactions: Biological Sciences* 351 (1346): 1413–1420.

128. Eagleman, D. (2015). *The Brain: The Story of You*, 224. New York: Pantheon Books.

129. Plutchik, R. and H. Kellerman. (1980). *Emotion: Theory, Research and Experience. Vol.* 1, 424. London, UK: Academic Press.

130. Coricelli, G., Dolan, R.J., and Sirigu, A. (2007). Brain, emotion and decision making: The paradigmatic example of regret. *Trends in Cognitive Sciences* 11 (6): 258–265.

131. Vogel, S. and Schwabe, L. (2016). Learning and memory under stress: Implications for the classroom. *npj Science of Learning* 1: 16011.

132. Alter, A.L. (2017). *Irresistible: The Rise of Addictive Technology and the Business of Keeping Us Hooked*, 370. New York: Penguin Press.

133. McGaugh, J.L. (2013). Making lasting memories: Remembering the significant. *Proceedings of the National Academy of Sciences, USA* 110 (Supplement 2): 10402–10407.

134. Kensinger, E.A. (2009) Remembering the details: Effects of emotion. *Emotion Review* 1 (2): 99–113.

135. di Pellegrino, G., Fadiga, L., Fogassi, L. et al. (1992). Understanding motor events: A neurophysiological study. *Experimental Brain Research* 91 (1): 176–180.

136. Dehaene, S., Changeux, J.P., Naccache, L. et al. (2006). Conscious, preconscious, and subliminal processing: A testable taxonomy. *Trends in Cognitive Sciences* 10 (5): 204–211.

137. Ledoux, J.E. (2016). *Anxious: Using the Brain to Understand and Treat Fear and Anxiety*, 428. New York: Penguin Books.

138. Burke, C. (2015). 100 customer service statistics you need to know. *InsightSquared* (22 April).

139. Maslow, A.H. (1943). A theory of human motivation. *Psychological Review* 50 (4): 370–396.

140. Maslow, A.H. (1968). *Toward a Psychology of Being*, 2e, 212. New York: Van Nostrand Reinhold.

141. Witt, U. (2001). Learning to consume – A theory of wants and the growth of demand. *Journal of Evolutionary Economics* 11 (1): 23–36.

142. Berns, G.S. and Moore, S.E. (2012). A neural predictor of cultural popularity. *Journal of Consumer Psychology* 22 (1): 154–160.

143. Du, P. and MacDonald, E.F. (2015). Products' shared visual features do not cancel in consumer decisions. *Journal of Mechanical Design* 137 (7): 071409-071409–411.

144. Cowan, N. (2010). The magical mystery four: How is working memory capacity limited, and why? *Current Directions in Psychological Science* 19 (1): 51–57.

145. Bromage, B.K. and Mayer, R. (1986). Quantitative and qualitative effects of repetition on learning from technical text. *Journal of Educational Psychology* 78 (4): 271–278.

146. Dimofte, C.V., Johansson, J.K., and Ronkainen, I.A. (2008). Cognitive and affective reactions of U.S. consumers to global brands. *Journal of International Marketing* 16 (4): 113–135.

147. Cowan, N. (2005). *Working Memory Capacity. Essays in Cognitive Psychology*, 246. New York: Psychology Press.

148. Gilchrist, A.L., Cowan, N., and Naveh-Benjamin, M. (2008). Working memory capacity for spoken sentences decreases with adult aging: Recall of fewer, but not smaller chunks in older adults. *Memory* (Hove, England) 16 (7): 773–787.

149. Smith, E.E. and Jonides, J. (1998). Neuroimaging analyses of human working memory. *Proceedings of the National Academy of Sciences, USA* 95 (20): 12061–12068.

150. Calder, B.J., Insko, C.A., and Yandell, B. (1974). The relation of cognitive and memorial processes to persuasion in a simulated jury trial. *Journal of Applied Social Psychology* 4 (1): 62–93.

151. Poppenk, J., Walia, G., McIntosh, A.R. et al. (2008). Why is the meaning of a sentence better remembered than its form? An fMRI study on the role of novelty-encoding processes. *Hippocampus* 18 (9): 909–918.

152. Alter, A.L. and Oppenheimer, D.M. (2006). Predicting short-term stock fluctuations by using processing fluency. *Proceedings of the National Academy of Sciences, USA* 103 (24): 9369–9372.

153. Filkuková, P. and Klempe, S.H. (20113). Rhyme as reason in commercial and social advertising. *Scandinavian Journal of Psychology* 54 (5): 423–431.

154. Novemsky, N., Dhar, R., Schwarz, N. et al. (2007). Preference fluency in choice. *Journal of Marketing Research* 44 (3): 347–356.

155. Reber, R. and Schwarz, N. (1999). Effects of perceptual fluency on judgments of truth. *Consciousness and Cognition* 8 (3): 338–342.

156. Shah, A.K. and Oppenheimer, D.M. (2007). Easy does it: The role of fluency in cue weighting. *Judgment and Decision Making* 2 (6): 371–379.

157. Reber, R., Schwarz, N., and Winkielman, P. (2004). Processing fluency and aesthetic pleasure: Is beauty in the perceiver's processing experience? *Personality and Social Psychology Review*, 8(4): 364–382.

158. Bernard, M. et al. (2002). A comparison of popular online fonts: Which size and type is best? *Usability News* (10 January).

159. Cialdini, R.B. (2016). *Pre-suasion: A Revolutionary Way to Influence and Persuade*, 413. New York: Simon & Schuster.

160. Deighton, J., Romer, D., and McQueen, J. (19890. Using drama to persuade. *Journal of Consumer Research* 16 (3): 335–343.

161. Monroe, K.B. and Lee, A.Y. (1999). Remembering versus knowing: *Issues in buyers' processing of price information. Journal of the Academy of Marketing Science* 27 (2): 207.

162. Algom, D., Dekel, A., and Pansky, A. (1996). The perception of number from the separability of the stimulus: The Stroop effect revisited. *Memory & Cognition* 24 (5): 557–572.

163. Karmarkar, U.R., Shiv, B., and Knutson, B. (2014). Cost conscious? The neural and behavioral impact of price primacy on decision making. *Journal of Marketing Research* 52 (4): 467–481.

164. Levy, M. (2010). Loss aversion and the price of risk. *Quantitative Finance* 10 (9): 1009–1022.

165. Abdellaoui, M., Bleichrodt, H., and l'Haridon, O. (2008). A tractable method to measure utility and loss aversion under prospect theory. *Journal of Risk and Uncertainty* 36 (245): 245–266.

166. Kadous, K., Koonce, L., and Towry, K.L. (2005). Quantification and persuasion in managerial judgement. *Contemporary Accounting Research* 22 (3): 643–686.

167. Cialdini, R.B. (1993). *Influence: The Psychology of Persuasion*, rev. ed., 320. New York: Morrow.

168. Fuller, R.G.C. and Sheehy-Skeffington, A. (1974). Effects of group laughter on responses to humourous material, a replication and extension. *Psychological Reports* 35 (1): 531–534.

169. Festinger, L. (1954). A theory of social comparison processes. *Human Relations* 7 (2): 117–140.

170. Smith, C.T., De Houwer, J., and Nosek, B.A. (2013). Consider the source: Persuasion of implicit evaluations is moderated by source credibility. *Personality and Social Psychology Bulletin* 39 (2): 193–205.

171. Yalch, R.F. and Elmore-Yalch, R. (1984). The effect of numbers on the route to persuasion. *Journal of Consumer Research* 11 (1): 522–527.

172. Dijksterhuis, A., Aarts, H., and Smith, P. (2006). The power of the subliminal: On subliminal persuasion and other potential applications. In: *The New Unconscious* (ed. R.R. Hassin, J.S. Uleman, and J.A. Bargh). Oxford, UK: Oxford University Press.

173. Simons, D.J. and Chabris, C.F. (1999). Gorillas in our midst: Sustained inattentional blindness for dynamic events. *Perception* 28 (9): 1059–1074.

174. Ricard, M. (2017). *Beyond the Self: Conversations Between Buddhism and Neuroscience*, 294. Cambridge, MA: MIT Press.

175. Singer, W. (1999). Neuronal synchrony: A versatile code for the definition of relations? *Neuron* 24 (1): 111–125.

176. Oishi, Y., Xu, Q., Wang, L. et al. (2017). Slow-wave sleep is controlled by a subset of nucleus accumbens core neurons in mice. *Nature Communications* 8 (1): 734.

177. Anderson, R.C., Pichert, J.W. and Shirey, L.L. (1983). Effects of the reader's schema at different points in time. *Journal of Educational Psychology* 75 (2): 271–279.

178. Pichert, J.W. and Anderson, R.C. (1977). Taking different perspectives on a story. *Journal of Educational Psychology* 69 (4): 309–315.

179. Gates, B. (2009). *Mosquitos, Malaria and Education*. TED Talk (4 February).

180. Rogers, T. and Milkman, K.L. (2016). Reminders through association. *Psychological Science* 27 (7): 973–986.

181. Stadler, M. and Ward, G.C. (2010). The effects of props on story retells in the classroom. *Reading Horizons* 50 (3): 169–192.

182. Handy, T.C., Grafton, S.T., Shroff, N.M. et al. (2003). Graspable objects grab attention when the potential for action is recognized. *Nature Neuroscience* 6 (4): 421–427.

183. Damasio, A.R. (2010). *Self Comes to Mind: Constructing the Conscious Brain*, 367. New York: Pantheon Books.

184. Gottschall, J. (2012). *The Storytelling Animal: How Stories Make Us Human*, 248. Boston, MA: Houghton Mifflin Harcourt.

185. van Laer, T., de Ruyter, K., Visconti, L.M. et al. (2014). The extended transportation-imagery model: A meta-analysis of the antecedents and consequences of consumers' narrative transportation. *Journal of Consumer Research* 40 (5): 797–817.

186. Mehrabian, A. (1972). *Nonverbal Communication*, 226. Chicago: Aldine-Atherton.

187. Huth, A.G., de Heer, W.A., Griffiths, T.L. et al. (2016). Natural speech reveals the semantic maps that tile human cerebral cortex. *Nature* 532 (7600): 453–458.

188. Johnson, D.A. (2016). *Newton in the Pulpit*, 184. New Sinai Press.

189. Auble, P.M., Franks, J.J., and Soraci, S.A. (1979). Effort toward comprehension: Elaboration or "aha"? *Memory & Cognition* 7 (6): 426–434.

190. Kember, D. (1996). The intention to both memorise and understand: Another approach to learning? *Higher Education* 31 (3): 341–354.

191. Carlson, K.A. and Shu, S.B. (2007). The rule of three: How the third event signals the emergence of a streak. *Organizational Behavior and Human Decision Processes* 104 (1): 113–121.

192. Wansink, B., Painter, J.E., and North, J. (2005). Bottomless bowls: Why visual cues of portion size may influence intake. *Obesity* 13 (1): 93–100.

193. Zeelenberg, M. (1999). Anticipated regret, expected feedback and behavioral decision making. *Journal of Behavioral Decision Making* 12 (2): 93–106.

194. Ten Brinke, L., Stimson, D., and Carney, D.R. (2014). Some evidence for unconscious lie detection. *Psychological Science* 25 (5): 1098–1105.

195. Mehrabian, A. and Wiener, M. (1967). Decoding of inconsistent communications. *Journal of Personality and Social Psychology* 6 (1): 109–114.

196. Moriarty, T. (1975). Crime, commitment, and the responsive bystander: Two field experiments. *Journal of Personality and Social Psychology* 31 (2): 370–376.

197. Cialdini, R.B. (1984). *Influence: How and Why People Agree to Things*, 302. New York: Morrow.

198. Howard, D.J. (1990). The influence of verbal responses to common greetings on compliance behavior: The foot-in-the-mouth effect. *Journal of Applied Social Psychology*, 20 (14): 1185–1196.

199. Freedman, J.L. and Fraser, S.C. (1966). Compliance without pressure: The foot-in-the-door technique. *Journal of Personality and Social Psychology*, 4 (2): 195–202.

200. Deutsch, M. and Gerard, H.B. (1955). A study of normative and informational social influences upon individual judgement. *Journal of Abnormal Psychology* 51 (3): 629–636.

201. Dunbar, R.I., Marriott, A., and Duncan, N.D. (1997). Human conversational behavior. *Human Nature* 8 (3): 231–246.

202. Tamir, D.I. and Mitchell, J.P. (2012). Disclosing information about the self is intrinsically rewarding. *Proceedings of the National Academy of Sciences, USA* 109 (21): 8038–8043.

203. Burnkrant, R. and Unnava, H. (1995). Effects of self-referencing on persuasion. *Journal of Consumer Research* 22 (1): 17–26.

204. Escalas, J.E. (2007). Self-referencing and persuasion: Narrative transportation versus analytical elaboration. *Journal of Consumer Research* 33 (4): 421–429.

205. Bargh, J.A. (2017). *Before You Know It: The Unconscious Reasons We Do What We Do*, 352. New York: Touchstone.

206. Buskist, W. and Saville, B.K. (2001). Creating positive emotional contexts for enhancing teaching and learning. *APS Observer* 14 (3): 12–13.

207. Tajfel, H., Billig, M.G., Bundy, R.P. et al. (1971). Social categorization and intergroup behaviour. *European Journal of Social Psychology* 1 (2): 149–178.

208. Tickle-Degnen, L. and Rosenthal, R. (1990). The nature of rapport and its nonverbal correlates. *Psychological Inquiry* 1(4): 285–293.

209. Wayne, A.H. and Brian, H.K. (1997). Establishing rapport: The secret business tool to success. *Managing Service Quality: An International Journal* 7 (4): 194–197.

210. Wood, J.A. (2006). NLP revisited: Nonverbal communications and signals of trustworthiness. *Journal of Personal Selling & Sales Management* 26 (2): 197–204.

211. Iacoboni, M. (2008). *Mirroring People: The New Science of How We Connect with Others*, 308. New York: Farrar, Straus and Giroux.

212. Preston, S.D., Bechara, A., Damasio, H. et al. (2007). The neural substrates of cognitive empathy. *Social Neuroscience*, 2 (3–4): 254–275.

213. Coch, D., Dawson, G., and Fisher, K.W. (2010). *Human Behavior Learning, and the Developing Brain*. London: Guilford Press.

214. Nygaard, L.C. and Queen, J.S. (2008). Communicating emotion: Linking affective prosody and word meaning. *Journal of Experimental Psychology, Human Perception and Performance*, 34 (4): 1017–1030.

215. Betts, K., (2009). Lost in translation: Importance of effective communication in online education. *Online Journal of Distance Learning Administration* 12 (2).

216. Rodriguez-Ferreiro, J., Gennari, S.P., Davies, R. et al. (2011). *Neural correlates of abstract verb processing. Journal of Cognitive Neuroscience* 23 (1): 106–118.

217. Jefferies, E., Frankish, C., and Noble, K. (2011). Strong and long: Effects of word length on phonological binding in verbal short-term memory. *The Quarterly Journal of Experimental Psychology* 64 (2): 241–260.

218. Sabsevitz, D.S., Medler, D.A., Seidenberg, M. et al. (2005). Modulation of the semantic system by word imageability. *Neuroimage* 27 (1): 188–200.

219. Nieuwland, M.S. and Kuperberg, G.R. (2008). When the truth is not too hard to handle: An event-related potential study on the pragmatics of negation. *Psychological Science* 19 (12): 1213–1218.

220. Larcker, D.F. and Zakolyukina, A.A. (2012). Detecting deceptive discussions in conference calls. *Journal of Accounting Research* 50 (2): 495–540.

221. Newberg, A.B. and Waldman, M.R. (2012). *Words Can Change Your Brain: 12 Conversation Strategies to Build Trust, Resolve Conflict, and Increase Intimacy*, 274. New York: Hudson Street Press.

222. Ludlow, C. (2005). Central nervous system control of the laryngeal muscles in humans. *Respiratory, Physiology, & Neurobiology* 147 (2–3): 205–222.

223. Tang, C., Hamilton, L.S., and Chang, E.F. (2017). Intonational speech prosody encoding in the human auditory cortex. *Science* 357 (6353): 797–801.

224. Schirmer, A. (2010). Mark my words: Tone of voice changes affective word representations in memory. *PLoS One* 5 (2): e9080.

225. Leaderbrand, K., Morey, A., and Tuma, L. (2008). The effects of voice pitch on perceptions of attractiveness: Do you sound hot or not? *Winona State University Psychology Student Journal* (January).

226. Bryant, G.A. and Haselton, M.G. (2009). Vocal cues of ovulation in human females. *Biology Letters* 5 (1): 12–15.

227. Cheng, J.T., Tracy, J.L., Ho, S. et al. (2016). Listen, follow me: Dynamic vocal signals of dominance predict emergent social rank in humans. *Journal of Experimental Psychology. General* 145 (5):536–547.

228. Ko, S.J., Sadler, M.S., and Galinsky, A.D. (2015). The sound of power: Conveying and detecting hierarchical rank through voice. *Psychological Science* 26 (1): 3–14.

229. Miller, N., Maruyama, G., Beaber, R.J. et al. (1976). Speed of speech and persuasion. *Journal of Personality and Social Psychology* 34 (4): 615–624.

230. Gibson, B.S., Eberhard, K.M., and Bryant, T.A. (2005). Linguistically mediated visual search: The critical role of speech rate. *Psychonomic Bulletin & Review* 12 (2): 276–281.

231. Kendall, T. (2013). *Speech Rate, Pause, and Sociolinguistic Variation: Studies in Corpus Sociophonetics*, 247. New York: Palgrave Macmillan.

232. MacGregor, L., Corley, M., and Donaldson, D.I., (2010). Listening to the sound of silence: Disfluent silent pauses in speech have consequences for listeners. *Neuropsychologia* 48 (14): 3982–3992.

233. Enos, F., Shriberg, E., Graciarena, M. et al. (2007). *Detecting Deception Using Critical Segments*. New York: Columbia University Academic Commons.

234. Peterson, R.A., Cannito, M.P., and Brown, S.P. (1995). An exploratory investigation of voice characteristics and selling effectiveness. *Journal of Personal Selling & Sales Management* 15 (1): 1–15.

235. Iyer, N., Brungart, D., and Simpson, B. (2010). Effects of target-masker contextual similarity on the multimasker penalty in a three-talker diotic listening task. *Journal of the Acoustical Society of America* 128 (5): 2998–3110.

236. Ljung, R., Sörqvist, P., and Hygge, S. (2009). Effects of traffic noise and irrelevant speech on children's reading and mathematical performance. *Noise Health* 11 (45): 194–198.

237. Marsh, J.E. and Jones, D.M. (2010). Cross-modal distraction by background speech: What role for meaning? *Noise Health*, 12 (49): 210–216.

238. Aune, R.K. and Kikuchi, T. (1993). Effects of language intensity similarity on perceptions of credibility relational attributions, and persuasion. *Journal of Language and Social Psychology* 12 (3): 224–238.

239. Dupuis, K. and Pichora-Fuller, M.K. (2010). Use of affective prosody by young and older adults. *Psychology and Aging* 25 (1): 16–29.

240. Ishii, K., Reyes, J., and Kitayama, S. (2003). Spontaneous attention to word content versus emotional tone: Differences among three cultures. *Psychological Science* 14 (1): 39–46.

241. Ekman, P. (2007). *Emotions Revealed: Recognizing Faces and Feelings to Improve Communication and Emotional Life*, 2e, 290. New York: Owl Books.

242. Ekman, P., Davidson, R.J., and Friesen, W.V. (1990). The Duchenne smile: Emotional expression and brain physiology II. *Journal of Personality and Social Psychology* 58 (2): 342–353.

243. Chaminade, T., Zecca, M., Blakemore, S.-J. et al. (2010). Brain response to a humanoid robot in areas implicated in the perception of human emotional gestures. *PLoS One* 5 (7): e11577.

244. Chang, L. and Tsao, D.Y.(2017). The code for facial identity in the primate brain. *Cell*, 169 (6): 1013–1028.e14.

245. Frumin, I., Perl, O., Endevelt-Shpaira, Y. et al. (2015). A social chemosignaling function for human handshaking. *Elife*, 4.

246. Senju, A. and Johnson, M.H. (2009). The eye contact effect: Mechanisms and development. *Trends in Cognitive Sciences* 13 (3): 127–134.

247. Itier, R.J. and Batty, M. (2009). Neural bases of eye and gaze processing: The core of social cognition. *Neuroscience and Biobehavioral Reviews* 33 (6): 843–863.

248. George, N. and Conty, L. (2008). Facing the gaze of others. *Neurophysiologie Clinique* 38 (3): 197–207.

249. Hietanen, J.K., Leppänen, J.M., Peltola, M.J. et al. (2008). Seeing direct and averted gaze activates the approach-avoidance motivational brain systems. *Neuropsychologia* 46 (9): 2423–2430.

250. Einav, S. and Hood, B.M. (2008). Tell-tale eyes: Children's attribution of gaze aversion as a lying cue. *Developmental Psychology* 44 (6): 1655–1667.

251. Schneier, F.R., Rodebaugh, T.L., Blanco, C. et al. (2011). Fear and avoidance of eye contact in social anxiety disorder. *Comprehensive Psychiatry* 52 (1): 81–87.

252. Gamer, M. and Buchel, C. (2009). Amygdala activation predicts gaze toward fearful eyes. *Journal of Neuroscience* 29 (28): 9123–9126.

253. Bateson, M., Nettle, D., and Roberts, G. (2006). Cues of being watched enhance cooperation in a real-world setting. *Biology Letters* 2 (3): 412–414.

254. Fehr, E. and Schneider, F. (2010). Eyes are on us, but nobody cares: Are eye cues relevant for strong reciprocity? *Proceedings: Biological Sciences* 277 (1686): 1315–1323.

255. Tombs, S. and Silverman, I. (2004). Pupillometry. *Evolution and Human Behavior* 25 (4): 221–228.

256. Goldman, M. and Fordyce, J. (1983). Prosocial behavior as affected by eye contact, touch, and voice expression. *Journal of Social Psychology* 121 (1): 125–129.

257. Sadr, J., Jarudi, I., and Sinha, P. (2003). The role of eyebrows in face recognition. *Perception* 32 (3): 285–293.

258. Enrici, I., Adenzato, M., Cappa, S. et al. (2010). Intention processing in communication: A common brain network for language and gestures. *Journal of Cognitive Neuroscience* 23 (9): 2415–2431.

259. Huang, L., Galinsky, A.D., Gruenfeld, D.H. et al. (2011). Powerful postures versus powerful roles: Which is the proximate correlate of thought and behavior? *Psychological Science* 22 (1): 95–102.

260. Cuddy, A. (2012). *Your body language may shape who you are.* TEDGlobal.

261. van Baaren, R., Janssen, L., Chartrand, T.L. et al. (2009). Where is the love? The social aspects of mimicry. *Philosophical Transactions of the Royal Society of London B: Biological Sciences* 364 (1528): 2381–2389.

262. Rhode, D.L. (2010). *The Beauty Bias: The Injustice of Appearance in Life and Law*, 252. New York: Oxford University Press.

263. Busetta, G. and Fiorillo, F. (2013). Will Ugly Betty ever find a job in Italy?, 391. *Quaderno Di Ricerca.*

264. Hamermesh, D.S. (2011). *Beauty Pays: Why Attractive People Are More Successful*, 216. Princeton, NJ; Oxford, UK: Princeton University Press.

265. Hill, A. and Scharff, L.V. (1997). Readability of screen displays with various foreground/background color combinations, font styles, and font types. *Proceedings of the Eleventh National Conference on Undergraduate Research*, II: 742–746.

266. Mackiewicz, J. (2007). Audience perception of fonts in projected PowerPoint slides. *Technical Communication* 54 (3): 295–307.

267. Ali, A.Z.M., Wahid, R., Samsudin, K. et al. (2013). Reading on the computer screen: Does font type have effects on web text readability? *International Education Studies* 6 (3): 26–35.

268. Breugst, N. and Patzelt, H. (2010). Entrepreneurs display of passion and employee's commitment to new ventures. *Academy of Management Annual Meeting Proceedings* 8 (1).

269. Mujica-Parodi, L.R., Strey, H.H., Frederick, B. et al. (2009). Chemosensory cues to conspecific emotional stress activate amygdala in humans. *PLoS One* 4 (7): e6415.

270. Wallechinsky, D., Wallace, I., and Wallace, A. (1977). *The People's Almanac Presents the Book of Lists*, 521. New York: Morrow.

271. Woo, J.W., Tam, J.K.C., Chan, D.S.G. et al. (2015). Uncovering what lies beneath a *Salmonella enterica* empyema. *BMJ Case Reports*, 2015.

272. Vrij, A. (2008). *Detecting Lies and Deceit: Pitfalls and Opportunities*, 2nd ed., 503. West Sussex, UK: Wiley.

273. Witkowski, T (2010). Thirty-five years of research on neuro-linguistic programming. NLP Research Data Base. State of the art or pseudoscientific decoration? *Polish Psychological Bulletin* 41 (2): 58–66.

274. Constantinidou, F. and Baker S. (2002). Stimulus modality and verbal learning performance in normal aging. *Brain Language* 82 (3): 296–311.

275. Brenda, S. (2009). Driving sales through shoppers' sense of sound, sight, smell and touch. *International Journal of Retail & Distribution Management* 37 (3): 286–298.

276. Olahut, M.R. and Ioan, P. (2013). The effects of ambient scent on consumer behavior: A review of the literature. *Annals of the University of Oradea, Economic Science Series* 22 (1): 1797–1806.

277. Velasco, C., Jones, R., King, S. et al. (2013). Assessing the influence of the multisensory environment on the whisky drinking experience. *Flavour* 2 (23).

278. brusspup. (2011). *Incredible Shade Illusion!* YouTube (11 August), https://www.youtube.com/watch?v=z9Sen1HTu5o.

279. TheRichest. (2015). *10 Mind Blowing Optical Illusions.* YouTube (5 March), https://www.youtube.com/watch?v=-IWk5NkxQF8.

280. Morrot, G., Brochet, F., and Dubourdieu, D. (2001). The color of odors. *Brain and Language*, 79 (2): 309–320.

281. Spence, C. (2012). Auditory contributions to flavour perception and feeding behaviour. *Physiology & Behavior* 107 (4): 505–515.

282. North, A.C., Hargreaves, D.J., and McKendrick, J. (1999). The influence of in-store music on wine selections. *Journal of Applied Psychology* 84 (2): 271–276.

283. Williams, L. and Ackerman J. (2011). Please touch the merchandise. *Harvard Business Review* (December 15).

284. Just, M.A., Newman, S.D., Keller, T.A. et al. (2004). Imagery in sentence comprehension: An fMRI study. *Neuroimage* 21 (1): 112–124.

285. Wilson, T.D. and Schooler, J.W. (1991). Thinking too much: Introspection can reduce the quality of preferences and decisions. *Journal of Personality and Social Psychology* 60 (2): 181–192.

286. WisdomLand (2017). Billboard scares the crap out of people crossing red light at intersection and takes their picture. YouTube (3 June), https://www.youtube.com/watch?v=vYWmeh6Q-Vk.

287. Thaler, R. and Sunstein, C. (2009). *NUDGE: Improving Decisions About Health, Wealth, and Happiness*, 312. New York: Penguin Books.

288. NeoFilmShop.com. (2014). MCL cinema Hong Kong Mobile phone car crash advertising effective. YouTube, 29 June, https://www.youtube.com/watch?v=5Gtio4V1L3o.

289. Kopp, F., Schroger, E., and Lipka, S. (2006). Synchronized brain activity during rehearsal and short-term memory disruption by irrelevant speech is affected by recall mode. *International Journal of Psychophysiology* 61 (2): 188–203.

290. Bastardi, A. and Shafir, E. (1998). On the pursuit and misuse of useless information. *Journal of Personality and Social Psychology* 75 (1): 19–32.

291. Johnson, E.J., Shu, S.B., Dellaert, B.G.C. et al. (2012). Beyond nudges: Tools of a choice architecture. *Marketing Letters* 23 (2): 487–504.

292. Rouhshad, A., Wigglesworth, G., and Storch, N. (2015). The nature of negotiations in face-to-face versus computer-mediated communication in pair interactions. *Language Teaching Research* 20 (4): 514–534.

293. Thaler, R., Sunstein, C., and Balz, J.P. (2013). Choice architecture. In: *The Behavioral Foundations of Public Policy* (ed. E. Shafir), 428–439. Princeton, NJ: Princeton University Press.

INDEX

Page references followed by *fig* indicate an illustrated figure; followed by *t* indicate a table.

Mirroring People: The New science of
How We Connect (Iacoboni), 234
Mirror neurons, 102, 247
MIT's Department of Brain and
Cognitive Sciences, 251–252
Momoamines, 61
Motivation
deficiency, 120
growth, 120
Maslow hierarchy of needs as theory
of, 120*fig*–121*fig*
Multiplying options bias, 54
Multisensory selling, 269

Needs
iceberg of decision drivers such as,
116–118
Maslow hierarchy of, 120*fig*–121*fig*
nature of, 119–121
Neocortex. *See* Rational brain
(neocortex)
Neomammalian complex, 62
Nervous system
central nervous system, 20, 21*fig*
illustrated diagram of, 21*fig*
parasympathetic, 21, 23*fig*
peripheral nervous system,
20–23
sympathetic, 21, 22*fig*
Neurobenchmarking multiple ads case
study, 11
NeuroIcons, 195
Neurolinguistic programming
(NLP), 266
NeuroMap
assessing how persuasion affects the
brain using the, 11
based on dominance of the primal
brain, 47–48*fig*
on bottom-up effect of persuasion,
47–48*fig*
as a brain-based persuasion model, 13
Cognitive Bias Codex categories as
explained by, 55–57

cognitive biases as explained by,
50–51
integrating the six stimuli, 105–110*t*
overview of the, 45–47
reviewing what you learned about,
285–288
unique research questions answered
by, 3, 5–6
varying teaching modalities using,
268–269
See also Persuasion theories; Primal
brain; SalesBrain
NeuroMap process
claims, 133, 166*fig*, 194–207
grabbers, 166*fig*–194
proof of gains, 141–162, 166*fig*,
214–217
See also Persuasion elements
NeuroMap Score, 35
Neuromarketing
advantages over traditional marketing
research, 4
how it can help prove value of
solution, 12–13
identifying gap between stated and
actual feelings, 8–9
SalesBrain customer testimonials on
ROI of, 13–17
unique research data provided by,
3, 5–6
Neuromarketing messages
attention getting using approach
of, 6
comparing the traditional rational
and, 48*fig*
helps prove value of solution, 12–13
See also Messages
Neuromarketing research matrix,
32–36*fig*
Neurons
anatomy of, 25*fig*
attention-grabbing, 26
description of, 7–8, 24
extending from limbic system, 96

on identifying attention-getting
  animal images, 6–7
on messages that engage the primal
  brain and working memory, 82
SalesBrain website
  colors and design of the, 90–91
  home page, 91*fig*
  opacity map of the, 92*fig*
Self-actualization, 120*fig*, 121*fig*
The Selfish Gene (Dawkins), 61, 65
Selfishness
  altruism contrasting with, 62, 63
  Dawkins on decisions driven
    by, 61, 65
  of the primal brain, 61–62
Self-refilling bowl test, 208–209
Semantic decoding, 236
Sensory memory, 80–81
Short-term memory, 81–82
Similarity factor, 233–235
Six stimuli
  in contract of Freud's
    psychoanalytical model, 64*fig*
  contrastable, 60*fig*, 68–73, 262–264*fig*
  emotional, 60*fig*, 95–105
  illustrated diagram on the, 60*fig*
  introduction to the, 59–60*t*
  memorable, 60*fig*, 78–83*fig*
  NeuroMap integrating the, 105–110*t*
  personal, 60*fig*, 61–68
  summary role of the, 106*fig*
  as a system of communication and
    language, 59
  tangible, 60*fig*, 73–78
  visual, 60*fig*, 84–94*fig*
  what to remember about the,
    111–112
  See also Stimulus
Smiling, 247
Social desirability bias, 8
Social norms bias, 53–54
Social proof (customer testimonials),
  13–17, 147–149, 215–217

Solutions
  compare your solution to your
    competitor's, 72, 131
  remind audience of pain before
    offering the, 66
  See also Claims
Speaking rate, 242, 243
*Speech Rate, Pause, and Corpus
  Sociophonetics* (Kendall), 243
Stage fright, 259–260
Stimulus
  Chabris and Simons's study on
    unexpected, 167
  definition of, 59
  Freud's psychoanalytical model on,
    63–65
  subliminal, 87–88
  Triune ethics model on, 62–63
  See also Six stimuli
Stories
  Business Storytelling For Dummies! on
    telling, 188
  Churchill's battle of Omdurman
    (1898), 186, 188, 218–219
  the don'ts of, 189
  the dos of, 187–189
  highlight positive side of objective
    using, 220
  introduction to effectiveness of,
    166*fig*, 183–185, 232
  the science of, 185–187
  what to remember about, 189
Storytelling
  be credible, 232–233
  body language when, 245
  body posture, 253–254
  the don'ts of using words for, 240
  eye communication, 250–253
  facial expressions when, 245–247
  use your similarity, 233–235
  using the right voice, 240–245
  using the right words and dos for,
    238–240